Between May 1949 and August 1954 the composers Pierre Boulez and John Cage exchanged a series of remarkable letters which reflect on their own music and the music and culture of the time. To this correspondence a further letter from 1962 has been added together with various other documents, including an unpublished lecture given by Boulez on Cage's music for prepared piano.

At the time, Cage and Boulez were great friends and these amicable letters reflect their differing ideas on the course new music should take. While Boulez was thinking about forms of serialism, Cage was moving in the direction of ever greater compositional freedom and chance procedures.

Professor Nattiez has written a full introduction to this collection of documents, and the meticulous and detailed annotation of every letter makes this a volume of extraordinary value for our understanding of the development of both Cage and Boulez and the music of their time.

THE BOULEZ–CAGE CORRESPONDENCE

THE BOULEZ–CAGE
Correspondence

Documents collected, edited and introduced by
Jean-Jacques Nattiez

with Francoise Davoine, Hans Oesch and
Robert Piencikowski

Translated and edited by
Robert Samuels

CAMBRIDGE
UNIVERSITY PRESS

Published by the Press Syndicate of the University of Cambridge
The Pitt Building, Trumpington Street, Cambridge CB2 1RP
40 West 20th Street, New York, NY 10011–4211, USA
10 Stamford Road, Oakleigh, Melbourne 3166, Australia

Originally published in French and English as *Pierre Boulez/John Cage:
Correspondance et documents* by Amadeus Verlag, Winterthur, Switzerland,
1990 and © 1990 by Paul Sacher Stiftung, Basel, Switzerland

First published in English by Cambridge University Press 1993 as
The Boulez–Cage Correspondence

English translation © Cambridge University Press 1993

Printed in Great Britain at the University Press, Cambridge

A catalogue record for this book is available from the British Library

Library of Congress cataloguing in publication data
Boulez, Pierre, 1925–
[Correspondence. English. Selections.]
Pierre Boulez and John Cage correspondence / documents collected,
edited, and introduced by Jean-Jacques Nattiez; translated and
edited by Robert Samuels ... [et al.]
p. cm.
'Originally published in French and English as *Pierre Boulez/John
Cage: Correspondance et documents* by Amadeus Verlag, Winterthur,
Switzerland, 1990' – T.p. verso.
Includes bibliographical references and index.
ISBN 0 521 40144 5 (hardback)
1. Cage, John – Correspondence. 2. Boulez, Pierre, 1925–
Correspondence. 3. Composers – Correspondence. I. Cage, John.
II. Nattiez, Jean Jacques. III. Title.
ML410.B773A413   1993
780'.92'2–dc20   92–36867   CIP   MN

ISBN 0 521 40144 5 hardback

Contents

Contents

Contents

Contents

Illustrations

Preface

In 1980, whilst I was working in Bayreuth editing Pierre Boulez's *Points de repère* (translated as *Orientations* (London: Faber, 1986)), I discovered the existence of an important sequence of letters between Pierre Boulez and John Cage, dating mainly from 1949 to 1954; I was able to have access to the letters from Cage received by Boulez. Thanks to the goodwill of Don L. Roberts, music librarian of Northwestern University at Evanston, I obtained the other half of the correspondence, the letters from Boulez, which Cage had placed there in order to make them available for research. These were then transcribed by Françoise Davoine, thanks to a grant from the Music Faculty of the University of Montreal, whilst I took charge of the letters from Cage to Boulez.

When the Paul Sacher Foundation in Basel acquired Boulez's manuscripts, and thus the letters from Cage, the late Dr Hans Oesch, the Foundation's director of research and musicological publications, gained the permission of the two composers for the publication of the correspondence. He then asked me to prepare a critical edition. This was published in 1990 as the first volume of the *Publications of the Paul Sacher Foundation*, by Amadeus Verlag of Winterthur.

For the original publication, Robert Piencikowski meticulously checked the transcription of Boulez's letters, and Hans Oesch read that of Cage's letters. John Holzaepfel contacted me with the translation by Cage of Boulez's letter no. 35, discovered in the David Tudor archives. I have published a French translation of this document in the French edition of this correspondence. A full critical edition of this letter, edited by John Holzaepfel, will appear in a later volume of the *Publications of the Paul Sacher Foundation*, dedicated to Boulez. Pierre Boulez, John Cage, Francis Dhomont, Dominique Jameux, Jean Nattiez, Marianne Souvtchinsky, and the archive administrators of Éditions Gallimard and the New York Philharmonic Orchestra provided me with invaluable information for the critical apparatus. Célestin Deliège, Paul Griffiths, and Robert Piencikowski read a first draft of the original edition and made many helpful comments, suggested additions and corrections, and gave crucial information now incorporated in the notes. Célestin Deliège in particular made several observations which enabled me to give the edition its final appearance. I am profoundly indebted to Frans van Rossum, who is working on a biography of Cage, and gave me much information relating to his career: this enabled me to complete my introduction and to correct several errors contained in the original and French editions.

Thanks once again go to Dr Paul Sacher for giving permission for this English edition and for the use of the music examples from the original edition.

Jean-Jacques Nattiez

Translator's introduction

In presenting the correspondence between Pierre Boulez and John Cage to an English-speaking audience, the aim has been to preserve as far as possible the familiar style of the letters. The original edition of the correspondence, published under the auspices of the Paul Sacher Foundation, published each letter in its original language, preserving the errors of each writer when using the language of the other and the numerous orthographical mistakes. This has been followed in the present edition, and orthography of numbers, abbreviations, and other inconsistent features have been retained, except where the result would be needlessly obscure. This accounts for most of the divergences between the version of part of no. 26 published in *Orientations* and that published here. English spelling errors have been preserved, except for proper names. American musical terms (e.g. "measure" and "quarter" for "bar" and "crotchet") have been used in the translations in order to conform with the untranslated English sections. Original punctuation has been preserved, except in one detail: Boulez uses dashes and full stops interchangeably, and so some dashes have been changed to full stops for the sake of clarity. In order to give consistent terminology in technical discussions, all quotations from Boulez's writings have been translated for this edition. However, page references to English editions of the sources are given where these exist.

The dating of the letters posed some problems. For the letters sent by Cage to Boulez on his tours, the addresses from the envelopes have been placed at the head of the letters; unfortunately, however, the stamps and postmarks are missing, cut off by the young Boulez for his parents' stamp collection. Conversely, Boulez's letters to Cage are rarely dated, and, unlike Cage, Boulez appears to have thrown away several letters from the latter part of the correspondence; dates have been deduced as far as possible from the contents. Fresh information has allowed more accurate dates to be assigned to some letters for this edition. Boulez's customary monogram with which he signs each letter has been rendered by the abbreviation PB throughout. In the rare cases where there is doubt over the transcription of the often cramped handwriting this is indicated by square brackets ([]). These brackets always indicate an editorial emendation.

A problem arose from the fact that several of the letters are written partly in

English and partly in French; given that Cage's French is considerably better than Boulez's English, it seemed desirable to mark on the page the portions that had been translated, without recourse to numerous footnotes. Thus *untranslated* sections have been italicised (i.e. sections originally in English). Since two thirds of the volume were in French originally, this seemed easiest on the eye. (The articles appearing as nos 5 and 32 are exceptions to this rule: they appear in roman font, although they were written originally in English.)

Several notes have been added to this translation compared with the version published by the Paul Sacher foundation (*Pierre Boulez / John Cage: Correspondance et Documents*, ed. J-J. Nattiez, Winterthur: Amadeus Verlag, 1990). These are indicated by (RS). In addition, a biographical glossary has been compiled in order to reduce the number of notes in the body of the text.

James Pritchett made many useful observations, particularly concerning the problematic letter no. 35. These have been acknowledged where possible, and his notes indicated by (JP).

My thanks go to Derrick Puffett for his comments on the draft of this edition, and in particular to Penny Souster of Cambridge University Press for her patience and advice during this first venture into translation and editing.

Robert Samuels

Abbreviations

The following abbreviations are used throughout the notes:

A John Cage Reader   P. Gend and J. Brent, eds, *A John Cage Reader* (New York: Peters, 1982)

Stocktakings   Pierre Boulez, *Stocktakings from an Apprenticeship* (Oxford: OUP, 1991). Translation by Stephen Walsh of *Relevés d'apprenti* (Paris: Seuil, 1966). Page references are to the English edition.

Jameux   Dominique Jameux, *Pierre Boulez* (Paris: Fayard, 1984); translated by Susan Bradshaw (London: Faber, 1991). Page references are to the English edition.

Orientations   Pierre Boulez, *Orientations*, ed. Jean-Jacques Nattiez and trans. Martin Cooper (London: Faber, 1982). Translation of *Points de repère* (Paris: Christian Bourgois éditeur, 1981). Page references are to the English edition.

Peyser   Joan Peyser, *Boulez* (New York/London: Schirmer Books, 1976)

Silence   John Cage, *Silence* (Middleton: Wesleyan University Press, 1961)

Introduction
Cage and Boulez: a chapter of music history

Introduction

Cage and Boulez: a chapter of music history

From time to time, in the history of culture, there are encounters which, because of the personalities and currents of thought that are brought together through them, take on symbolic value and may even acquire the status of myth. Such are the visits made by Nietzsche to the Wagners at Tribschen and Bayreuth; such is the handshake between Sartre and Aron on the steps of the Palais de l'Elysée. The encounter between Cage and Boulez is less well known,[1] doubtless because the documentary evidence has hitherto been published only in a very fragmentary form.[2] However, the intensity of their correspondence from that time takes on in retrospect a surprising and significant status, since today they embody two radically opposed streams of post-war music history.

Where, then, were the characters before they went on stage?

In 1949 Pierre Boulez, the younger, was twenty-four.[3] His studies at the Paris Conservatoire had been brief; between 1943 and 1945, he had taken harmony with Georges Dandelot and studied the major principles of analysis with Messiaen. In private, he had learnt counterpoint with Andrée Vaurabourg-Honegger, and "a bit of piano" with Mme François, assistant to Jean Doyen. Boulez may not have been gifted enough on the instrument to be admitted to the top class, but he was nevertheless able enough to give the first performance, a little later, of his Third Piano Sonata and to play his *Structures* for two pianos with, variously, David Tudor, Olivier Messiaen and Yvonne Loriod. Although prior to 1949 he wrote several pieces now withdrawn from the catalogue (*Notations* for piano (1945); *Trois psalmodies* for piano (1945); Variations for piano left hand (1945)); Quartet for Ondes Martenot (1945–6), which became the Sonata for two pianos (1948); he also had five works to his credit which are still performed today and whose

---

[1] Nevertheless see Peyser, pp. 60–2; and Jameux, pp. 72–3.

[2] "The system exposed", in *Orientations*, pp. 129–42. Peyser has published a facsimile of the last page of one of Boulez's letters (Peyser p. 87) and included short extracts from various others.

[3] Dominique Jameux is to be thanked here for the large amount of information given by his work on Boulez: he greatly facilitated the setting up of this publication. His catalogue of Boulez's works (Jameux pp. 369–72) will be used for references throughout, with additions or corrections where necessary.

importance is generally acknowledged: the Sonatine for flute and piano (1946), the First Piano Sonata (1946), *Le visage nuptial* (1946–7) in its first version (Jameux Catalogue no. 7a), *Le soleil des eaux* in the version for performance on the radio (Jameux no. 9a), *Livre pour quatuor* (1948–9), Jameux no. 10a), and the Second Piano Sonata (1946–8).

In 1949 John Cage, on the other hand, was thirty-six. He had studied the piano from 1920 to 1928, and had drifted from poetry to architecture and music. At the end of 1931 Cage returned from his first trip to Europe. In April 1932 he began to study composition with Richard Buhlig, who advised him in September 1933 to continue his studies with Henry Cowell. Cowell taught him composition and "dissonant counterpoint" from the end of 1933 to April 1934. In order to prepare him for his studies with Schoenberg, Cowell arranged for Cage to study with Adolph Weiss – himself a Schoenberg pupil – in New York, which he did from April 1933. At the same time, Cage attended Cowell's classes in contemporary harmony, rhythm, and music from oral traditions, and a survey course on contemporary music, all at the New School for Social Research. In December 1934 Cowell and Cage returned to Los Angeles together. From March 1935 to the summer of 1937 Cage studied counterpoint and analysis with Schoenberg, first at the University of Southern California and then at the University of California in Los Angeles. However, Schoenberg never accepted him as a composition pupil.

This already makes it easier to see what drew Boulez and Cage together at this time: to some extent, their backgrounds shared similar influences. Thus during the thirties Cage developed a method of composition according to which the repetition of each individual sound in a series of twenty-five was avoided as far as possible. Through his friendship with a film producer, Oscar von Fischinger, he became interested in noise, in percussion notation, and in rhythm. In the autumn of 1938, at the Cornish School in Seattle, where he held the position of composer and accompanist, he met the choreographer Merce Cunningham, with whom he was to enjoy a lifelong collaboration. At this time Cunningham was attending courses in dance at the Cornish School whilst studying drama. During 1939 Cage moved to New York to begin work with the Martha Graham Dance Company. In the same year he composed *Imaginary Landscape No. 1*, which uses muted piano, cymbal, and variable-speed turntable and requires a recording studio for its performance; it was the first work in the history of music to combine 'live' electronics with an aleatory component. The same year saw *First Construction (in Metal)* for percussion sextet. These two works were premièred on 9 December 1939, as part of an evening of dance at the Cornish School. At the same venue on 28 April 1940 Cage's first piece of prepared piano, *Bacchanale*, received its première. At this time Cage considered the creation of a centre for experimental music, and tried to interest both Mills College and the Cornish School in the project. In 1941 he taught at the Chicago School of Design, where several of the Bauhaus School artists had been reunited. At the end of spring 1942, Cage and

4

Cunningham met again at Bennington College (Vermont). With *Credo in Us* their collaboration began. The choreography was by Jean Erdmann and Cunningham, and Cage wrote the music. Cage used James Joyce's *Finnegans Wake* in *The Wonderful Widow of Eighteen Springs*, met Marcel Duchamp, and in 1943 organized a percussion concert at the New York Museum of Modern Art. Cage's interest in Indian philosophy stemmed from his encounter with an Indian musician, Gita Sarabhai, in New York in August 1946. As a consequence, he composed *Sonatas and Interludes* for prepared piano, the success of which enabled him in 1949 to obtain a grant from the Guggenheim Foundation and an award from the American Academy and National Institute of Arts and Letters to spend six months in Europe. Merce Cunningham took the trip as well.

Cage left New York on a boat for Amsterdam on 23 March 1949. During his stay in Paris – he stayed at a hotel on the Île de la cité – he studied the life and works of Erik Satie at the Bibliothèque Nationale. During the summer he played *Amores* (parts 1 and 4) at the Vieux Colombier theatre as accompaniment to the ballet of the same name, as well as *A Valentine Out of Season* for *Effusions avant l'heure*, both choreographed by Cunningham. He also began to compose a string quartet.

At the suggestion of Virgil Thompson (according to Joan Peyser) or Roger Désormière (according to Boulez) Cage knocked at Boulez's door in the Rue Beautreillis shortly after his arrival in Paris. The two became friends. Boulez introduced Cage to Messiaen, who invited him to play his *Sonatas and Interludes* to his pupils at the Salle Gounod of the Paris Conservatoire, Rue de Madrid, on 7 June. Cage moved among the close circle of Boulez's friends: the painter Bernard Saby, the playwright Armand Gatti, the novelist Pierre Jouffroy and Pierre Souvtchinsky, the last of whom enabled Boulez to meet Suzanne Tézenas, the future president of the Domaine musical. For his part, Cage introduced Boulez to the younger man's first two publishers: Amphion would publish the Sonatine for flute and piano and the First Piano Sonata, and Heugel *Le visage nuptial*, *Le soleil des eaux*, the *Livre pour quatuor*, and the Second Piano Sonata.

The present collection begins with an important document (no. 1): the text of Boulez's introductory talk on the *Sonatas and Interludes* for prepared piano, given at Suzanne Tézenas's salon in 1949.[4] Peyser, in a book of often questionable tone, has given a colourful description of the occasion on the basis of various accounts collected by her:

The afternoon of the performance, Cage spent three hours carefully inserting objects into the piano that he had chosen for the work. Something was not in order with the *una corda* pedal and Suzanne Tézenas watched with apprehension as Cage poured cognac into her Bechstein to weaken the glue between the strings

[4] In a letter to his parents dated 1 June, Cage says that the presentation with Boulez at Suzanne Tézenas's will take place on 17 June. (JP)

so he could move the hammers in a way that would secure the effect he had in mind. Cage worked with cardboard underneath his materials in order not to damage the soundboard. He says he always leaves a piano in better condition than he finds it. The evening of the performance the living room was jammed. Chairs were set up close together and Cunningham lay stretched out on the floor between the foyer and the living room.[5]

Boulez did not forget the text of that introductory talk. He probably had it in front of him in the summer of 1951 (see no. 27) when he wrote his important article "Possibly . .", in which he outlines the theory of total serialism. He mentions Cage there in identical terms to those used in 1949 (cf. no. 37).

Between Cage's return to New York, probably in November 1949, and the visit made by Boulez to that city from 11 November 1952 onwards (when Boulez accompanied the Compagnie Renaud-Barrault on its second tour of South America), an intense correspondence started up. This makes up the bulk of the present collection (nos 3 to 41).

What is recreated through these documents is first and foremost the musical climate of the times, a difficult climate for these two illustrious representatives of the avant-garde. On the one hand, Boulez lived in musical isolation. Given the works he already had behind him, and given the eminently *new* universe that he was carrying within himself – this was the time (between 1950 and 1952) when, as this correspondence shows, he was working on the principles of total serialism in *Polyphonie X* and *Structures* for two pianos and when he was beginning *Le marteau sans maître* – one can well understand his distancing himself from Leibowitz, Jolivet or Dallapiccola (never mind Copland!). He did this through what was to become his familiar polemical style, razor sharp yet crystal clear. Now, from a distance, like Boulez himself (who was away on tour in South America with Barrault), we can be present at the first, relatively mediocre, performance of the Second Sonata – an occasion that the composer seems to make fun of (see no. 13) – and the first performance of *Le soleil des eaux* in its first version, which by contrast did not go unnoticed and the success of which reverberated as far as New York.

Throughout Cage's letters, the context that emerges is naturally that of America, dominated by routine and neoclassicism. Cage was no longer a very young man, and was already fairly well known; but there was no one of Boulez's stature in his immediate circle for him to talk to. "The great trouble with our life here is the absence of an intellectual life," he writes in January 1950 (see no. 7), "no one has an idea." What Cage had, instead of an equal, was several disciples – Brown, Wolff, Tudor, Feldman – who appear as the letters progress, even if, with the unfaltering delicacy typical of his side of the correspondence, Cage does not underline the fact. On the contrary, it is he, the elder of the two, who places himself in the rôle of pupil to the other. He

[5] Peyser, p. 61.

admits that in Paris he did not dare to show Boulez his string quartet (see no. 7).

Cage was himself in search of matrices with which to organize works, particularly their rhythmic structure, and he avows admiration for the detailed technical explanations with which Boulez supplies him at his request (see nos 26, 31 and 35): "The long letter you sent me with the details about your work was magnificent" (no. 28). Indeed the second letter on technical matters (no. 31) so impressed him that he translated the bulk of it and had it published in the journal *Transformations*, alongside "statements" by Feldman, Wolff, and himself, which are included here to give the full context of the intellectual debate (see no. 32).

In addition, Cage made himself the proselyte of Boulez in the United States. He arranged the American première of the Second Piano Sonata, a première which was at first planned with William Masselos in mind, but finally given by David Tudor, whom Boulez would later invite to the Domaine Musical.[6] Cage also tried unsuccessfully to put on the first performance of the *Livre pour quatuor* and arranged repeat performances of the First Piano Sonata and Boulez's two *musique concrète* Études. He seemed to be constantly on the lookout for any recognition of his friend, ready to be of help.

Cage did even more than this: he went to great lengths to have Boulez brought to the States, using the opportunity provided by Jean-Louis Barrault's South American tour. A whole portion of the correspondence (letters 12 to 24) describes the ups and downs of this project, which came to grief over a technicality. Cage's bitterness can be felt, although it is modestly expressed (see letter 23), but despite the circumstances he did not give up the idea. When the possibility of another meeting becomes a certainty with Barrault's 1952 tour to Canada and the U.S.A., Boulez's letters display undisguised enthusiasm (see nos 36, 39, 40 and 41).

For his part, Cage was working throughout this period on a number of works which he sometimes explains at length (the relevant document numbers will be given below): music for a film on Calder (no. 28), the *String Quartet in Four Parts* (nos 9 and 28), the Concerto for prepared piano and chamber orchestra (no. 28), the *Six Melodies for Violin and Keyboard* (No. 28), the Sixteen Dances for flute, trumpet, four percussion players, piano, violin and cello (no. 28), *Imaginary Landscape No. 4* (no. 28), the *Music of Changes*, *Imaginary Landscape No. 5* (no. 38) and *Williams Mix* (no. 43). In no. 7 Cage also talks of *First Construction (in Metal)*, which dates back to 1939. If this information is compared with that given by Cage in his first collection of articles, *Silence*,[7] this correspondence provides

---

[6] He accompanies Severino Gazzelloni in the first recording of the Sonatine for flute and piano, performed under the auspices of the Domaine Musical (Vega C30 A139).

[7] One of the chapters of *Silence*, "To describe the process of composition used in *Music of Changes* and *Imaginary Landscape No. 4*" (pp. 57–9) is taken from an article included in

indispensable material for the understanding of the techniques involved in Cage's compositions of the period.

There was, then, a desire on both sides to know what the other man was doing, thinking and inventing. Given the radically differing stances later adopted by the two friends, who came to represent the two most divergent streams of contemporary music, the question arises as to what could ever have made them take such interest in each other in the first place: "This seems a puzzling, even eccentric thing to have done," writes Jameux; "it is hard to see what could possibly have interested Cage in this computerized passion, harder still to understand Boulez's indulgence towards the contemplative tinkering of the *Sonatas and Interludes*."[8] In his book, Jameux sums up the basic reasons for this reciprocal curiosity.[9] However, the correspondence and the juxtaposition of texts allows this analysis to be refined, emphasizing in particular – as will be shown with reference to Boulez's 1949 talk on Cage – that on Boulez's side, the worm was in the bud right from the beginning.

Boulez's thought is characterized by a relatively small number of pivotal ideas, which are identifiable from very early on and which can be traced throughout his career until the point where they find a satisfying musical fulfilment.

Amongst these ideas is the questioning of received acoustical notions: "Instead of producing what one might term pure sounds ... John Cage's prepared piano provides us with frequency complexes," he says in the 1949 lecture. To this end, the traditional function of instruments must be put in question. In "Possibly..." of 1951[10] his ideas have not changed: "[Cage] has proved that it is possible to create non-tempered sound spaces, even using existing instruments."[11] It must not be forgotten that even in the (earlier) *Visage nuptial*, as well as in the soon to be undertaken *Polyphonie X*, Boulez was experimenting with microtonal intervals (quarter-tone series). In 1953 he wrote, in "Tendencies in recent music":[12]

What remains to be discovered is still non-tempered sound worlds ... How can one at present solve the problem posed by sound production? John Cage's prepared piano provides a solution which is pragmatic and embryonic, but nevertheless plausible. In any case, the prepared piano has the enormous merit of making concrete here and now the sound worlds which we would have had to give

this edition (no. 32), with alterations given in the notes. Cage had earlier described many of these methods in a letter to Boulez (no. 28). (RS)

8 Jameux, p. 54.

9 Jameux, pp. 44–5, 52–5.

10 "Éventuellement...", *Revue musicale*, no. 212 (May 1952), pp. 117–48; reprinted as "Possibly ...", *Stocktakings*, pp. 111–40.

11 *Stocktakings*, p. 134 [cf. no. 37].

12 "Tendances de la musique récente", *Revue musicale*, no. 236 (1957), pp. 28–35; reprinted as "Tendencies in recent music", *Stocktakings*, pp. 173–80. Robert Piencikowski points out that this article had been written by 1953 (personal communication).

up provisionally, given the difficulty in realizing them ... This shows the way towards a future evolution of music where instruments can aid in the creation of a new sound system which both needs and calls for them, thanks to the development of progressively more perfect notations.[13]

For the aborted Mallarmé *Coup de dés* project of 1951, he is already imagining having a machine built (see no. 26). Later he would be able to use the halaphon[14] in *...explosante/fixe...* (1972, Jameux no. 31b), and the IRCAM 4X computer in *Répons*. Indeed, it is not impossible to see the foundation of IRCAM in 1974 – along with a similar idea of Varèse, the studios in Cologne and Milan, and even the enterprises of Xenakis – as the final realization of Cage's vision of a centre for experimental music, mentioned in Boulez's 1949 lecture, which he, Cage, had already written about in 1937:

Centers of experimental music must be established. In these centers, the new materials, oscillators, turntables, generators, means for amplifying small sounds, film phonographs, etc., available for use. Composers at work using 20th century means for making music. Organization of sound for extra-musical purposes (theatre, dance, radio, film).[15]

"Instead of employing pure sounds, he makes use of sound complexes," Boulez says again in the 1949 lecture. Cage admitted to Henry Cowell, "My influence on him is that he accepts my idea of aggregates."[16] The same note is struck in "Possibly...": "We owe the idea of sound complexes to John Cage." And in 1953: "The piano will become, by way of a do-it-yourself tuning system [*une tablature artisanale*], an instrument capable of producing frequency complexes."[17] In a letter of January 1950 (see no. 6), Boulez is still more explicit. He declares concerning *Le soleil des eaux*:

I plan to put into practice in it some ideas derived from your pieces and what I explained to you about complex sounds ... you are the only person who has added an anxiety about the sound materials I use ... I have explored nothing as yet and everything remains to be looked for in fields as varied as sound, rhythm; orchestra, voices; architecture.

Again, an echo of Cage is to be heard in Boulez's article "Chord" for the *Encylopédie Fasquelle* (1958):

[13] *Stocktakings*, p. 176.
[14] The halaphon is a piece of equipment that enables a sound to pass from one loudspeaker to another. It was invented by a German engineer, Lawo, for the Freiburg studio following an idea by the then head of the studio, Hans-Peter Haller.
[15] "The future of music: credo", in *Silence*, p. 6. He would return to this theme in "Where are we going? and what are we doing?", in *Silence*, pp. 233ff.
[16] Cf. no. 30, note 1.
[17] *Stocktakings*, p. 176.

More recently, the chord, having gradually lost its structural functions, has become a sonic aggregate; it is chosen for its own sake, for its internal capacities of tension or relaxation, according to its registral disposition and the intervals it puts into play. Thus its structural function is both diminished and sharpened, which tends to demonstrate that the truly harmonic era of Western European music is at an end.[18]

Boulez's 1949 lecture also indicates the second strand of his interest in Cage: "When Cage got rid of the twelve-tone series, a strongly characterized rhythmic structure became necessary to him as a support for the musical argument." Even here, at the beginning of their relationship, a divergence is apparent which will become progressively more pronounced. Cage "wishes to give each sound a prominent individuality". For the time being, Boulez admits that Cage cannot organize pitches, since these are "scrambled" [*brouillées*] by the different objects inserted into the prepared piano. But he maintains that Cage is working with a kind of alternative organization. This important point undoubtedly explains the curiosity that each of the two friends had concerning the other's work between 1949 and 1952. Cage could not but be fascinated by the complexity of total serialism (see nos 26, 31 and 35), by which Boulez sought a method of organizing sound aggregates. For his part, Boulez observes that Cage spent much time sketching models of temporal organization during a period when he had not yet given chance a pre-eminent place or transformed concerts into "happenings". This aspect of Boulez's interest in Cage's preoccupations deserves comment. He declares himself extremely interested (see no. 29) by the long descriptions Cage provides him of the Quartet, the Calder film music, the *Six Melodies for Violin and Keyboard*, the Concerto for prepared piano and orchestra, the Sixteen Dances and *Imaginary Landscape No. 4* (see no. 28). He writes, concerning *Music of Changes*:

> I was absolutely charmed by this development in your style. And I am with you all the way. It is certainly my favourite amongst everything you have done.... In any case you cannot know how much I agree with you – I can tell you this enthusiastically. (no. 39)

This letter gives the lie entirely to Peyser, who goes as far as calling *Music of Changes* "the very work that had precipitated Boulez's break from Cage".[19] On the contrary, it was to be the one work of Cage's that Boulez would programme in a Domaine Musical concert, on 15 December 1956, when relations between the two had already cooled.

Nevertheless, it is worth wondering what it was that "charmed" Boulez in this piece. It appears a transitional work in Cage's output, and Boulez would

[18] Reprinted in *Stocktakings*, p. 281.
[19] Peyser, p. 121.

only take from it that which Cage would soon leave behind. Even if the distribution of silences and sound aggregates results from chance operations, Cage still clings to the concept of structuration in this piece, though it is practically the last time he does so. And the structuration is even a twelve-tone one. Cage writes:

> Charts were ... used for the *Music of Changes*, but in contrast to the method which involved chance operations, these charts were subjected to a rational control: of the sixty-four elements in a square chart eight times eight (made in this way in order to interpret as sounds the coin oracle of the Chinese *Book of Changes*) thirty-two were sounds, thirty-two silences. The thirty-two sounds were arranged in two squares one above the other, each four by four. Whether the charts were mobile or immobile, *all twelve tones were present*[20] in any four elements of a given chart, whether a line of the chart was read horizontally or vertically. Once this dodecaphonic requirement was satisfied, noises and repetitions of tones were used with freedom. One may conclude from this that in *Music of Changes* the effect of the chance operations on the structure (making very apparent its anachronistic character) was balanced by a *control* of the materials.[21]

One can clearly see the control to which chance must be subjected, and this is something which Boulez was not able to reject.

Certainly Cage would soon realize from experience that he could dispense with these structuring and controlling operations. Earlier in the same letter he emphasizes what *Music of Changes* owes to the dialectic of order and freedom,[22] corresponding respectively to what elsewhere he calls structure – "divisibility into successive parts, from phrases to long sections" – and method – "the means of controlling the continuity from note to note."[23] Since syntactic progression in this piece is established by the chance of heads or tails, method, in Cage's terms, comes to resent the rigour of structure: "what happened came about only through the tossing of coins. It became clear, therefore, that structure was not necessary. And, in *Music for Piano*, and subsequent pieces, indeed, structure is no longer a part of the composition means."[24] But Boulez did not have cause to worry about this yet. For the moment, he heard a result in sound of the intervention of chance operations at the level of the composer, but not at the level of the interpreter's performance.[25] Thus *Music of Changes* has the attractions of an atonal work which is Webernian in inspiration – indeed, even more Webernian than Boulez's own, in the dominating role played by silences. Moreover, in Cage's renunciation here of the seductions of the prepared piano, Boulez must surely have found the radical athematicism, violence apart, of his earliest

---

[20] My italics.
[21] In "Changes" (1958), *Silence*, pp. 25–6.
[22] *Ibid.*, p. 20.
[23] In "Forerunners of modern music" (1949), (see no. 5).
[24] In "Changes", *Silence*, p. 22.
[25] Cf. "Indeterminacy",, in *Silence*, p. 36.

compositions, notably the abstract purity of his Second Sonata. Finally, *Music of Changes*, following the model of *Sonatas and Interludes*, takes up an entire concert, a project which would preoccupy Boulez constantly from *Pli selon pli* to *Répons*.

As Jameux has rightly emphasized,[26] the anonymous personality that found realization in Cage's charts and diagrams exerted a fascination over Boulez. "Cage came to the conclusion that in order to build this construction, a purely formal, impersonal idea was required: that of numerical relations ... In this way an *a priori* numerical structure arises which the composer describes as prismatic and which I should prefer to call a crystallized structure" (1949 lecture). Boulez takes up almost exactly the same terms again in "Possibly...".[27] In 1949 he emphasizes Cage's use of whole numbers – which he too adopts, as is little known, for the structuring of the tempos of "Constellation-Miroir" in the Third Piano Sonata – as well as fractions. In 1952 he emphasizes "[Cage's] way of conceiving rhythmic construction, which is based on the idea of real time, as is evidenced by the numerical relations *where the personal coefficient is not involved*."[28] (The 1949 lecture gives further technical details on this point.) And Boulez's article of 1952 is specific: "More recently [cf. Cage's letter no. 28], which definitely considers itself a crucial document] he [Cage] is concerned with creating structural relations between the different components of a sound, and to this end he employs tables, organizing each of them according to parallel but autonomous divisions. The direction of research pursued by John Cage is too close to our own for us not to take it into account."[29]

So much for public recognition. But ordering the correspondence chronologically reveals more. The invention of total serialism has always been attributed to Messiaen, in his *Mode de valeurs et d'intensités*,[30] and Boulez reinforced this link by choosing the series of this work as that of his *Structures* for two pianos.[31] This correspondence irrefutably establishes that Cage's ideas – if not his works – partially contributed to the development of the total serial technique, though not to the concept itself.

In his 1949 talk, Boulez already points out that the prepared piano leads to "the *necessity*[32] of modifying duration, amplitude, frequency, and timbre, in other words, the four characteristics of a sound" (document 1). But during the summer of 1951, the time when he was working on both the *Structures* for two pianos and the article "Possibly...", he writes (in no. 27):

In this series of works, I have attempted to realize the serial organization at all levels: arrangement of the pitches, the dynamics, the attacks and the dur-

---

26 Jameux, p. 44–5.
27 *Stocktakings*, p. 135 [see no. 37].
28 *Ibid.*, My italics.
29 *Ibid.*
30 Begun at Darmstadt in 1949 and finished during winter 1950 in Paris.
31 He indicates this in no. 31.
32 My italics.

ations.... I've taken over your chess-board system for my own purposes, by making it serve on dissociated, antagonistic, and parallel or anti-parallel levels.[33]

This is the system that Cage had explained to him at length in his letter of 22 May 1951 (no. 28), to which Boulez had responded; "[Your last letter] was absolutely absorbing. We are at the same stage of research" (no. 29). For his part, Cage would write to Boulez, "I am full of admiration ... for the way in which you have generalized the concept of the series" (no. 38).

Did Boulez learn more than his elder from this encounter? A single work – *Music of Changes* – really elicited his admiration, and all he knew of Cage's activities was the theoretical explanations given in the letters. It must be emphasized that the roots of the later divergence extend back to 1949. Boulez's reservations, courteously expressed, were to increase as chance rapidly overtook organization in Cage's work and contributed to the decisive alienation of the younger man from the elder.

Firstly, in his 1949 talk, Boulez rejected neoclassicism:

the structure of these sonatas brings together a pre-classical structure and a rhythmic structure which belong to two entirely different worlds; this combination cannot possibly be imagined without recourse to an extra-musical dialectic, a breeding-ground for dangerous ambiguities. (no. 1)

This is the same criticism that Boulez would make of Schoenberg (in the famous "Schoenberg is dead" of February 1952).[34] He reproaches the latter for placing the revolutionary procedure of the series within a formal, rhythmic and metrical mould which remains inspired by tonality. Indeed it was precisely in order to make a decisive break with the tonal character of parameters other than pitch that Boulez was to throw himself into the radical enterprise of total serialism, despite the fact that it proved to be a dead end, as he himself soon came to recognise.[35]

Secondly, Boulez was worried from the first by Cage's liking for the individuality of sound: "One might overdo it and fall into the very trap that one wanted to avoid at all costs" (no. 1). And Boulez already affirmed that Webern's option was superior to Cage's: "If each sound is treated as absolutely neutral – as for example in Webern – the context causes each sound to

---

[33] My italics.

[34] "Schoenberg is dead", *Stocktaking*, pp. 209–14.

[35] "Webern only organized pitch; we organize rhythm, timbre, dynamics; everything is grist to this monstrous all-purpose mill, and we had better abandon it quickly if we are not be be condemned to deafness." ("Current investigations" [1954] in *Stocktakings*, p. 16)

"The four [ways of generation] all seem to me to bring into relief the specific properties of pitch and time which are of fundamental importance to all music, and which are capable on their own of generating a sound universe, whereas dynamics and timbre are important, certainly, but could never assume such a responsibility." ("... Near and far", *Stocktakings*, p. 154)

take on a different individuality each time that it appears" (no. 1). Boulez repeats this statement word for word in the 1952 "Possibly...".[36]

A document from another source gives a fairly precise picture of Cage's ideas in 1949, at the time he met Boulez. This is an article entitled "Forerunners of modern music" which appeared in America in *The Tiger's Eye* (March 1949), and shortly afterwards in France in *Contrepoints* (see no. 5), under the title "Raison d'être de la musique moderne",[37] after Cage's return to the U.S.A. Boulez takes it into account in his letter of 3 January 1950 (no. 6).[38] Boulez could in the main agree with Cage's definitions of structure and form; but in contrast to his attitude in the *First Construction (in Metal)* (1939), where structure, method and material are submitted to organization, Cage here takes pains to add,

> Whereas form wants only freedom to be. It belongs to the heart; and the law it observes, if indeed it submits to any, has never been and never will be written.[39]

In several of his writings, Cage limits the function of the series. For example, "The 12-tone row is a method. A method is a control of each single note."[40]

For Boulez, the follower of Webern, writing serial music involved more than being able to count up to twelve. It was, rather, a principle of construction which also governed the form. This was to be expressed very clearly in "Bach's moment" (1951):

> In Webern, the *aural effect* is produced by making the structure arise from the material. By this is meant the fact that the architecture of a work is directly derived from the order of the series.[41]

For his part, Cage looked on Schoenberg's invention from the social point of view, an attitude which would always be alien to Boulez. In 1937 he wrote: "Schoenberg's method is analogous to a society in which the emphasis is on the group and the integration of the individual in the group." In his own practice, by contrast, "any sound is acceptable to the composer of percussion music."[42] In the *Tiger's Eye* article of 1949 he writes: "Music is edifying, for from time to time it sets the soul in operation. The soul is the gatherer-together of the disparate elements (Meister Eckhardt), and its work fills one with peace and love."[43]

---

[36] *Stocktakings*, p. 135.
[37] *Contrepoints*, no. 6, 1949, pp. 55–61; *Silence*, pp. 62–66.
[38] Cage's article appeared at the same time as one by Boulez, "Trajectories – Ravel, Stravinsky, Schoenberg" (reprinted in *Stocktakings*, pp. 188–205).
[39] *Silence*, p. 62.
[40] in "45' for a speaker" (1954), *Silence*, p. 153.
[41] *Stocktakings*, p. 8.
[42] in "The future of music: credo", *Silence*, p. 5.
[43] in "Forerunners of modern music" (see no. 5).

This article by Cage gives the key to the ambiguous nature of his encounter with Boulez: right up to 1952, Cage was seeking to organize what he called the structure of his pieces. Pitch had long since ceased to be determined by the series, and he was especially concerned to organize rhythm and temporal intervals. For his part, Boulez discovered in Cage a pursuit of sonorities behind which there was still some control. From this sprang their interest in each other's work and the possibility of their areas of investigation overlapping. However, everything toppled after 1952: chance grew from the status of compositional method (*Music of Changes*) to that of interpretation (*Williams Mix*) and would later transform the musical work into a "Happening". By contrast, Boulez reinforced the element of control and extended serial principles to all aspects of composition.

How then may Boulez's attitude towards Cage between 1949 and 1952 be described? Whilst expressing interest in and admiration for his friend's discoveries – the bringing into being of a non-tempered sound world through the physical modification of the piano, the use of sound aggregates, the organization of rhythmic structure – he takes hold of these completely new ideas in order to make them bear fruit but only in the context of a musical language and morphology which was no longer that of Cage from the moment the two men met. Boulez's style was already following well-defined paths in 1949, even if there was some distance between the First and Second Piano Sonatas. Cage's ideas became integrated by Boulez in a sound world that Cage himself had renounced long before. Thus similar techniques of construction took on very different meanings: Cage was concerned to organise the temporal unfolding of the work in a context where chance already rules, for reasons that are more social than musical, whereas total serialism allowed Boulez to rid the new sound world of what remnants of tonality it was still harbouring. In aesthetic terms, the two men's encounter could not have been anything other than a misunderstanding. The case is a little like that of Wagner, who borrowed melodic figures or harmonic ideas from Weber, Mendelssohn, Meyerbeer or Liszt, and indeed from the whole corpus of grand opera, and confronted them with a new world in which they could acquire an unsuspected and transcendental scope. On the other side, though, did Cage learn anything from Boulez? Everything in his behaviour towards Boulez does after all bear witness to his admiration for the younger man's formal rigour.

Here the most controversial and delicate point in this encounter is reached. When Henry Cowell asked Cage what he owed to Boulez, he replied with the apparently surprising words: "Boulez influenced me with his concept of mobility."[44] Thus in a sense Boulez owed total serialism to Cage, and Cage the concept of chance to Boulez?! One of Jameux's remarks tends in the same direction: "The depersonalization sought by Boulez in *Structure Ia* is even

[44] January 1952. Cf. no. 30, note 1.

closer in 1951 to a conception of chance than that which Cage had reached to this date."[45] As Boulez often recognized later, the automatism of total serialism is certain to engender an anarchy, which was described by Boulez as "statistical", and might more technically be described as "entropic", one which connects with chance procedures "by the back door". However, it is uncertain whether this consequence would have influenced Cage in his development.

One must be careful here. First of all, what is this "mobility"? Confining discussion to those documents at our disposal and taking account of the fact that the word does not appear in the letters, there is only one occurrence of it in the articles written by Boulez before January 1952 (the date when Cage's statement to Cowell was published). In "Propositions" (published in 1948), before he met Cage,[46] Boulez writes,

> We must now define what is meant by dynamism or stasis in the scale of sounds. It seems imperative to me that in twelve-tone technique, entirely different procedures must be used to obtain equivalents of tonal values such as modulation; these procedures must be founded on the mobility or fixity of notes. In other words, mobility means that a note will apear in a different register on each of its occurrences; whilst fixity means that the contrapuntal line exists within a certain disposition of the twelve sounds in which each has its own determined place.[47]

This concept of mobility has nothing to do with the introduction of chance into the compositional process; it is concerned with the freedom that the composer gives himself regarding the registral disposition of each note in the series. It is its placing in relation to the rest of the series which remains fixed. In *Silence,* Cage makes several allusions to the dialectic of mobility and immobility which is put into practice by the correlation tables that organize all his works up to *Williams Mix*:

> The principle called mobility-immobility is this: everything is changing but while some things are changing others are not. Eventually those that were not changing begin suddenly to change et vice versa ad infinitum.[48]

A little later in the same text, he states that from then (October 1954) onwards, this principle was no longer of interest to him.[49] The use of chance, which was to upset relations between Cage and Boulez, therefore remained an aesthetic question for Boulez, whilst moving to the more psychological level of precompositional planning for Cage.

[45] Jameux, p. 54.
[46] "Propositions", *Polyphonie*, 2ᵉ cahier, 1948, pp. 65–72. Reprinted as "Proposals" in *Stocktakings*, pp. 47–54.
[47] "Proposals", *Stocktakings*, p. 50.
[48] "45′ for a speaker", *Silence*, p. 154.
[49] *Ibid.*, p. 159.

In January 1950, that is, on returning from Paris, Cage wrote concerning his experiments with tape recorders, "the adventure was halted by machines which are too perfect nowadays. They are stupid ... Chance comes in here to give us the unknown" (no. 7). Chance may have intervened in compositional planning only with *Music of Changes* (1952), but it already figures in Cage's work when he uses "two variable speed turntables" in *Imaginary Landscape No. 1* (1939), or when in *Bacchanale* of 1940 the objects in the prepared piano transform the normal sonority in ways that cannot be controlled by notation, or when a radio broadcast functions aleatorically in *Credo in Us* (1942). Cage's attraction to chance processes dates from well before 1951. It is just that he has not yet made it the main basis of his aesthetic.

In a letter probably written at the end of 1951 (no. 35), a long commentary on a work by Feldman gives a clear picture of what it is that separates Boulez from American music inspired by Cage. For the first time, he takes a firm stance against Cage's conception of chance. Concerning *Music of Changes* he writes:

> The only thing, forgive me, which I am not happy with, is the method of absolute chance (*by tossing the coins*). On the contrary, I believe that chance must be extremely controlled: by using tables in general, or series of tables, I believe that it would be possible to direct the phenomenon of the automatism of chance, whether written down or not ... there is already quite enough of the unknown.[50]

Boulez later gave a marvellously poetic description of the part played by the unknown in the creative process: "The unforeseeable surges forth from these given ideas which we have studied in detail ... Creativity resides solely in the passage from the unforeseeable to the necessary."[51] According to the accounts of the 1952 meeting collected by Peyser, in particular that of David Tudor,[52] Boulez distanced himself from the question of chance. But contrary to her statement,[53] Boulez did not cease writing to Cage after that trip. However, he does emphasize their differences more and more strongly. In 1953:

> I will have a discussion with you about the *Tape-Music* [*Williams Mix*]. For that will revive our conversations, which have already been animated, and seem certain once more to turn on the necessity of chance (no. 44).

In the following letters, Boulez mainly gives Cage news of his activities and of European artistic life. It is moreover symptomatic that after the New York

---

[50] This letter does not appear in the collection given to Northwestern Library. For the history of its transcription, see letter 35, note 1. Peyser quotes the passage as follows: "by temperament I cannot toss a coin ... Chance must be very controlled. Il y a suffisamment d'inconnu" (Peyser, p. 82).

[51] "Possibly ...", *Stocktakings*, p. 133.

[52] Peyser, p. 82.

[53] *Ibid.*, p. 85.

meeting Boulez kept only one of Cage's letters (no. 43). In June(?) 1954, just before plunging into the composition of *Le marteau sans maître*, Boulez is very clear about his orientation (no. 44). He refers to the end of an article which appeared in the Cahiers Renaud-Barrault:[54]

⌐We should see the work as a sequence of refusals in the midst of so many probabilities; a choice has to be made, and therein lies the difficulty which the expressed desire of 'objectivity' had conjured away so effectively ... The compositional act will never be assimilable to the fact of juxtaposing coincidences which are established in an immense statistical field.[55]

In the context of the article, this is clearly a self-criticism. Boulez is rejecting the unexpectedly chance-like character that results from the automatism of total serialism. Did Cage, in a letter now lost, think that these remarks were aimed at him? In any case, Boulez had not at this date formulated the type of aleatory form that he could not only tolerate but aspire to; he writes to Cage, "Obviously we disagree as far as that goes – I do not admit – and I believe I never will admit – chance as a component of a completed work. I am widening the possibilities of *strict* or *free* music (constrained or not). But as for chance, the thought of it is unbearable!" (no. 45). Boulez states that he is about to take up the theme of the last part of his article again in another text. This probably refers to "Alea",[56] but that had to wait three years; what he turned to immediately was the experimental Third Sonata, composed between 1955 and 1957 (Jameux no. 19).

Although Boulez speaks only of "adventurous research with chance" in the entry on Cage in the *Encyclopédie Fasquelle* (1958),[57] emphasizing Cage's contribution to the field of acoustic research proper, he does not mince words in the article "Alea":

At present, contemporary composers seem constantly preoccupied, not to say obsessed, by chance ... The most elementary form of chance transformation goes along with a philosophy tinged with orientalism, which covers up a basic weakness of compositional technique ... This experimenting with chance I term carelessness.[58]

Boulez makes an opposition between this use of chance – the refusal to choose and the transfer of responsibility to the performer[59] – and a "supervised

---

54 "... Auprès et au loin", *Cahiers de la Compagnie Madeleine Renaud Jean-Louis Barrault*, Year 2, no. 3, 1954, pp. 7–24; reprinted as "... Near and far", *Stocktakings*, pp. 141–57.
55 "... Near and Far", *Stocktakings*, p. 157.
56 "Alea", *Nouvelle revue française*, no. 59, 1 November 1957, pp. 839–57; reprinted in *Stocktakings*, pp. 26–38.
57 This article was not reprinted in *Stocktakings*. This is undoubtedly why it is little known. See document 47.
58 "Alea", *Stocktakings*, p. 26.
59 *Ibid.*, p. 28.

parting of the ways", "a sort of labyrinth with several paths",[60] an evolving form,[61] a "directed chance".[62] The Third Piano Sonata illustrates his concept of aleatory form.

As is often Boulez's way, "Alea" does not mention anyone by name; Cage was not however deceived. If Joan Peyser's account is to be trusted, he reacted very badly: "After having repeatedly claimed that one could not do what I set out to do, Boulez discovered that Mallarmé *Livre*. It was a chance operation down to the last detail. With me the principle had to be rejected outright; with Mallarmé it suddenly became acceptable to him. Now Boulez was promoting chance, only it had to be *his* kind of chance."[63] There was still a big difference in practice; whereas Cage had given over a large part of the creative responsibility to the performer, Boulez continued to define each component of the musical texture down to the last detail. As he wrote to Cage in 1954, he proposed a music that would be "free" at the level of the courses it might follow (no. 45).

But must the *Livre* by Mallarmé, which came off the presses on 13 March 1957 in a volume collected by Jacques Schérer, be held to have had a decisive influence on the Third Sonata? Later, in "Sonate, que me veux-tu" (1960), Boulez would write:

> I reached the principle that I required [for the composition of the Third Sonata] when a book appeared which contained Mallarmé's posthumous notes for a projected 'Book', preceded by an excellent study of Mallarmé's intentions by Jacques Schérer. This was a revelation for me, in the strongest sense of the word ... More than being a confirmation, Mallarmé's *Livre* was final proof of the urgent necessity for poetic, aesthetic and formal renewal.[64]

To judge by the quantity of sketch material for the work held at the Paul Sacher Stiftung, it is most unlikely that Boulez could have conceived and written the Sonata between March and September 1957, when it was premièred at Darmstadt. On the other hand, it is not at all impossible that he had the idea of making the components movable after reading Schérer: since chance would only affect the ordering of blocks whose text would be otherwise entirely fixed, a few elements would suffice to make them mobile. It remains an open question. Boulez claimed in conversation with Deliège, "When I composed my Third Sonata in 1956–7, I had not yet read Mallarmé's *Livre*, since it was published at the end of 1957."[65] This is not accurate.

---

[60] *Ibid.*, p. 29.
[61] *Ibid.*
[62] *Ibid.*, p. 31.
[63] Peyser, p. 129.
[64] "Sonate, que me veux-tu", *Orientations*, pp. 143–55.
[65] *Par volonté et par hasard* (Paris: Seuil, 1975), p. 64; translated as *Conversations with Célestin Deliège* (London: Eulenberg, 1976).

Cage accuses Boulez of trying to appropriate the notion of chance for his own ends. And Joan Peyser, in her account of this stage in their relationship, explains everything in terms of Boulez's desire always to be the first. All this is fair, but is it not the right of any creative artist who is both active and aware of his own innovations? Witness Cage: "As contemporary music goes on changing in the way I am changing it what will be done is to more and more completely liberate sounds ... I am talking and contemporary music is changing."[66]

From a historical point of view, the scenario seems more complicated. By all accounts Cage sparked off a craze for chance, openness and indeterminacy in which sociopolitical and ideological factors were mixed with aesthetic and musical criteria. From 1952, all Cage's disciples – Wolff, Feldman, Brown – threw themselves into the adventure. Then there was Stockhausen, whom Boulez certainly admired more than Cage from this period on, and who had known how to reconcile rigour of composition with the use of chance in *Zeitmasse* (1955–6) and *Klavierstück XI* (1956). Boulez applied himself to the task of giving *his* response to the question of the open work in the face of this movement. But he did it without giving up in the slightest either his basic options or his personality. On the contrary, if the dialectic of formalism and a certain degree of indeterminacy is entirely consonant with the binary oscillations that can be observed throughout his thought and work, the choice of an aleatory form was a response to two problems of composition particular to Boulez: firstly, opposing the "chance through oversight" that is engendered by the mechanism of total serialism with a very controlled use of chance; and secondly, using the bias of the performer's choices to create a perpetual non-fixity of form so that it can never give way to fixed and recognizable stereotypes which would therefore be reproducible.

How did Cage react publicly to all this? With humour and irony, and without aggression. Brief allusions are scattered through the texts collected in *Silence*!

Cage clearly alludes to Boulez, without mentioning him by name, in *45' for a speaker* (1954):

Have you not lost your friend? No, sir, I have not lost my friend either. Is it interesting? It is and it isn't. But one thing is certain. They are with respect to counterpoint melody harmony rhythm and any other musical methods, *pointless*. All that is necessary is an empty space of time and letting it act in its magnetic way. Eventually there will be so much in it that it whistles. In order to apply it to all of these various characteristics he necessarily reduces it to numbers. He has also found a mathematical way of making a correspondence between rows. I remember as a child loving all the sounds even the unprepared ones; I liked them especially when itself in the jaws cheeks and tongue and the commentary says 'The most superficial way of trying to influence others is through talk that has

[66] "45' for a speaker", *Silence*, pp. 161 and 181.

nothing real behind it.' The influence produced by such mere tongue-wagging must necessarily remain insignificant.... *I believe* that one can arrive at directing the phenomenon of the automatism of Chance which I mistrust as a facility which is not absolutely necessary. For, in the end, in interpolations and interferences between different rows (when one of them passes from time-lengths to pitches, at the same time that another passes from intensities to attacks, etc.) there is already a sufficiency of the unknown.[67]

In *Music Lover's Field companion* (1954), Cage mixes the memory of his meetings in the Rue Beautreillis with a visit to an exhibition of mushrooms,[68] and then makes reference to the publication of Boulez's article "Recherches maintenant": "My friend Pierre Boulez ... is interested in music and parentheses and *italics*! This combination of interests seems to me excessive in number. I prefer my own choice of the mushroom. Furthermore it is avant-garde."[69]

Four years later (1958) – "Alea" had been published in the meantime – Cage's tone is more cutting: "Who's interested in Satie nowadays anyway? Not Pierre Boulez:[70] he has the twelve tones, governs la Domaine musicale [sic], whereas Satie had only the Group of Six and was called Le Maître d'Arcueil."[71] And from the same year:

Do you agree with Boulez when he says what he says? Are you getting hungry? Twelve. Why should you (you know more or less what you're going to get)? Will Boulez be there or did he go away when I wasn't looking? Why do you suppose the number 12 was given up but the idea of the series wasn't? Or was it? And if not, why not?[72]

In the same text, he makes a detailed comparison of European and American tendencies:

[67] *Ibid.*, pp. 177–8. The end of the passage quotes the beginning of Boulez's letter 35. Cf. note 49 above and letter 35, note 1. James Pritchett points out that this text is a collage of quotations from various sources, juxtaposed by chance procedures (which accounts for the strange grammar and apparent non sequiturs; the procedures are described in *Silence* pp. 146–7). The sources are as follows:
  "Have you not lost ... my friend either." ("Lecture on nothing", *Silence*, p. 118)
  "Is it interesting? ... is certain." (source unknown)
  "They are with respect ... *pointless*." ("Juilliard lecture", *A Year from Monday*, p. 100)
  "All that is necessary ... between rows." (new material)
  "I remember as a child ... especially when" ("Lecture on nothing", *Silence*, p. 115)
  "itself in the jaws ... insignificant." ("Communication", *Silence*, p. 45)
  "I believe ... sufficiency of the unknown." (no. 35 below)
  (RS)
[68] *Silence*, p. 275.
[69] *Ibid.*, p. 276.
[70] Boulez wrote in a fairly ironic manner on Satie in the article *Chien flasque* which appeared in 1952 in the *Revue musicale* no. 214, pp. 153–4. It is reprinted in *Orientations*, pp. 323–5.
[71] "Erik Satie" (1958), *Silence*, p. 77.
[72] "Communication" (1958), *Silence*, p. 48.

The american avant-garde, recognizing the provocative character of certain european works, of Pierre Boulez, Karlheinz Stockhausen, Henri Pousseur, Bo Nilsson, Bengt Hambraeus, has in its concerts presented them in performances, notably by David Tudor, pianist. That these works are serial in method diminishes somewhat the interest they enjoin. But the thoroughness of the method's application bringing a situation removed from conventional expectation frequently opens the ear. However, the european works present a harmoniousness, a drama, or a poetry which, referring more to their composers than to their hearers, moves in directions not shared by the american ones. Many of the american works envisage each auditor as central, so that the physical circumstances of a concert do not oppose audience to performers but dispose the latter around-among the former, bringing a unique acoustical experience to each pair of ears. Admittedly, a situation of this complexity is beyond control, yet it resembles a listener's situation before and after a concert – daily experience, that is, it appears such a continuum is not part of the european objective, since it dissolves the difference between 'art' and 'life'. To the unexperienced, the difference between the europeans and the americans lies in that the latter include more silence in their works. In this view the music of Nilsson appears as intermediate, that of Boulez and of the author as in opposition. This superficial difference is also profound, when silence, generally speaking, is not in evidence, the will of the composer is. Inherent silence is equivalent to denial of the will. 'Taking a nap, I pound the rice.' Nevertheless, constant activity may occur having no dominance of will in it. Neither as syntax nor structure, but analogous to the sum of nature, it will have arisen purposelessly.[73]

A 1959 article written by Cage for the *Darmstädter Beiträge* is even more radical; the author does not escape a certain triumphalism in his conviction that Boulez has merely taken up Cage's idea of chance for his own ends:

> The vitality that characterizes the current European musical scene follows from the activites of Boulez, Nono, Maderna, Pousseur, Berio, etc. There is in all of this activity an element of tradition, continuity with the past, which is expressed in each work as an interest in continuity whether in terms of discourse or organization. By critics this activity is termed post-Webernian. However, this term apparently means only music written after that of Webern, not music written *because* of that of Webern; there is no sign of *klangarbenmelodie*, no concern for discontinuity – rather a surprising acceptance of even the most banal of continuity devices; ascending or descending linear passages, crescendi and diminuendi, passages from tape to orchestra that are made imperceptible. The skills that are required to bring such events about are taught in the academies. However, this scene will change. The silences of American experimental music and even its technical involvements with chance operations are being introduced into new European music. It will not be easy, however, for Europe to give up Europe. It will, nevertheless, and must; for the world is one world now.[74]

---

[73] *Ibid.*, p. 53.
[74] "History of experimental music in the United States" (1959), *Silence*, pp. 74–5.

Happily, this correspondence ends well. Overcoming their aesthetic disagreements, Boulez wrote a last letter to Cage for his fiftieth birthday in September 1962 (no. 48). It can be gathered that Cage had written to him in order to get himself invited to Paris – but Boulez takes the opportunity to emphasize his old pal's birthday in a humorous and somewhat surrealistic letter, of the sort he had occasionally written to him before, and the numerological character of which perhaps alludes to their discussions in the fifties.

Aesthetically, for Boulez, the matter was closed. In 1970 he told Claude Samuel in a France-Culture broadcast:

> John Cage is responsible just as Satie is responsible. He had a beneficial influence to the extent that he helped to burst the fetters of 1950s discipline. He did it with ingenuity and naivety. There was much humour in his work, and this ingenuity in wanting to break down discipline by showing up its absurdity and academicism. But after that, he hardly had anything but imitations. Now, to imitate an act is to be just a performing monkey. No thought is involved, but only acts which repeat themselves. And it is tiresome to see what are practically always the same acts done again and again for twelve years.

And to Célestin Deliège concerning Cage in 1975:

> There are some things you must not want to do. What exactly is the an-aesthetic or anti-aesthetic programme? It is the passive acceptance of what is; it is a concept of abandonment ... The anti-social implications of such a position are so obvious for me that by that time one is fit for the fascist-type societies which leave you a coin to put in the slot. In my opinion, it is like wanting voluntarily to play the king's fool ... Indeed, I find it a truly repulsive state of mind, both wanting to play the king's fool in all his abject state, the fool of society, and giving that society a pretext for becoming a closed society with fascist tendencies.[75]

The last occasions on which Boulez and Cage met were strictly professional. In 1976 Boulez conducted the New York Philharmonic Orchestra in *Apartment House 1776*, "Material for a musicircus in observance of the bicentennial of the U.S.A.". In 1979 he invited Cage to IRCAM to perform another "——, —— —— Circus on ——", described as "a means of translating any book into music. *Roaratorio, an Irish Circus on Finnegans Wake* is a realization of this piece by John Cage and John Fulleman."[76] It is not impossible that, years later, *Roaratorio* represents a response on Cage's part, half ironic and half good-natured, to Boulez, who wrote concerning the Third Piano Sonata – the bone of contention –

> What drove me to write such a "sonata" for piano? It was more my literary experiences than musical considerations. In the final analysis, my current mode of thought took shape more as a result of reflection on literature than on music.[77]

[75] *Conversations with Célestin Deliège*, p. 111.
[76] *A John Cage Reader'*, p. 199.
[77] "Sonate, que me veux-tu", p. 143.

Whilst Cage moved more and more beyond chance towards the concept of the "happening", Boulez was never, throughout this exchange, going to disavow his responsibilities as composer. After the "blind alley" of total serialism, he pursued in turn each path of development available to him: he caused the creation of the institution and instrumental facilities for the performance of a large work in which all the parameters, shorn of their last links with tonality, are strictly related to one another. *Répons* can thus be seen in a long-term historical perspective as the final outcome of the conversations of 1949, a time when a young man of twenty-four heard of an aborted project for an experimental music centre and saw how a pragmatic machine could distort traditional parameters. But already at that time, with the Sonatine for flute and piano, the First and Second Piano Sonatas and the *Livre pour quatuor*, there was no question of giving up creative self-expression. For as far as responsibility goes, the opposition of Boulez and Cage rests essentially on the establishment of a fact that is rather forgotten by the advocates of chance: in the immediacy of improvisation, the musician can all too easily fall back on memory and stylistic cliché. In an unpublished letter, Boulez writes that

> All renewal in music – even renewal of materials – passes through the reorganization of compositional practice. I was quite alone in thinking that at the moment of dissemination and diaspora. Much was – and is – spoken of freedom; whilst this so-called freedom is nothing but a perfumed subjection to memory. The illusion in the cave.[78]

To sum up, it would seem that the tangential encounter between Boulez and Cage was based on a misunderstanding explicable by the context of the period. As Boulez wrote in 1990,

> At that time, there really wasn't anything apart from the asphyxiating academicism of Leibowitz. Messiaen had taken me to a certain point, and it was necessary to go beyond. And on the other hand, it is difficult to imagine today what attraction there was then in North America. Indeed, it was the same for Cage; the attraction of a continent to discover. The war had shattered its remoteness, and brought an immense prestige for whatever had to do with the future. USSR stood for ideology, US for modernity. Seen in retrospect, what a curious pair of alternatives![79]

Jean-Jacques Nattiez
University of Montreal

---

[78] Letter to J.-J. Nattiez, February 1985.
[79] Letter to J.-J. Nattiez, March 1990.

Letters and Documents

I

Pierre Boulez's introduction to
Sonatas and Interludes for prepared piano by
John Cage at Suzanne Tézenas's salon.[1]
probably 17 June 1949

Ladies and Gentlemen,

One's first reaction on hearing about John Cage's prepared piano might well be curiosity verging on amused scepticism. Some demented inventor can easily be pictured, a "piano de-tuner" doing his best to clothe the strings with metallicizing vegetation. More seriously, one thinks of a subtle and ingenious soundsmith, drawing new possibilities from the percussive aspects of the piano. The reality has more to do with questioning acoustic ideas received in the course of the evolution of Western music, ideas on which the most radical and challenging works are still based. Instead of giving what might be called pure sounds – fundamentals and natural harmonics – John Cage's prepared piano supplies us with complexes of frequencies. Moreover, we can find a precedent for this use of complex sounds in the central African instruments called *sanzas*. Immediately, a primordial question arises: does the traditional education which we have received – or submitted to – deprive us of a more refined acoustic sense?

The logic of the path that Cage has followed lies in his refusal to accept the currently received acoustic system as definitive, when the problem of how to create music arises.

John Cage was at first self-taught, and during that anarchistic period he set about destroying the notion of the octave and avoiding the successive repetition of any one note in two- and three-part counterpoint, using scales of twenty-five chromatic tones.[2] These essays took place at the same time as explorations in the field of abstract painting.

He abandoned painting to give himself over entirely to music. His ideas about how sounds might acquire a value in themselves through the refusal to use the octave or repetition led him to work under Schoenberg's supervision for three years.[3] It should be pointed out at once that Cage did not study

---

[1] The Paul Sacher Stiftung possesses a rough draft of this lecture in addition to the manuscript.

[2] The draft adds: "so that each sound is individualized and at least 9 sounds occur between repetitions". Cage's early twenty-five-note pieces include the Sonata for Two Voices (1933), Composition for Three Voices (1934) and Solo with Obbligato Accompaniment (1933–4) (information from JP).

[3] Draft: "Coincidence with Schönberg's ideas: don't repeat notes." The draft specifies that Cage also worked with one of Schoenberg's pupils, Adolph Weiss.

serial technique with him. In fact, when Schoenberg's pupil asked him to analyze his own works, Schoenberg replied: "That's none of your business!" Despite this off-putting response, Cage took up dodecaphonic composition. Between 1934 and 1937 he wrote several works using this method: five movements for piano entitled *Metamorphoses*, three movements for wind instruments, four movements for piano, and two pieces for flute duo.[4]

One feature of the use of the series in these works that should be noted here is that from the beginning it is divided up into static, rhythmically defined motives.[5] This is perhaps reminiscent of the division of the series into cells favoured by Webern.

In the course of composing these twelve-tone works, Cage came to realize that no matter how carefully the clichés of the old tonal language are avoided, the responsibility for them remains, for a large part, with our instruments which were created according to the requirements of that language. He therefore turned towards percussion, which was still under-explored and (with the exception of a few brief experiments) used only in a fairly rudimentary way. However, in order to organize a world of sounds of indefinite pitch, the composer could no longer rely upon the series: rhythm is the only architectonic element powerful enough to permit valid, non-improvised constructions. On the other hand, the composer suffers in terms of practical realization from the lack of numerous or varied instruments, being able to use only the traditional orchestral percussion section.

There are, therefore, two parts to Cage's research. Firstly, the writing of more or less abstract works, without specific instrumental composition; then, experimental essays in every area of struck sound. The instrumentation of these abstract works therefore stems from experimental discovery.[6] From this period dates a collection of objects all with interesting percussive properties, found by chance during various travels; with a small number of amateur colleagues, Cage founded a group and gave concerts devoted to his own works and those of the composers who responded to his call. A few names: Varèse, Russell, Lou Harrison, Johanna Beyer, Gerald Strang, Henry Cowell, José Ardevol, Amadeo Roldan, and Ray Green. So between 1938 and 1943 fifteen concerts took place in major cities of the United States. Here we should single out two very interesting projects: in Los Angeles Cage tried to set up a centre for experimental music where technicians and musicians would collaborate in acoustic research of all sorts, including the field of electronics, and at the

---

[4] The first two works referred to here are *Metamorphosis* for piano (1938) and *Music for Wind Instruments* for wind quintet (1938). The "four movements for piano" must refer to Two Pieces for piano (1935), and the "two pieces for flute duo" must be the Three Pieces for flute duet (1935) (information from JP).

[5] The draft specifies: "The series never appears in the works."

[6] The draft adds: "Ideas of rhythmic structure begin in 1938. Directs and writes music for dancers at the Cornish School (Washington) (Electronic Laboratory – work for electronic instrument and percussion)." At the Cornish School in Seattle, Cage met Merce Cunningham. The work in question was probably *Imaginary Landscape No. 1* for "two variable speed playbacks, frequency recordings, muted piano and cymbal" (1939).

Bauhaus, exiled by Nazism to Chicago, he taught a course entitled "Class in experiments with sound".

The works he composed at this time have titles such as the following: firstly the abstract works already mentioned: a quartet in four movements and a trio in nine movements.[7] Then came three *Constructions*: the first for metal instruments, the second for various instruments, and the third for non-resonant percussion and blown conch shell.[8] Then three *Imaginary Landscapes* for percussion and electronics, which can only be heard as recordings, since they have to be mixed.[9] This series of works culminates in the only deliberate attempt at collective music that I know of, called *Double Music* and composed in collaboration with Lou Harrison.[10] Wanting to revive the anonymity of medieval sculptors, the two composers decided the general plan and structural features of the work they were to write, shared out the task by giving themselves precise instructions and separated, working in complete isolation since they lived in different towns. John Cage has told me that when they put their respective scores together, absolutely nothing had to be changed in the resulting whole.

This is a curious fact, for it recalls – though with a quite different intent, which need not be spelt out – the experiments of certain French poets during the explosive period of surrealism.[11]

In 1940 Cage again came to distrust the external effects of noise, and realized the necessity for a more inward-looking music.[12] Noise does indeed have a very great immediate physical effect, but utilizing this is dangerous, since its novelty rapidly wears off. Once accustomed, the ear then has needs that are much more difficult to satisfy, because less immediate. A hackneyed dialectic between sound and silence is therefore found irreducibly at the root of writing music. At this point in his development Cage turned – half by chance, half by necessity[13] – to the piano, which he had dreamt of before, but still in a primitive way, from 1938 onwards. In 1942–3, his research narrowed and gradually produced the prepared piano such as you are going to hear today. After many cautious experiments[14] Cage tried to establish what objects

---

7 Quartet for four percussion instruments (1935); Trio for three percussionists (1936), but in three movements, not nine.

8 The first *Construction* (1939) is for percussion sextet, the second (1940) for percussion quartet and the third (1941) for percussion quartet.

9 See note 6 for *Imaginary Landscape No. 1. No. 2* is for percussion quintet, *No. 3* for percussion sextet.

10 For percussion quartet (1941).

11 The draft refers to the percussion orchestra founded by Lou Harrison and to the concert given by amateur players at the Museum of Modern Art in New York.

12 The draft specifies: "Because of international and social events."

13 The resort to the prepared piano (beginning with *Totem Ancestor* in 1942) is explained in the draft by the difficulty in engaging professional musicians to accompany dance productions.

14 The draft has: "Discovery of the prepared piano by chance, during experimental research. A black female dancer created an African dance, using elementary rhythms. Since the theatre did not have an orchestral pit, a piano was required." The process by

could remain stable between the strings of a piano,[15] what were the materials to use and how they should be placed; from this he deduced the necessity of modifying duration, amplitude, frequency, and timbre – in other words, the four characteristics of a sound. To facilitate realization, he used everyday objects such as screws, nails, nuts, felt, rubber, and pennies wedged vertically between two strings or horizontally straddling the three strings relating to a key.

Using the *una corda* pedal would therefore also modify the pitches, since the hammer, shifted sideways, would strike only two strings out of three.

The four characteristics of a sound having been altered in this way, each one is given a new individuality. Obviously, anyone can exercise his ingenuity to enrich this as yet largely unexplored realm with new possibilities. John Cage himself varies the preparation of the piano with each new work.

John Cage began writing for prepared piano, though only dance pieces, from 1938 onwards, whilst he was composing works for percussion. Chamber music pieces date only from 1943: of these I shall mention *A Book of Music*[16] for two pianos, written for the two American pianists Robert Fizdale and Arthur Gold; Three Dances, also for two pianos,[17] recorded by Maro Ajemian and William Masselos; and finally the collection of sixteen sonatas and four interludes[18] that you are about to hear. John Cage interrupted work on these sonatas in order to write a ballet for conventional orchestra.[19] For this, he transferred the principle of the prepared piano to the orchestra, though obviously not by preparing every instrument, as many might jokingly have assumed. Instead of employing pure sounds, he makes use of sound complexes. To put it more clearly, John Cage writes chords in place of notes, each chord having no harmonic function but acting essentially as a resonance-amalgam of superimposed frequencies. A peculiar way to write, but linked entirely logically to his preceding experiments in tackling the normal orchestra.

I have so far spoken only of Cage's research in the realm of sound materials. I should like also to follow his progress as a composer. First of all, as we have seen, it was a question of negating the traditional harmonic system based on the repetition of different scales at the distance on an octave. Then came the desire to give each sound a prominent individuality.[20] As is well known, harmonic structure is the underlying principle of all classical construction. Ever since Debussy and Wagner, composers have had to give it up.

which Cage came to develop the prepared piano is described by him in "How the piano came to be prepared", *Empty Words*, pp. 7–9. (JP)

[15] The draft adds: "The resonance displacing the objects".

[16] *A Book of Music*, for two prepared pianos (1944).

[17] Three Dances, for two prepared pianos (1945). Recorded on DISC 643 (issued in 1949).

[18] Written between 1946 and 1948.

[19] The title of the ballet is *The Seasons* (1949); it also exists in a piano version.

[20] The draft mentions "chamber music works" dated in 1943 by Boulez: *Amores*, two solos for prepared piano with two trios for percussion, *A Room* for piano or prepared piano and *The Perilous Night* for prepared piano (1944).

When Cage got rid of the twelve-tone series, a strongly characterized rhythmic structure became necessary to him as a support for the musical argument. John Cage came to the conclusion that in order to build this construction, a purely formal, impersonal idea was required: that of numerical relations. To take a simple example, a primary section of ten bars has a corresponding development of ten times ten bars, where primary section and development may both be divided irregularly. Further, the proportions of the primary section are replicated in the development: in other words, a given number of one-bar units will give rise to an equal number of units in the development. Finally, these structures take account as exactly as possible of the passing of real time: that is, two bars at a slow tempo, for instance, will be made to correspond to four or five bars in a faster tempo. In this way an *a priori* numerical structure arises which the composer describes as prismatic and which I should prefer to call a crystallized structure. In his first works to make use of these structures, John Cage uses whole numbers.

In the *Sonatas and Interludes*, though, he uses fractions. Moreover, he tries to combine the *a priori* structure of his earlier works with the simplest classical structure, that of two repeated halves, as in Scarlatti. In a desire to avoid academic formalism, he has not taken up the architecture of the pre-classical sonata exactly; here the two parts are in opposition to each other, mainly through contrasts, a feature which also recalls the two themes of a Beethovenian exposition. So we see cross-breeding taking place within a pre-classical architectural design, in which the main part is played not by tonal logic (tonic-dominant, dominant-tonic), but rather by an *a priori* rhythmic structure. Finally, to avoid obvious repetitions of passages – and relating to the constant variation of the twelve-tone method – John Cage uses the idea of constant invention, which avoids the idea of classical development, since in this way everything becomes development, or, if you like, everything is thematic. This freedom of invention thus operates in contrast to the invariant factors, the rhythmic structure and the musical scale.

I would not wish to draw conclusions about this work before you have heard it: that would be rather silly and sloppy. Nevertheless, I will go so far as to point out two fairly important facts. The first, as the composer himself recognizes, is that the structure of these sonatas brings together a pre-classical structure and a rhythmic structure which belong to two entirely different worlds; this combination cannot possibly be imagined without recourse to an extra-musical dialectic, a breeding-ground for dangerous ambiguities.

The second point I would like to comment on is the question of giving <u>at the outset</u> an individuality to each sound. If this individuality is unvarying for the whole of an extended work, a global and hierarchical neutrality results in the scale of frequencies because of their repetition over time. In other words, a mode of multiple frequencies arises; and one might overdo it and fall into the very trap that one wanted to avoid at all costs. Here I would remark, however, that this polarization is already richer with two pianos prepared differently, given the interference patterns – of sorts – created by the two modes so established. By contrast, if each sound is treated as absolutely neutral – as for example in Webern – the context causes each sound to take on a different individuality each time that it appears.[21]

This sort of reversibility of cause and effect might perhaps be the basis for a discussion – and what a perilous one! – of the opportunity, effectiveness and, I would gladly say, the necessity for reform to which the sonatas that you are about to hear bear witness.[22]

I should like to announce in closing that you will be able to hear a performance of the first of John Cage's Three Dances by Arthur Gold and Robert Fizdale, as part of their concert at the Salle Gaveau at 9 p.m. on the 24th of June.[23]

PB

2

Letter from Pierre Boulez to John Cage
between 20 and 24 May 1949

My dear friend,

I am writing in a hurry. Because the time and place for listening to the recordings of your music have been changed.[1]

It won't be on Thursday evening – I forgot that it is Ascension and these friends are not available. Instead we will be at one of the group's house on Friday afternoon at 3 p.m. Here is his address:

Maurice Jarre.
16 rue Henri-Tariel.
Issy-les-Moulineaux.
(Metro: Mairie d'Issy on the North-South line).

---

[21] The draft adds: "Each sound having to become an individual entity. This comes from Debussy: freedom of scales."

[22] The draft gives, in conclusion: "Function of music: personal integration. Harder to listen to music than to write music."

[23] The last sentence has been added in pencil. In places the manuscript includes brackets added in pencil which are not reproduced in this edition: {} from the last sentence of paragraph three to the first of paragraph four (These essays ... entirely to music), a single bracket, {, in the last sentence of paragraph seven, before "electronic", and another bracket, {, in paragraph fifteen before "multiplied".

[1] These recordings must have included the *First Construction (in Metal)*, which Boulez owned, and the Three Dances for two prepared pianos (cf. no. 6 and no. 8, note 3).

As getting there is a bit complicated, I shall call for you at your hotel around 2.15 on Friday afternoon.

Best wishes,

PB

P. Boulez – 4. rue Beautreillis.

3

Letter from Pierre Boulez to John Cage
November 1949[1]

[upside down:] *Perhaps, you will have the visit of Nicole Henriot, a very good young pianist, who is a good friend of Souvtchinsky and myself. I have gived your adress and your telephone-number. She is very wonderful, and very nice (that is always a pleasure!).*

My dear John,
What are the news on your travel? Gatti, Joffroy, Souvtchinsky etc ..., we should be very glad to know what you became since your return in U.S.A. I hope you have found your home and you are working very hard, perhaps! It is probably the reason of your silence, maybe! (Excuse my very bad english!)

Here, nothing! or a little only. However, I have heared (?) Pierrot Lunaire, in a very wonderful performance by Marya Freund, and Italian musicians under Pietro Scarpini. I remember these are who have played in Palermo. I had made a great "paper" on Ravel, Stravinsky, Schönberg for "Contrepoints"[2] and I added a little text to say many good things on Marya Freund (in opposition with

---

[1] This letter was only sent to Cage in January 1950. It can be dated from Boulez's remarks in no. 6.

[2] This refers to "Trajectoires", published in *Contrepoints*, no. 6 (1949), pp. 122–42. Reprinted as "Trajectories: Ravel, Stravinsky, Schoenberg" in *Stocktakings*, pp. 188–205. In the later version, Boulez excised everything that gave the 1949 article the character of an up-to-the-moment review, and changed "I" to "we". The original text is prefaced by the following long note:

> The performance took place last July, at the Salle de Géographie, and it was indeed "something to make us listen" ... In fact, we watched a person – whom I would not have the audacity to call a conductor – with aggressive shoulders and flexed knees, sweat profusely, with no great apparent result; we pretended to hear singing; and we applauded the skills of the soloists of the Orchestre National unreservedly, so evident were their exceptional qualities despite these impedimenta which did little to exploit them.
>
> I might be accused of being too easily inclined to blasphemous exaggeration: nevertheless, I should be allowed to doubt the musicality of a "conductor" who lets

Leibowitz!) and Scarpini. We had also the "Erwartung" of Schönberg for his "75 geburstage" (the madness of the birthdays in Vienna School). But I want hear it, because I was at Marigny for the money.[3] In the next days (—middle of December, we will have Wozzek, the complete work. (not on a stage, but only in a performance). Nothing of Webern for the moment.

Do you remember Scelsi, the italian musician, with whom we eated on 1 evening of July, before going to see Marina Scriabine(!!) and Boris de Schloezer? and of whom we heared the stringquartet with Souvtchinsky? Désormière plays a "Cantate" by him; the title is "Naissance du Verbe"; you must not understand

the piano drift a quarter-tone out of tune with the other instruments; who bothers so little about orchestral balance that the instrumental ensemble seemed faulty in its conception; who is very probably not at all disturbed by *Sprechstimme*, to surmise from the fact that it was constantly magicked away. We could add many other complaints, if we were not left with a certain feeling of pity – even if quite misplaced – which bids us remain silent about this sort of adventure which combines the demonstration of physical culture with a ceremony of cremation: M Leibowitz is in the habit, indeed, of having one of his pupils read out, at the beginning of the concert, a juicy "obituary", in which technique, poetics, and philosophy interweave in the dustiest garlands, with not the happiest of results. All this means that each of M Leibowitz's concerts remind me of one of La Fontaine's fables about a bear, an amateur gardener, a fly, and a paving slab.

And here is the postscript which Boulez mentions to Cage:

Nevertheless, an exceptional performance of *Pierrot Lunaire* – by Marya Freund and the Rome Philharmonic Ensemble conducted by Pietro Scarpini – exceptional in quality and in cohesion, obliged us to recognize the mastery of sound and the unquestionable effectiveness of the "feel" of this work, and this despite the distance – of which I have spoken – that separates us from the aesthetic of its elaboration, at the same time post-romantic and expressionist.

The real, immediate emotion seems to me to stem especially from the use of *Sprechstimme*; in keeping with the original destination of the work (which was commissioned from Schoenberg by the actress Albertine Zehme), Marya Freund candidly exploits the diction of its text, without thereby neglecting the perfect accuracy of spoken intervals: thus enabling herself to be perfectly happy with the marked tempo and with a tessitura which at first sight might seem difficult and even inaccessible. It gives one an impression of naturalness: the instrumental ensemble comes to have the pre-eminent position, and the voice, situating itself on a different (acoustic) plane, doesn't have to struggle for power in the same (musical) domain.

Moreover, the technical perfection of this instrumental ensemble – honed over many months by continual work – and its perfect ease in face of performance difficulties, can enable it to achieve a transparency and balance of sound which can put over the many variations of shading in *Pierrot Lunaire*.

However transitional the character of this work – as in the realm of its language as in that of its implied aesthetic –, nevertheless one is still confronted by a musical fact whose unique success is undeniable. Even after this hearing, it still seems to me that the best pieces are not the ones intended humorously in the third cycle, nor certain "over-dramatic" pieces; my preferences lie with the "half-tint" pieces, where the expression is realized by musical means of perhaps greater flexibility. (In particular I would note the first piece of the first cycle, and, in its stark purity, the seventh, for flute and voice).

This "unique" character justifies, once and for all, the privileged – indeed symbolic – rôle which has been given to it in the evolution of musical writing even though its language, in the final analysis, is not very different from that of the works that surround it.

[3] Boulez was musical director for the Compagnie Renaud-Barrault (1946–56).

must not understand the word *"Verbe"* as λογος *(in Apocalypse!)*, but only as birth of the words! – The first movement is for the unarticulated sounds and *"Voyelles"*; the second for the *"consonnes"*; and the third for the ensemble of these various elements. As you can see, it is very happy! But no funny! But I criticize it before having heared! and I go to-morrow to the repetition [i.e. rehearsal].

For the publication,[4] it is *"on the road" (in the ways?)*. I went to Heugel rue Vivienne, and I saw the printer, who had some difficulties with the number of quaver or semi-quaver *(I don't remember exactly)*.

But it is, now, for me not very interesting. I do not put, at the end, the poem of Michaux[5] for writing my next work for *(various)* voices and *(various)* orchestras! – I have returned to my first loves, that is the *"Poème pulvérisé"* of René Char, to which I have thinked since a year. It will be a *"great work"!!* *(firework or water music)*.[6] But with all these *"hesitations"*, I have not written only a dirty little thing. I have translated *(am translating – more correctly! –)* songs of Char *(written three years ago)*, entitled *"Visage Nuptial"* for large orchestra and voice.[7] I remake the instrumental combinations. It is interesting, but hard! I rather like compose. But I <u>must</u> do that ... and my symphony![8]

Perhaps, – it is not very sure indeed – I come in South America during three months *(May, June, July 1950)* with J. L. Barrault! I dream over that; I would

---

4 This refers to the Second Piano Sonata, published by Heugel in 1950.

5 Boulez did not compose *Poésie pour pouvoir* until 1958, but it is noteworthy that this collection of poems, published by Drouin in 1949, was in fact available to him when this letter was written.

6 *Le soleil des eaux* went through four versions (Jameux 9a–9d). The first version, a piece for radio premièred in April 1948, did not have the two poems contained in the suite: "La complainte du lézard amoureux", and "La sorgue. Chanson pour Yvonne", which belong to two special collections (and not to the text of the piece); "Les matinaux" (first published by Gallimard, 20 January 1950); and "Fureur et mystère" (Gallimard, 14 September 1948). At the time of writing this letter, Boulez could not have known "La complainte". It is therefore probable that he was looking for texts for the new concert version of *Le soleil* in *Le poème pulvérisé*, published by Éditions Fontaine on 2 May 1947. The fact that Boulez refers to what was to be the second version of *Le soleil des eaux*, first performed on 18 July 1950 (cf. no. 8, note 9, and no. 24), seems borne out by the Handelian pun he allows himself here.

7 *Le visage nuptial* had first existed in a two-movement version for soprano, contralto, two Ondes Martenot, piano and percussion in 1946–7, first performed in 1947 and not published. The version referred to by Boulez here (for soprano, contralto, women's choir, and large orchestra) was not to be premièred until 4 December 1957. This letter and nos. 13 and 24 suggest earlier dates of composition for this work than 1951–2 (given as Jameux no. 7). Four of the work's five movements were the subject of later revisions (1986–7) and were first performed in their new form in London on 25 January 1988. The complete revised version was given in Metz on 16 November 1989, then at the Autumn Festival in Paris on 17, in Milan on 19, and in London on 23 November.

8 This refers to the 1947 *Symphonie concertante* for piano and orchestra, lost in 1954 (Jameux no. 8). Boulez quotes four bars from it in his 1948 article "Proposals" (see *Stocktakings*, p. 52). The Paul Sacher Foundation possesses four pages of sketches and two pages of short score, and a single page of sketches is found with the manuscript of the Second Piano Sonata in the Boulez archive given by Cage to Northwestern University.

like very much a long travel (15 days on a boat for going – and id. for the return; i.e. "a month on the sea"; a good title for a charming song as one of Frank Sinatra!). We go, may be, in the great towns of Bresil, Argentine, Chili etc ... with Hamlet,[9] Le Procès,[10] etc ... what do you think of that? It is not wonderful? I am not very "Flying ... man", but for one time only, why not?

A propos, the C.C.C. (Cercle Culturel du Conservatoire), organisation for young composers and more generally young people which is working at the conservatoire, has asked me to show your records of music for percussion and to explain your rhythmic Constructions. I would like you send me a table of all the instruments you have used and the manner to use. I shall say on you that I have said when you have played in Lady Tézenas'sssss house.[11] But I would like can tell you much more with the precision And the C.C.C. asked me also to say the experiences of myself, in a "parallele" way with yours. I think I shall talk about that during January or February. Send me all the documents necessary for that.

Have you seen Messiaen in New-York? I believe it is actually at Boston for the first performance of Turangalila[12] (by a music composer and rhythmician!), this symphony in many movements and being longer (increasing) in few years. (until the people becomes whole crazy). Have you heared the famous (??!) concerto for Martenot by Jolivet?[13] It is absolutely zero.

Gatti, Saby, Joffroy, Souvtchinsky send to you the better remember, and are weeping (or tearing? I want say: pleurer) after your very parisian figure. – For you, you must give the "good day" – a frenchicism! – to all the friends (a friendicism!) whom you have known in Paris, Merce Cunningham, Maro Ajemian, Gold, Fizdale, Heliker, Brown[14], etc ..., etc ... I hope you don't forget us! as we don't forget you! With this word seeming as a holy word of holy book, I send to you my better thinking. And you can say that my very bad english linguage has been a very hard – labour! As for the "Assimili", you must send me

---

9 André Gide's translation of *Hamlet* was performed by the Compagnie Renaud-Barrault at the Marigny theatre from 17 October 1946. It is noteworthy that Barrault specifies in his *Souvenirs pour demain* (Paris: Seuil, 1972, p. 192) that the accompanying music consisted of a combination of recorded and instrumental sounds, and that it was signed Maurice Jarre-Pierre Boulez (no catalogue of Boulez's works gives a specific composition for this production).

10 This refers to André Gide and Jean-Louis Barrault's adaptation of Kafka's novel *The Trial*, published by Gallimard in 1947. The work was first performed by the Compagnie Renaud-Barrault at the Marigny theatre on 10 October 1947.

11 Cf. no. 1.

12 The American première of Messiaen's *Turangalîla Symphony* was given by the Boston Symphony orchestra on 2 December 1949, with Yvonne Loriod as solo pianist, conducted by Leonard Bernstein.

13 The Concerto for Ondes Martenots by André Jolivet (1947).

14 This is Merton Brown, not to be confused with Earle Brown, whose name is frequently associated with Cage, but whom Cage did not meet until a tour with Cunningham in 1951 (personal communication from John Holzaepfel).

my letter after having written all the mistakes!!! And I will buy a grammar and a dictionnary.
Your old fellow, now.

PB

4

Letter from John Cage to Pierre Boulez

Sunday, 4 December [1949]

My dear friend,

A few days ago, I met a Parisian from the Salabert Company (Rouart Lerolle?), and after we had been talking a little, he told me that he wants to see your Sonata for 2 Pianos.[1] If it is not published in Paris, we could always get it published here.

More good news: the "League of Composers" wishes to put on your music here 'for the first time'. I think they have chosen the Second Piano Sonata[2] and that William Masselos is keen to work on it.

I have returned to an apartment which has been demolished (luckily, though, because now it is new). The man who was here decided to study the piano. In order to accomplish this simple project he wrote the names of the notes on the ivories using 'crayons' (in English that means children's colours, – they are most free of the effects of time, – permanent (Pompei)). Etc. etc. you can see what I mean by the word "demolished".

At the moment I am writing some film music (Calder's mobiles).[3] I think constantly of my friends in Paris, of you and your music, of Gatti, wife, child

---

[1] Gerald Bennett gives the information that part of the first (radio) version of *Le soleil des eaux* already existed as a movement for two pianos ("Passacaglia. Variations"), which, combined with the two movements of the Quartet for four Ondes Martenots of 1945–6, formed the Sonata for two pianos of 1948 (G. Bennett, "The early works", in *Pierre Boulez, a Symposium*, ed. W. Glock. London: Eulenberg, 1986, p. 66). These two works (Jameux no. 4) have been withdrawn from the catalogue.

[2] The Second Piano Sonata (Jameux no. 11) was composed between May 1946 and 1948 and first performed on 29 April 1950 by Yvette Grimaud at the École Normale de Musique concert hall in Paris. Therefore the work had not yet been performed in public when Cage was planning the American première. Boulez gave him the sketches and autograph (see no. 25, note 2).

[3] This refers to the music for Herbert Matter's film *Works of Calder*. The music won first prize at the Woodstock Film Festival in 1951. The producer was Burgess Meredith, later a well-known actor. (personal communication by Frans van Rossum)

and poetry, Saby and Souvtchinsky. Give my regards to all but especially to yourself.

John

*I would like
to hear something about
'sound space'.*[4]

326 Monroe St., New York 2, N.Y.

5

Article by John Cage 'Forerunners of modern music'
March 1949[1]

The purpose of music

Music is edifying, for from time to time it sets the soul in operation. The soul is the gatherer-together of the disparate elements (Meister Eckhart), and its work fills one with peace and love.

Definitions

Structure in music is its divisibility into successive parts from phrases to long sections. Form is content, the continuity. Method is the means of controlling the continuity from note to note. The material of music is sound and silence. Integrating these is composing.

Strategy

As is repeated below schematically (Fig. 1), structure is properly mind-controlled. Both delight in precision, clarity, and the observance of rules. Whereas, form wants only freedom to be. It belongs to the heart; and the law it observes, if indeed it submits to any, has never been and never will be

[4] Cage may be referring here to the essays in spatialisation of sound in the earliest experiments in *musique concrète* that Boulez was soon to embark on. He tells Cage about these from the following month onwards (see no. 6 note 4).

[1] This article first appeared in the March 1949 issue of *The Tiger's Eye*, a journal edited by Ruth and John Stephan from Bleecker Street in New York. It was translated into French by Frederick Goldbeck, who changed the title to *Raison d'être de la musique moderne*. This was published in *Contrepoints* (Paris) later in the same year. It appeared again, without the diagram, in *Silence*, pp. 62–6. Footnotes 2–16 of this document are by John Cage.

written.[2] Method may be planned or improvised (it makes no difference: in one case, the emphasis shifts towards thinking, in the other towards feeling; a piece for radios as instruments would give up the matter of method to accident). Likewise, material may be controlled or not, as one chooses. Normally the choice of sounds is determined by what is pleasing and attractive to the ear: delight in the giving or receiving of pain being an indication of sickness.

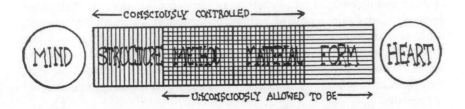

Refrain

Activity involving in a single process the many, turning them, even though some seem to be opposites, towards oneness, contributes to a good way of life.

The plot thickens

> *When asked why, God being good, there was evil in the world, Sri Ramakrishna said: To thicken the plot.*

The aspect of composition that can properly be discussed with the end in view of general agreement is structure, for it is devoid of mystery. Analysis is at home here.

Schools teach the making of structures by means of classical harmony. Outside school, however (e.g., Satie and Webern), a different and correct[3] structural means reappears: one based on lengths of time[4,5].

In the Orient, harmonic structure is traditionally unknown, and unknown

---

[2] Any attempt to exclude the 'irrational' is irrational. Any composing strategy which is wholly 'rational' is irrational in the extreme.

[3] Sound has four characteristics: pitch, timbre, loudness and duration. The opposite and necessary coexistent of sound is silence. Of the four characteristics of sound, only duration involves both sound and silence. Therefore, a structure based on durations (rhythmic: phrase, time-lengths) is correct (corresponds with the nature of the material), whereas harmonic structure is incorrect (derived from pitch which has no being in silence).

[4] This never disappeared from jazz and folk-music. On the other hand, it never developed in them, for they are not cultivated species, growing best when left wild.

[5] Tala is based on pulsation; western rhythmic structure on phraseology.

with us in our pre-Renaissance culture. Harmonic structure is a recent Occidental phenomenon, for the past century in a process of disintegration[6].

Tonality[7] has happened

The disintegration of harmonic structure is commonly known as atonality. All that is meant is that two necessary elements in harmonic structure, the cadence, and modulating means, have lost their edge. Increasingly, they have become ambiguous, whereas their very existence as structural elements demands clarity (singleness of reference). Atonality is simply the maintenance of an ambiguous tonal state of affairs. It is the denial of harmony as a structural means. The problem of a composer in a musical world in this state is precisely to supply another structural means[8], just as in a bombed-out city, the opportunity to build again exists[9]. This way one finds courage and a sense of necessity.

"But one must achieve this unselfconsciousness by means of transformed knowledge. This ignorance does not come from lack of knowledge but rather it is from knowledge that one may achieve this ignorance. Then we shall be informed by the divine unconsciousness and in that our ignorance will be ennobled and adorned with supernatural knowledge. It is by reason of this fact that we are made perfect by what happens to us rather than by what we do."

At random

Music means nothing as a thing.

A finished work is exactly that, requires resurrection.

The responsibility of the artist consists in perfecting his work so that it may become attractively disinteresting.

---

[6] For an interesting detailed proof of this, see Casella's book on the cadence.

[7] The term, atonality, makes no sense. Schoenberg substitutes 'pantonality,' Lou Harrison (to my mind and experience the preferable term), 'proto-tonality.' This last term suggests what is actually the case: present even in a random multiplicity of tones (or, better, sounds [so as to include noises]), is a gravity, original and natural, 'proto,' to that particular situation. Elementary composition consists in discovering the ground of the sounds employed, and then letting life take place both on land and in the air.

[8] Neither Schoenberg nor Stravinsky did this. The twelve tone row does not offer a structural means; it is a method, a control, not of the parts, large and small, of a composition, but only of the minute, note-to-note procedure. It usurps the place of counterpoint, which, as Carl Ruggles, Lou Harrison, and Merton Brown have shown, is perfectly capable of functioning in a chromatic situation. Neo-classicism, in reverting to the past, avoids, by refusing to recognize, the contemporary need for another structure, gives a new look to structural harmony. This automatically deprives it of the sense of adventure, essential to creative action.

[9] The twelve tone row offers brick-layers [changed to "bricks" in *Silence*], but no plan. The neo-classicists advise building it the way it was before, but surfaced fashionably.

It is better to make a piece of music than to perform one, better to perform one than to listen to one, better to listen to one than to misuse it as a means of distraction, entertainment, or acquisition of 'culture'.

Use any means to keep from being a genius, all means to become one.

Is counterpoint good? "The soul itself is so simple that it cannot have more than one idea at a time of anything.... A person cannot be more single in attention." (Eckhart)

Freed from structural responsibility, harmony becomes a formal element (serves expression).

Imitating either oneself or others, care should be taken to imitate structure not form (also structural materials and structural methods not formal materials and formal methods), disciplines, not dreams; thus, one remains "innocent and free to receive anew with each Now-movement a heavenly gift." (Eckhart)

If the mind is disciplined, the heart turns quickly from fear towards love.

Before making a structure by means of rhythm, it is necessary to decide what rhythm is.

This could be a difficult decision to make if the concern were formal (expressive) or to do with method (point to point procedure); but since the concern is structural (to do with divisibility of a composition into parts large and small), the decision is easily reached: rhythm in the structural instance is relationships of lengths of time.[10] Such matters, then, as accents on or off the beat, regularly recurring or not, pulsation with or without accent, steady or unsteady, durations motivically conceived (either static or to be varied), are matters for formal (expressive) use, or, if thought about, to be considered as material (in its 'textural' aspect) or as serving method. In the case of a year, rhythmic structure is a matter of seasons, months, weeks, and days. Other time-lengths such as that taken by a fire or the playing of a piece of music occur accidentally or freely without explicit recognition of an all-embracing order, but, nevertheless, necessarily within that order. Coincidences of free events with structural time points have a special luminous character, because the paradoxical nature of truth is at such moments made apparent. Caesurae on the other hand are expressive of the independence (accidental or willed) of freedom from law, law from freedom.

Claim

Any sounds of any qualities and pitches (known or unknown, definite or indefinite), any contexts of these, simple or multiple, are natural and conceivable within a rhythmic structure which equally embraces silence. Such a

---

10 Measure is literally measure, nothing more, for example, than the inch on a ruler, thus permitting the existence of any durations, any amplitude relations (metre, accent), any silences.

claim is remarkably like the claims to be found in patent-specifications for and articles about technological musical means (see early issues of Modern Music and the Journal of the Acoustical Society of America). From different beginning points, towards possibly different goals, technologists and artists (seemingly by accident) meet by intersection, becoming aware of the otherwise unknowable (conjunction of the in and the out), imagining brightly a common goal in the world and in the quietness within each human being.

For instance:

Just as art as sand-painting (art for the now-moment[11] rather than for posterity's museum-civilization) becomes a held point of view, adventurous workers in the field of synthetic music (e.g. Norman McLaren) find that for practical and economic reasons work with magnetic wires (any music so made can quickly and easily be erased, rubbed-off) is preferable to that with film.[12]

The use of technological means[13] requires the close anonymous collaboration of a number of workers. We are on the point of being in a cultural situation[14], without having made any special effort to get into one[15] (if one can discount lamentation).

The in-the-heart path of music leads now to self-knowledge through self-denial, and its in-the-world path leads likewise to selflessness.[16] The heights that now are reached by single individuals at special moments may soon be densely populated.

---

[11] This is the very nature of the dance, of the performance of music, or any other art requiring performance (for this reason, the term, sand-painting, is used: there is a tendency in painting (permanent pigments), as in poetry (printing, binding), (e.g.), to be secure in the thingness of a work, and thus to overlook, and place nearly insurmountable obstacles in the path of, instantaneous ecstasy).

[12] 24 or n frames per second is the 'canvas' upon which this music is written; thus, in a very obvious way, the material itself demonstrates the necessity for time (rhythmic) structure. With magnetic means, freedom from the frame of film means exists, but the principle of rhythmic structure should hold over as, in geometry, a more elementary theorem remains as a premise to make possible the obtaining of those more advanced.

[13] "I want to be thought new-born, knowing nothing, absolutely nothing about Europe." (Paul Klee).

[14] Replete with new concert halls: the movie houses (vacated by home television fans, and too numerous for a Hollywood whose only alternative is 'seriousness').

[15] Painting in becoming literally (actually) realistic (this is the 20th century) seen from above, the earth, snow-covered, a composition of order super-imposed on the "spontaneous" (Cummings) or of the latter letting order be (from above, so together, the opposites, they fuse) (one has only to fly (highways and topography, Mila-repa, Henry Ford) to know) automatically will reach the same point (step by step) the soul leapt to.

[16] The machine fathers mothers heroes saints of the mythological order (works only when it meets with acquiescence (cf. The King and the Corpse, Zimmer-Campbell).

6

Letter from Pierre Boulez to John Cage
3, 11 and 12 January 1950—
attached to letter of November 1949 (no. 3) and sent with it

My dear John,

I must seem a right sod not to have thanked you for Finnegan's [sic] Wake, which I enjoyed so much; nor to have told you any news; nor to have replied to you. I shall never get to the end of the grievances mounting against me. You should know that I wrote a first letter, wholly in English – you will appreciate such a worthy effort – and that I found it amongst my papers when I thought I had already sent it. I didn't date it, but it must be from the end of November. Since it is now 3 January, I realize that I really am very late.

I am sending it to you anyway, as evidence that I have thought of you since you left, and that the lack of news is due to a reparable – if annoying – oversight.

This letter won't be in English because that really is very tiring, and my grammar is still too shaky. Anyway, here is some news.

First of all, publication is still moving ahead. I have corrected the first proofs of my Second Sonata. A second lot of corrections will, I think, be needed; then it may be publishable. You will be the first to know, with a complimentary copy!

No. 6 of "Contrepoints" has just come out,[1] and you are sure to get it soon if you have not already done so; I read your article in it[2] which I liked a lot, and where I met your approach to form and method again. It made me go and read Meister Eckhardt.

I am taking up this letter again after several days' interruption for it is now 11 January!

I have just had news of you from P. Souvtchinsky and it made me feel all the more wretched because Gatti wrote to you some time ago and I am the only one who hasn't. This is quite inexcusable!

What can I tell you that is really new about my activities? Nothing of any importance. I have just embarked on the preparatory phase of my new work, which will indeed (as I indicated in my first letter) be Char's *Poème pulvérisé*.[3] I plan to put into practice in it some ideas derived from your pieces and what I explained to you about complex sounds – (using a grid of quarter-tones placed across the series: a grid which is the series in prime, inversion,

---

[1] See no. 3, note 2.
[2] See no. 5.
[3] I.e. *Le soleil des eaux* (cf. no. 3, note 6).

retrograde, retrog. inversion all a quarter tone below or above the original series or even more. This gives an infinite number of combinations for complex sounds. In addition, I am applying myself to an increasingly individualized kind of orchestration, with the result that the overall mass will arise from a series of extremely diverse constituents. I reckon that the percussion will have a most important role, taking part in the construction via the same phenomenon of rhythmic cells. As for the voices, they too will be extremely versatile, both in their deployment and in their relation to the text. The whole contained in a great architectural complex.

Keep me in touch with your own experiments, as much in the prepared piano field as with electronics etc... As for me, I may be going to try some experiments with P. Schaeffer.[4]

On that subject, I have met up with Woronow, the Belgian musician whom you mentioned to me. But he didn't have any music with him. Here's how we met. At Liège and Brussels there is a group of Belgian musicians, more or less all pupils or friends of Souris, who were in Paris for a few days, and, through Boris de Schloezer and Marina Scriabine, they asked to see me. So I showed them my quartet and I played them your percussion records and your prepared piano records, which none of them knew. They were bowled over by them, and sometime during February I have to go to Liège to give a lecture on your research and mine. I shall play some of your records (they were particularly struck by Construction in Metal).[5] In order to present these discs in a precise manner, I should like to be able to say exactly what instruments and rhythmic construction you used. If you could send me the score, that would be fine; but if not, you must send me the exact nomenclature of all the percussion instruments you used and indicate in what way you used them. (The gongs submerged in water; the piano with the iron cylinders to produce these rising glissandi during the resonance. I should like to know just how you get those rubbing effects, which sound to me like an iron whip or brush on the surface of a gong). I very much regret that we did not write down the nomenclature when you were in Paris.

After a lengthy consideration of your percussion research, I shall move on to the prepared piano, and with the disc and scores I shall be able to explain clearly what is involved. And when we have heard your discs, I shall play my second Sonata (two movements of it, at any rate), explaining what may link us in researching a work's structure by means of rhythmic structures. Is all that to your liking? Send me your suggestions, and don't forget to tell me what you

---

[4] Boulez had in fact written two *musique concrète* pieces, a study on a single sound and a study on a seven-sound chord (1951–2, Jameux nos. 13a and 13b). The second was released on a Barclay record. On the performances of the pieces in France, see no. 36, and in America, no. 40. On the structure of the first piece, see no. 35.

[5] *First Construction (in Metal)*, for percussion sextet and assistant, goes back to 1939. It was recorded on a "New music distribution service' disc by the Manhattan Percussion Ensemble, directed by Paul Price.

think is important about your work if I have left anything out, or about the two of us.

On that subject, let me tell you that you are the only person who has added an anxiety about the sound materials I use. Meeting you made me end a "classical" period with my quartet,[6] which is well behind me now. Now we have to tackle <u>real</u> "delirium" in sound and experiment with sounds as Joyce does with words. Basically – as I am pleased to discover – I have explored nothing as yet and everything remains to be looked for in fields as varied as sound, rhythm; orchestra, voices; architecture. We have to achieve an "alchemy" in sound (see Rimbaud) to which all I have done so far is merely a prelude and which you have greatly clarified for me.

As for concerts during all this time, we have not been spoiled. <u>Nothing at all</u> worth bothering about.

If you get "Contrepoints,", tell me what you think of my article "Trajectoires". I am writing one for the second issue on Bach and his importance for today.[7] This will be 1) an attack on all the official fossilized teaching claiming to derive from Bach but actually going against him –; 2) a violent attack on all neoclassicism and the return to "pure music", which camouflages an inexcusable indigence –; 3) this will on the other hand focus on the parallel that Berg made between Bach and Schönberg (regarding historical position, –; 4) which will then be an attempt to analyze what of value one might draw today from Bach's œuvre: a certain <u>unitary</u> technique, existing alongside an essentially variable form, despite all appearances.

But I come back to your article which, I repeat, interested me a lot; and which, if you had stayed, would have occasioned numerous discussions and round trips right along the Ile St Louis as far as the Rue Beautreillis! For I don't agree with what you say about the sort of series which is a means of generating structure (see Webern). And obviously, I don't agree with you about Satie: but if we spent a whole century together, I don't suppose we would ever resolve this disagreement.

It is more and more likely that I shall be in South America from April to August. What a marvellous trip!

Where has your film on Calder[8] got to? And when shall we see it here?

Hoping to hear from you, I reaffirm my friendship and hope that these five full pages make up for my long silence.

Best wishes to all your friends in New York.

PB

see P.S. over   4 rue Beautreillis – Paris (4e)

<u>P.S.</u> I almost forgot to tell you that Ansermet, the conductor, has sent me an

---

6 This refers to *Livre pour quatuor* (Jameux no. 10a), composed in 1948–9.

7 "Moment de Jean-Sébastien Bach", *Contrepoints*, no. 7 (1951), pp. 72–86. Reprinted as "Bach's moment", in *Stocktakings*, pp. 3–14.

8 See no. 4, note 3.

enormous letter concerning one of my scores. He is very up in philosophical jargon which rings rather hollow: e.g.: "the 'cadence' being the form of our internal time – 'cadencification' [*cadenciation*] without which music remains a mere object of 'contemplation', levelled on the single metrical succession" ... all this and better. And he ends by saying that what I have written will never be "performed" in the sense in which he means "perform". I shall keep it to re-read in a few years' time: it will be even funnier.

All the best

PB

Once again a thousand thanks for Finnegan's [sic] Wake. You can't imagine how much I enjoyed that book. It is almost a "totem"! Indeed, reading it was slower than slow, given the difficulty of deciphering it.

Superb photo of you sent to Souvtchinsky! I really liked the window looking out to the stars and the comment: that is rare for New York! Lucky asteroid citizen!

12 January 5.30 p.m.

I have just seen Baron Mollet who brought me Sonia Sekula; they greatly reproached me for still not having written to you. But I don't feel guilty any more!

7

Letter from John Cage to Pierre Boulez

17 January [1950]

My dear Pierre,

Your letter has just arrived here at home. I cannot tell you how overjoyed I was to get it. Without news of you I am without news of music, and you know I love music with all my heart.

You write English admirably. (Thanks)

The trip to South America must be marvellous! Now it must be made even better by coming down to New York. I shall try to arrange concerts, lectures (I can talk to Copland about Tanglewood, etc.); and you can stay at home here and make use of an un-nailed piano(!). Everyone here is talking about you (pronouncing the Z) but no one has heard your music (exceptions: Copland, Thomson). The musical atmosphere is ready – everyone full of desire. We even really need the vitality which you could give. Because our musical life is not very lively at present. We have some Schoenberg (Serenade, conducted

1 John Cage in New York, 1949. This photograph was sent to Pierre Souvtchinsky by his American friend (see letter 6, second postscript).

by Mitropoulos, etc.) and there are some "young ones" who are taking up the Stravinsky question again (Mavra, etc) But the date is now 1950, I believe. There is Jolivet, but not for me (I heard the recording in Paris, and the work doesn't interest me). Messiaen was here; – I love him for his ideas about rhythm. Almost everyone was against him because of his half-religious half-Hollywood spirit. I invited him here (big reception, dinner, and music), and he explained his Turangalila score to some composers.

Since knowing you, our music sounds feeble to me. In truth, it is only you who interests me. I have heard STEFAN WOLPE's Sonata (violin and piano)[1] and some of BEN WEBER's works. That's all; and both tend towards Berg rather than Webern. And what is amazing, we have two composers writing pentatonic music! Poor Merton Brown is beginning to see psychoanalysts. People talk about a Kirchner (Léon). One of these days I am going to hear the music of MILTON BABBITT, who is the most Webernian. He has talked to me about rhythmic inversions. He takes a duration, and he inverts the fractions (corresponding to the octave and interval inversion). But he looks like a musicologist.

William Masselos is going to play your sonata (2nd piano) but he has asked for a year to work on it. He is very busy. Two quartets now want to play your quartet.[2] I have said two years to work on it (to put some fear into them, which is good for the health).

I have just finished recording my cinema music.[3] I started that piece of work in a dream: I wanted to write without musical ideas (unrelated sounds) and record the results 4 times, changing the position of the nails[4] each time. That way, I wanted to get subtle changes of frequency (mobility), timbre, duration (by writing notes too difficult to play exactly) and amplitude (electronically altered each time). But I found musical ideas all about me, and the result will be (I mean "would have been") no more than simple or perhaps Japanese canons. I abandoned the dream and I wrote some music. Also the adventure was halted by machines which are too perfect nowadays. They are stupid. Even so I had fun in the 2nd part by recording noises synthetically (without performers). Chance comes in here to give us the unknown. Apparently the film will be seen in Paris (as soon as I know the date, I'll let you know).

Cunningham gave his dance concert on the 15th of January. It was a great success. I'm sending you the programme.

I am going to have lunch with Nicole Henriot on the 18th. We will talk about you which will be a great pleasure to me.

(Whilst you are in Brazil, get some cotton for your ears so that you're not Milhauded.[5])

[1] Stefan Wolpe's Sonata for piano and violin dates from 1949.
[2] See no. 6, note 6.
[3] The music for the film about Calder. See no. 4, note 3.
[4] I.e. the nails used on the soundboard in preparing the piano.
[5] A reference to works by Darius Milhaud: *Saudades do Brasil* (1920–1) and *Scaramouche* (1937).

Tomorrow I have to play the Sonatas and Interludes for Henry Cowell's pupils. The class is going to come to my place. I should rather remain alone and quiet working on the quartet[6] which I began in Paris and which (I want to say, which I didn't have the courage to show you).

Virgil Thomson liked your article in Polyphonie: "Propositions" a lot. He told me he is going to write an article on your ideas about rhythm.[7]

Now something about the Construction in Metal.[8] The rhythmic structure is 4, 3, 2, 3, 4. (16×16). You can see that the first number (4) equals the number of figures that follow it. This first number is divided 1, 1, 1, 1, and first I present the ideas that are developed in the 3, then those in the 2, etc. Regarding the method: there are 16 rhythmic motives divided 4, 4, 4, 4, conceived as circular series

$$\begin{array}{ccccccc}
 & 1 & & & & 1 & \\
4 & ① & 2 & \qquad & 4 & ② & 2 \\
 & 3 & & & & 3 &
\end{array}$$

When you are on 1, you can go 1 2 3 4 1 or retrograde. You can repeat (e.g. 1122344322 etc.) But you cannot go 2↔4 or 1↔3. when you are on 2, you can not only use the same idea but you can go back to 1 using the "doorways" 1 or 4. (Very simple games.) Equally there are 16 instruments for each player. (Fixation with the figure 16) But (funnily enough) there are only 6 players! I don't know why (perhaps I only had 6 players at the time). And the relationships between the instruments (in the method) are similar to those between rhythms (circle-series), according to which the work is written in 4/4 (*four measures, 3 measures, 2 measures, 3 measures, 4 measures, the whole lot 16 times*). The score isn't here at home but I shall now try to give you the names of the instruments. (in English)

---

6 *String Quartet in Four Parts* (1950).

7 Virgil Thompson in fact published an article, "Atonality today", which appeared in two parts in the *New York Herald Tribune*, on 29 January and 5 February 1950. In it he writes:
   The ideal of nonmetrical rhythm, like that of atonality, is a symmetry. Pierre Boulez states it as *d'éviter la carrure*, that is to say, the avoidance of everything square. This means that metrical repeating patterns are out and that even the rhythmic canon by inversion, the hardest to hear of all rhythmic imitations, requires violation of its exactitude by means of the Hindu added dot. There are problems of rhythmic construction too that require solution, though conservative twelve-tone composers like René Leibowitz consider them subsidiary to tonal relations and not soluble independently. John Cage employs a numerical ratio in any piece between the phrase, the period, and the whole, the phrase occupying a time measure which is the square root of the whole time and the periods occupying times proportional to those of the different rhythmic motifs within the phrase. This procedure, though it allows for a symmetry within the phrase and period, produces a tight symmetry in the whole composition and is not therefore quite the rendering of spontaneous emotion that the European atonalists hope to achieve.
   This is reprinted in *A Virgil Thompson Reader* (Boston: Houghton Mifflin Company, 1981), pp. 339–40.

8 From here, Cage is replying to the specific request for information about this work that Boulez made in the preceding letter.

1st performer		*Thundersheet, orchestral bells*
2nd	"	*Piano* (The pianist has an assistant who uses metal cylinders on the strings; the pianist plays trills; the assistant turns them into glissandi.)
3rd	"	*12 graduated Sleigh or oxen bells, suspended sleigh bells, thundersheet.*
4th	"	*4 brake drums (from the wheels of automobiles)* *8 cowbells* *3 Japanese Temple gongs, Thundersheet*
5th	"	*Thundersheet, 4 Turkish cymbals* *8 anvils or pipe lengths* *4 Chinese cymbals*
6th	"	*Thundersheet, 4 muted gongs* *1 suspended gong* *water gong* *Tam Tam*

The number 16 occurs in some cases in considering changing the method of striking (difference of sonority).

You know that with exposition and development (without recapitulation) and with the form (climax, apotheosis (?)) etc., this Construction is 19th century. Your ideas for the lectures are very good. I have nothing to add. Suzuki's works[9] on Zen Buddhism are about to be published. I seem a bit empty. I have come from the film work and the Cunningham concert and I have to play the Sonatas tomorrow morning and I am still not properly started as far as the Quartet goes. And I am tired.

English part:
Gatti's letter was marvellous and by now there must be a new Gatti. Give my love to them all and say I am writing to him tomorrow. I think of you all almost every day and I miss you deeply. Tell Saby that I am very fond of his drawing that he gave me.

The great trouble with our life here is the absence of an intellectual life. No one has an idea. And should one by accident get one, no one would have the time to consider it. That must account for the pentatonic music.

I know you will enjoy travelling to South America; It must be very beautiful. I have never been there. Please keep me well-informed about your plans so that should the Tanglewood idea go through, you could always be reached.

I forgot to mention that the New Music Edition is publishing one of Woronow's pieces (the Sonnet to Dallapiccola) I must write and tell him so.

I am starting a society called "Capitalists Inc" (so that we will not be accused

---

9 At this date, Cage's knowledge of Suzuki would have been entirely through his writings, many of which, dating from the 20s and 30s, were republished between 1949 and 1951. Suzuki lectured on Zen at Columbia University, New York in 1951. (JP).

of being Communists); everyone who joins has to show that he has destroyed not less than 100 disks of music or one sound recording device; also everyone who joins automatically becomes President. We will have connections with 2 other organizations, that for the implementation of nonsense (anyone wanting to do something absurd will be financed to do it) and that Against Progress. If the American influence gets too strong in France I am sure you will want to join.

Very affectionately

your friend

John

8

Letter from Pierre Boulez to John Cage
April 1950

My dear John.

I am replying very late to your long letter of January which I much appreciated – and particularly its *humour with the English part. (and your 'society of Capitalists'!). I want to join – of course – your organization for the implementation of nonsense.*

But I must write more seriously because I have a great birth to say you: the Gatti's son is born three weeks ago; and we could not call him Annalivia, but only Stephen (not Dedalus, indeed).[1] *His name really, is: "Civil War".* But the mayor did not want to register this odd Christian name. *Gatti must tell you the birth of his son, but he has forgotten, with the new works to make, because the baby!.*

I travel to South America. The contract is all wrapped up. *We go on the 28th of April; we go to Buenos-Ayres, Rio-de-Janeiro, Montevideo, and perhaps Santiago & Valparaiso. I shall tell you all the countries in what we shall be. I must buy a great hat* (a sombrero) *to look very South American!* (I will try not to come back as Milhaud!).

And if it is possible, I should be very glad to go to New-York after this travel. The last day in South-America is the 28th of July. I am free after this day.

A propos, I have received yesterday, the Piano Variation[2] *by Copland "with the compliments of the composer". It is the best work I know of him. It is evidently under the Strawinsky's influence. But is the good Strawinsky, i.e. a good*

---

[1] Reference to the character in Joyce's *Ulysses*.
[2] This refers to a fairly old work by Copland, the Piano Variations of 1931.

*influence. And there was a "violence" which seems to me very good (once more!).
What do you think about these variations?*

*Many thanks for your letter about your constructions en métal. I went not in
Belgium. But, more important, I gave your records (the construction en métal and
the first writing of the Dances for two pianos,[3] very well recorded and very well
performed) for the National-Broadcasting. The title of the broadcastings was*
"What they were ... what they are now – history of musical instruments"; *it
was organized by Yvette Grimaud. And your Construction en métal was very
noisy among the specialists. I think we must give it again. And I am very glad of
this "résultat"* [i.e. outcome]. *Of course, because it was a broadcasting for many
people, (the more important of the organization of the French Broadcasting, la
chaîne nationale), we could not give all the indications you sent me. But the more
important was that the recordings are heared.*

I have written myself, three Essays for percussion skin-wood-metal.[4] *But I
had only three players! It was very few. And one repetition* [i.e. rehearsal; and
below] *of three years (excuse this Joyce-lapsus for three hours!!!)[5] for repeating and recording: too very few. Consequently, the recordings are very bad.
And I want not keep that.* Alongside yours, they make a pretty shabby
sight.

Could you find "Contrepoints" no. 6? If you have, tell me that [sic] *you think
of my paper. A propos, in the Musical Quarterly, Goldbeck has written a Note on
me.[6] You will remark a: "possibly, a sense of humour"!! which had enjoyed me. –
I have not known all the things he says, but I suppose when my technique of the
English is too deficient.*

*I will use your precisions on the rythm for writing an article on you; and your
ideas on the sound itself.[7] – When you know the date of the parution of the
Calder's film in Paris, you tell me.*

And this quatuor, is it coming? If I travel to New-York, I hope you show me.

---

[3] For details of these recordings, see no. 1, note 16, and no. 6, note 5.

[4] This abandoned project does not appear in the Jameux catalogue. The Paul Sacher
Stiftung possesses sketches and an outline. According to Pierre Boulez, its rhythmic
organization is re-used in *Oubli signal lapidé* (personal communication). See also no. 36,
note 6.

[5] This parenthesis has been added above the paragraph.

[6] Frédéric Goldbeck's biography appeared in *The Musical Quarterly*, 36 2 (April 1950),
pp. 291–5. Having described Boulez as the most individual and least pretentious of the
young French composers, Goldbeck writes concerning the manuscript of the Second
Sonata:

> His handwriting is most typical ... and would enable a tone-deaf graphologist to give
> a quite satisfactory account of his style: notes like pinpoints, the marks between the
> staves diminutive; on the front page no capitals used, not even for the author's
> initials. A tiny, wiry, angular lettering, difficult to read, yet uncommonly precise. No
> fat at all, little flesh, plenty of sinews. A spiritualized character, yet strangely
> matter-of-fact. A doggedly indefatigable Ariel with, possibly, a sense of humour, and
> certainly a strong sense of geometry.

[7] Boulez apparently never devoted an entire article to Cage, but he was about to write
"Possibly ... " in which a whole section is concerned with his innovations (this extract
forms No. 37 below).

Tell to W. Masselos I shall send him the score of my 2d Piano Sonata when I shall have it. I.e., in a few weeks. But you will have the first.

I am very glad that you have seen Nicole Henriot. She is a very good pianist, and a very good friend. And I found your three-letter very splendid.

I have heared some works by Dallapiccola; either dodecaphonist or not dodeca-phonist, they were very bad in all ways! The Italian lyricism! ...

If it was possible, when could you give me an answer for an eventual travel to New-York for me? – In your letter, don't forget that. I should be so glad to see you and your friends! but especially you, naturally. There will be lots of things to tell each other and get straight since our discussions in the Rue Beautreillis!

Many thanks for the program of concert of Merce Cunningham. You tell him my good souvenir. (I don't know the correct form of words in modern letter-writing. Excuse my ignorance). *I am very glad that this concert was very "réussi"* [i.e. successful]. *And I am sure that was marvellous.*

Here, for me, two concerts in preparation. One organized by Heugel; among the works, there will be my second Piano Sonata played by Yvette Grimaud. (the 24th or 29th of April).[8] *And another one, organized by Souvtchinsky and Désormière; "Le Soleil des Eaux",*[9] *two poems by René Char; will be songed by Irène Joachim with the National Orchestra. (of the Radio). (it will be the 18th of July: I will not be in Paris).*[10]

I was forgetting to say I have heared the music recording of Joyce's voice in few pages of "Finnegan's [sic] *Wake". You know it, certainly. It is a friend of Gatti who has it. For compensation* [i.e. in return], *I have gived to hear the recordings of your music.* They impressed him a lot.

Saby is always drawing. Chi va piano, va sano ... and the second part!

We had recently the performance of the six Bartók's String Quartets; a very good performance by the Végh Quartett. But the music itself is very "décevante" [i.e. disappointing]. *And in the time when you see this music is so poor – the 4th str. quart. excepted –, all the musical people of Paris enjoys with it. Which makes you seem perverse!*

In a week, we have the performance of the Kammersymphonie of Schönberg and of his Suite op 29 – Conducted by Max Deutsch (a pupil of Schönberg). And also in the same concert the "Jardins Suspendus" poem [i.e., Das Buch der hängenden Gärten], *by Stefan George – music Schönberg, of course.*

Send me a great letter to give me your news! Hello to all your New York

[8] This refers to the first performance of the Second Sonata, which in fact took place on 29 April 1950 at the concert hall of the École Normale de Musique in Paris. See no. 13, note 4.

[9] Another première. This refers to the withdrawn version of *Le soleil des eaux* (Jameux no. 9b), for soprano, tenor, bass and chamber orchestra, performed at the Théâtre des Champs-Elysées on 18 July 1950 by the Orchestre National conducted by Roger Désormière, with soloists Irène Joachim, Pierre Mollet and Joseph Payron. On this première, see nos 24 and 25, and for the recording, no. 25, note 6.

[10] Boulez was to be on the Compagnie Renaud-Barrault tour of South America.

friends (including the psychoanalysts whom Merton Brown has been to consult!) – All your Paris friends send their best wishes – with me at their head, of course.

Excuse this letter's charabia, *written in english (?!)* and in French. But that requires and demonstrates an effort on both sides!.

PB

9

Letter from John Cage to Pierre Boulez
February 1950

My dear Pierre

I have just 'phoned Copland and he has told me that all the tutors for the summer at Tanglewood have already been selected. You can blame me for being too late. Copland said that if you find yourself in the States he could arrange a lecture, but the money for that is not enough to pay for your travel.

I imagine that the best plan will be to go a little slowly and arrange things for next year. It is naturally with regret that I say this.

Your letter is full of good news. I am overjoyed to hear of Gatti's son and of your concerts. I would like to send Stephan [sic] a gift (what would he like?). I have not yet written to Gatti, and each day I grow more embarrassed because I have not. Life here is full of unconsequential complexities.

Fizdale and Gold are going to give another concert in Paris (in November) followed by the same one here in New York. They will play your Sonata.[1] Which reminds me of two things I want to say.

a. Virgil Thomson thinks your coming here should be preceded by hearing your music here. And next season I am hoping not only for performances of the 2 piano Sonata but of the 2nd piano Sonata (Masselos) and the Quartet. Virgil T. has published 2 articles[2] about your article in Polyphonie[3] (rhythm as the contemporary 12 tone problem). (I will send these to you shortly; you may not agree with them but they serve to get people talking and thinking).

b. I am trying to get the 2 piano Sonata published by Salabert. They will certainly get in touch with you; otherwise the New Music Edition wants to publish it. We will shortly publish Woronow's Sonnet.

I have finished my Quartet. 4 parts: quietly flowing along, gently rocking,

---

[1] This probably refers to the Sonata for two pianos (1948) now withdrawn (Jameux no. 4).

[2] See no. 7, note 7.

[3] "Propositions", *Polyphonie*, 2, 1948, pp. 65–72. Reprinted as "Proposals" in *Stocktakings* pp. 47–54.

nearly stationary, and Quodlibet. It uses throughout a gamut of assorted sounds, single and accords, which are always played on the same strings of the same instruments. There is no counterpoint and no harmony. Only a line in rhythmic space. (2½·1½ 2·3 6·5 ½·1½) The whole lasts 17½ minutes and is in one tempo throughout! The third part (which is long: 8¾ minutes) is a canon (retrograde & inversion), which is quite interesting because of the variations resulting from the rhythmic structure and the asymmetry of the gamut. I shall be terrified to show you this work. Nevertheless, I love it. *Now I shall start work on a concerto for prepared piano, percussion orchestra and strings plus perhaps a few of the other instruments.*[4] *After the Quartet I write a few bad pieces for Violin and piano, – but I shall discard them – at least for the time being.*

Maro[5] *will play my Sonatas again on March 7 and after that I go to Virginia for a few days to accompany Cunningham who will dance there. When I return I will start the Concerto.*

Naturally I agree with you about the Copland Variations, they are certainly his best work.

I should very much like to see your Essays for percussion.

Your article in Contrepoints[6] *was magnificent. I shall reread it many times.*

The Webern Symphony Op. 21 was our music of this season as far as I am concerned. I was deeply moved. Also I copied it since it was nowhere to be bought.

I am very sorry not to have succeeded with the Tanglewood business. Perhaps something will come up at the last moment.

Another thing I hope for (since as President of Capitalists Inc. I must undermine the organization) is a recording of your music available here. Perhaps through Heugel or some one here recordings could be made of the Char songs and Grimaud playing the piano sonata.

Forgive this hasty letter (and mostly in English); I will write again soon.

Very affectionately,

John

---

[4] The Concerto for prepared piano and chamber orchestra (1951).
[5] This is Maro Ajemian.
[6] This must refer to "Trajectories", since Cage had not yet received "Bach's moment" (see no. 12).

IO

Letter from John Cage to Pierre Boulez
before April 1950

My dear Pierre,

I have just received the Sonata (2nd) and it has given me enormous pleasure. But imagine my distress at not being able to read the last word you wrote on the "frontispiece" (title page).

A week ago I invited Philippe Heugel round and he brought me a copy, but I gave that copy to Virgil Thompson because I knew you would send me another one.

Every note leaps off the page. I am in a state of ecstasy and sentimentality. Masselos already has a copy of the two mixes (selections). And someone here (Ross Russell) may be going to record it. If you like Grimaud's "performance", it could be recorded in Paris. But Heugel thought that a man would be better (Masselos). I am still working on the possibility of seeing you here in New York after South America. And Virgil Thompson agrees with the scheme now. He is talking to music professors in the universities (colleges). We shall see. You mustn't get too interested, because it may not come off. But, – still give me the itinerary so that I can write to you, – if something comes up. My god, it would be good to see you again!

A young dodecaphonist is here at the moment, – Monod. He showed me some scores. I find them small and *"travaillés" ("labored",* in English). What do you think of him? He asked me to introduce him to the musicians here, and I've helped him get to know Harrison, and Weber. They didn't like him. But they haven't seen the music, either. He (Monod) wants us to put on some concerts of music by him and his friends, – Casanova, Duhamel(?), etc. He doesn't know your music yet. That will come! His attitude seems puerile (childish) to me.

Maro Ajemian is going to give a concert next Sunday. She is coming here to play it for a few friends this evening. Monod was scandalized *[scandalisé]* by your article in Contrepoints. But scandalized in advance, because he never read it. (My god, my French!)[1] I showed him my Quartet, and he was scandalized again – in English, *"nonplussed"*. He asked me, "Where are you trying to get to?" and I replied, "Nowhere." He didn't understand. The day I show you my new works, I shall be full of dread. It is better to keep them out of your sight.

I have a wonderful pupil. He is sixteen and his favorite composer is

---

[1] Cage has just written *il n'a jamais été le lu*; correct French would be *il ne l'a jamais lu*. (RS)

Webern. He has great intelligence and sensitivity. What's more, he was born in France. His name is Christian Wolff.

Currently I have the problem of writing a study of Virgil Thompson's works for a book.[2] I would like to send Stéphan a present. What would be suitable? I know nothing when it comes to children. Have Salabert & Co. got on to you (about printing the Sonata for 2 pianos)? If not, we want to publish it here (New Music); and ask Yvette to send me her music too. We can print it here.

Kindest regards (which grow every day) and my regards to Souvtchinsky, Gatti, Saby, Joffroy and everyone.

John

P.S. I have just finished the 4th part of a Suite for Violin and Piano (6 parts).[3]

P.S. I am sending the articles in which Virgil Thompson mentions you.[4] Ignore my notes in pencil. But you know that I don't entirely agree with Virgil Thompson. But after my study of his works I understand him better. A lot of his ideas (pronouncements) on other people's music are actually his idea of his own work.

Many thanks again for the Sonata and I hope that we meet again soon.

and BON VOYAGE!

I I

Letter from Pierre Boulez to John Cage
May 1950

Ambassador Hotel
R. Senador Dantas, 25
Rio de Janeiro

My dear John,

Here I am, already Saudading in Brazil.[1] You must surely be wondering how I have managed to leave your letters unanswered for so long. And I go on

---

[2] In no. 12, Cage says that in the end, he did not draft this article. He did, however, work for years on a book on Thompson's life and works, of which only the lengthy section on the music was published, as the second part of *Virgil Thompson. His Life and Music* by Kathleen O'Donnell Hoover and John Cage (New York/London: Thomas Yseloff, 1959) (communication from Frans von Rossum).

[3] *Six Melodies for Violin and Keyboard* (1950).

[4] See no. 7, note 7.

[1] An allusion to Milhaud. Cf. no. 7, note 5.

at myself more every day for not having written. Remorse succeeds remorse, and still I don't write. It has to be said here that the great mitigating circumstance is the voyage with its preparations and postparations! *and so on and so on.* Then during the voyage, you just live and don't feel at all the need to write. And after the voyage, you no longer feel the need to write down what you have lived through, because everything has been carried off by insignificance.

Shall I describe the country to you? You must see it for yourself. It is very warm because it is autumn, and it has the warmth of the French summer (which makes you think about summer here!); evening falls very early at about 5 p.m. but it remains warm nevertheless. The first few days are exhausting; then you acclimatise. The country is amazingly beautiful, bursting forth everywhere; luxurious vegetation takes hold in every last possible place. It would be marvellous to be able to get to the interior of this land; but the performances mean that we can hardly move from the area around Rio.

I have had news from Gatti, Joffroy, Souvtchinsky and Yvette Grimaud telling me how the first hearing of my Sonata published by Heugel went. It was fairly badly received, and some fairly unpleasant remarks have come from various quarters.[2] You will certainly agree with me anyway that all this is unimportant. I still haven't replied to you over the Tanglewood question. Please don't put yourself out. If it doesn't happen this year, it will next year and that is no catastrophe.

On the subject, if you see Morton Feldman, tell him that I am most ashamed not to have responded either to his letter or to his sending me his manuscripts. Tell him that I did not have the time, because his manuscripts only arrived two days before I left France. But I shall write to him soon. For myself, if you know these works, I find his piano piece "Illusion"[3] very finely developed. In the Oboe Quintet,[4] which is more adventurous, one gets the sense that he doesn't yet have a feel for counterpoint and architecture. But that will undoubtedly come. Anyway, he wrote me such a nice letter that I feel really guilty not to have replied. If there are any complimentary copies of my Sonata left, have one given to him. If there are none left, I shall write to Heugel to get it seen to.

What is your news? I imagine you are hard at work. As for me, in the midst of all these distractions, I have a hard battle to safeguard my own work and not submit to complete dispersal.

I have not met any young musicians here. For we are mainly moving in society circles. But I am still hoping, although I haven't got any addresses. For someone here who knows some young composers promised to phone me soon to organize a get-together. I hope he will.

---

[2] For a fairly uncomplimentary account of this première, see no. 13, note 5.

[3] *Illusion* for piano (1949).

[4] There is no quintet including oboe in the catalogue of Feldman's works, but *Projection II* (1951) is scored for flute, trumpet, piano, violin and cello.

2 Pierre Boulez in the early 1950s

Thank you for the Virgil Thompson articles. I had heard of them indirectly via P. Souvtchinsky and Nicole Henriot. Have you been sent the last issue of Contrepoints where I wrote "Moment de J. S. Bach", a study of contemporary "classicism"?[5] I hope to hear from you soon. I shall cut this letter short and excuse myself, because I must go to dinner and then off to the theatre.

With very best wishes,

PB

[In the margin:]
I apologize for writing in French. But in trying to learn Portuguese (which I am however failing to do) I have lost the little English I thought I had!!!
  You can write to me at the Hotel Ambassador
                    Rua Senador Dantas, 25
up to 10 June.
  I am depending on getting a letter (Don't follow my bad example)

12

Letter from John Cage to Pierre Boulez
5 June 1950

Monsieur P.B.
Ambassador Hotel
R. Senador Dantas 25
Rio de Janeiro, Brazil

My dear Pierre,

I have just voyaged through your letter; I saw the Brazilian colours of the envelope while it was still in the letterbox. Many thanks (I am eager for the next one).

Gatti also sent me a letter, with news of your concert and a photo of Stéphane. I have sent Stéphane several presents, and that the concert should have been a scandal seems quite traditional to me. That's how the musical world's mind develops.

I am about to embark on a new work, but I find myself stupid, without sensibility, etc. The same old story. It's probably string orchestra and

[5] See no. 6, note 7.

prepared piano.[1] I have just written Six Melodies for Violin and Keyboard[2] (using the same gamut that you hear in the Quartet).

You are invited to spend two weeks in Middlebury, Vermont in August (all expenses paid and 85 dollars on top – not a lot); it's a "Composers' Conference". I can't say whether it is interesting because I've never been there. But if you tell me how much money we need in order to have your presence in the Capitalist States, I shall look for funds again. You know that as far as all that goes I am completely egocentric: I very much want to see you again.

I have spent several weeks studying Virgil Thomson's works. I had been asked for a study of them. But in the end I said no.[3]

I haven't seen the Contrepoint article you mention; I hope I shall see it. I have subscribed, but the mail is slow.

In the last week of June I go to New Orleans for a concert. Otherwise I shall stay here for the whole summer.

William Masselos does want to work on the 2nd Sonata. It will be for one of the League of Composers' programmes.

I have nothing to report: musical life here is outwardly almost dead; and inwardly I am meeting invisible obstacles.

I have two gifted pupils: one is Polish and the other was born in France, the son of a German who used to play with Paul Klee in the evenings (violin and piano). The son is called Christian Wolff. I don't know the Pole's name, it is too difficult.

I hope you will write soon

With all best wishes,

John

P.S. I have a Sarabhai here: Geera.[4]

---

[1] This refers to the Concerto for prepared piano and chamber orchestra.
[2] Mentioned in no. 10.
[3] See no. 10, note 2.
[4] Cage had been studying Indian philosophy and classical music with Gita Sarabhai since 1946.

13

Letter from Pierre Boulez to John Cage
June 1950

Lord Hotel
Av. São João, 1173
Sao Paulo, Brazil

[Upside down:]
For the Mallarmé[1], I have brought all the Bach vocal works.[2] What nourishment! It's an incredible intimidation.

Dear John,

Thank you for your letter which caught up with me in Rio. – And for the excellent news you gave me. Extraordinary!! You work out whether the 85 dollars will be enough when I arrive in New York and whether it will be that much. But I want you to clarify a few things.

(The Cartesian spirit?!)

1) The exact dates of the Middlebury event. Because it may create complications. We may have to extend our travels to Chile (we would cross the Andes cordillera by plane, which would be wonderful!!) and thus extend the length of the tour by a fortnight. We will be fixed up in three or four days at the outside. I shall send you another letter.

2) What I would do there. Should I prepare lectures? On what subject? To give you an idea, I have with me the Berg Chamber Concerto, the two last Webern Cantatas, the Webern String Quartet. As for my manuscripts, I have the Visage Nuptial (Char) and the beginning of my Symphony (in short score), and obviously my 2nd Sonata from Heugel.

3) How would I travel? Is the fare covered by air or by sea? And where

---

[1] This undoubtedly refers not to the later *Pli selon pli* but to *Un coup de dés*, a work for choir and large orchestra on the Mallarmé poem of the same title (referred to again in nos 26 and 28). This was an aborted project that should come between nos 11 and 12 in the Jameux catalogue.

[2] Boulez had just finished a discussion of the chorale *Vor Deinen Thron tret' ich hiermit* in his article "Bach's moment" (see no. 6, note 7). He writes:

> It has not been sufficiently clearly shown that the structure of the chorale melody gives rise to the structure of the chorale itself ... This can be summed up by saying that here the "tune" gives rise to all the figuration of its development and its own architecture, the latter flowing from the former.

He goes on to state that "what we need most of all from research into Bach's work" is "a powerfully unitary formal technique, indeed a *uterine* relationship, between the writing itself and the architecture". (*Stocktakings*, p. 12)

would I leave from? New York? I hope anyway that you will wait for me and give me some guidance, because I shall feel quite lost.

4) How long will I be able to stay in New York with the small amount of money that I shall have, and is it necessary to ask about a place on a New York – Paris ship immediately?

I think that makes a detailed and precise questionnaire to which I hope you will reply in even more precise and detailed terms!! – I am really excited at the thought of this trip.

Another minor geographical question: where is Vermont? (You will blush at my ignorance!)

I am very pleased that Dante[3] wrote to you. He should have done so ages ago! Now you know Stéphane! As for the concert in which my sonata was performed, I don't give a damn about it. I don't believe Yvette Grimaud played it well, she must have played it in too feminine a manner.[4] But anyway, I was already on the boat to South America. And that's the important thing.

[3] Dante here is Armand Gatti's nickname.

[4] In her book on Boulez, Joan Peyser publishes anonymously the letter from a friend of Boulez's to Cage that contains an account of this première:
> The interpretation, while quite decent, was pitiful. I heard at least 25 times the main passage of this sonata played by Pierre. I assure you it was very different in the hands of this pianist. "Lento", "dolce", "soave", "addormentato", from the beginning to the end. Not a single forte. Not a single sustained note. A river (like the tranquil Seine) from the beginning to the end. According to Souvtchinsky she took seven minutes longer to play the entire piece than it normally requires. But all this did not warrant in any way the reactions of the audience. From the very first bars, three quarters of the audience smiled with already prepared smiles and shrugging of shoulders. Already in the first movement I felt compelled to call two women utter fools and to threaten another with knocking her block off. That was nothing. The rest of the audience only increased by tenfold the hostility already rampant. The women were exultant. Sighs of boredom, invitation cards that they were passing along to each other on which they had put next to Boulez's name the number ZERO. At one point a few respectable musicians (and they do exist here and there in the world) felt the need to shout vehemently and indignantly, "Have you quite finished your stupid antics?" (The music being performed then was that of Boulez.) I felt compelled to intervene with invective of my own.... Fortunately for the performance Max Deutsch demanded silence in imperative tones and obtained it. The scene ended with some exaggeratedly heavy applause (provided by a few of Boulez's friends) and a general lethargy on the part of a slightly amused audience. I went out without hearing the rest of the concert, shouting all the coarsest language I could muster. A short while later Joffroy met me, accompanied by Saby and Souvtchinsky. We spent the night going from one bistro to the next to get rid of some of the bitterness we felt. We tippled until we were completely drunk. Joffroy rid himself of his hostilities by breaking a considerable number of glasses. Not a single music critic in any one of the daily papers thought it wise to discuss the work. The few who bothered with it at all were to a one surprised that the public did not boo. Quite the contrary, they were full of encomiums – as was the public, moreover, for this poor ass Martinet whose sorry "fugue" sounded like a song by Edith Piaf. The whole affair made me ill for two days. Now things have fallen into perspective and I view it all with more equanimity. Unfortunately this poor lady must play the Second Sonata again at the Sorbonne around the end of the month. The only felicitous aspect of this story is that Pierre, having left the day before for South America (with Barrault and company) did not attend the circus that accompanied the performance of his piece and the irremediable mess that was made of his work. (Peyser, pp. 63–4)

All the same, tell William Masselos that I am very happy for him to work on it. Perhaps I shall meet him in August in New York.

I was about to forget something very important: Reply to me as soon as possible at:

Compagnie Mad. Renaud-J.L. Barrault

Teatro Solis

Montevideo (Uruguay) before 28 June

And after that at Compagnie M. Renaud-J.L. Barrault

Teatro Odeon

Buenos Aires (Argentina)

As you can see from these addresses, we are still travelling. It is very nice to empty oneself completely and live in the midst of a fog of words which one can't understand. – and that brings unexpected meetings. You know someone called Nogueira whose mother was in Amsterdam last year, and who is one of your close friends; you know that we had dinner together at Mabillon, the first day that I went to your place; with Mollet and the rest of that lot. Can you believe that I met him here last night, in Sao Paulo, in a nightclub called Nick Bar, quite by chance. You have to admit that that's pretty good as coincidences go!

As you can gather, with this atmosphere of travelling, work has slowed right up. I am mainly orchestrating old things. A task, after all, which requires less concentration than composition proper. Nevertheless, I am not moving an inch away from my Mallarmé![5]

I think – just between us – that you did the right thing in giving up the project of writing a book on the works of Virgil Thomson. He may be an interesting character; at least that is the impression I've had, since I don't know him. But as for the works, I find them rather inconsistent. *Do you think so?*

So you are off on travels too, since you are going to New Orleans. It sounds like a marvellous city. (One is always thirsty for what one doesn't know).

This evening I have been to a demonstration of the Hammond Organ and the Solovox with added tremolo, and I had to give a little Martenot "show" in exchange. Pity me with this cheap rubbish.

I've had some letters from friends in Paris since I left. But I have to say that I've hardly written. Impressions of the journey always tend towards the Perrichon sort (cf. Labiche[6] etc. . . . . etc. . . . .).

Whilst I have been here, I've been very sinusoidal and have become increasingly bloody-minded. It's the only way. Keep your shell waterproof!

Looking forward to hearing from you soon with news and information. – Best wishes as ever.

PB

---

[5] See note 1 above.
[6] This alludes to Eugène Labiche's work *Le voyage de Monsieur Perrichon*.

14

Letter from John Cage to Pierre Boulez
21 June 1950

P.B.
Compagnie Mad. Renaud-J.L. Barrault
Teatro Solis
Montevideo, Uruguay

My dear Pierre
   I cannot answer all your questions at present because I only have a few minutes but I have fantastic (*Boulezversant*) news.[1] I am a member of a 'Selection Committee' which chooses composers to spend 3 months in the United States under the patronage of the "Institut d'éducation internationale" paid $175 per month and an extra $175 for travel <u>within</u> the United States. All applications have to go through *Leslie Brady, Cultural Officer, American Embassy, Paris*. But since you are in Brazil, I have just written to Brady asking him to let me send you the application form direct and for you to return it directly to me. Because time is short for the decision. The important things you must do at once are to study English, and to find out if it is possible to swap the Rio-Paris voyage for a Rio-N.Y. one.
   Until tomorrow (I shall write to you tomorrow). All the best

                                                                John

---

[1] Cage is making a pun on *bouleversant* (overwhelming).

15

Letter from John Cage to Pierre Boulez
June 1950

P.B.
Compagnie Mad. Renaud-J.L. Barrault
Teatro Solis
Montevideo, Uruguay

Dear Pierre,
Here are the *"Application Blanks"*. You can begin by answering the awkward questions. But let's wait for Leslie Brady to reply to my letter before sending back the *"Applications"*. Maybe you will have to send them here or to Paris, – I don't know yet, – whichever.

I am continuing the correspondence with Middlesbury. I said you could give lectures on "Rhythm and its relation to Dodecaphony"; "Ravel, Schoenberg and Stravinsky"; *"Achievement of Anton Webern"* and that you could play and analyse your Second Sonata. But actually you can say what you want to do. I am also going to try to arrange a lecture for you at Tanglewood (which means A. Copland).

All is going amazingly well. You will notice that you need 3 "References"; in order to save time which is short and "fugitando", I took the liberty of sending 3 *"blanks"* to Goldbeck, de Schloezer and Souvtchinsky (thinking that they would also be your choices). (Be so good as to put down their names as referees).[1]

Concerning travel expenses, first of all you must try to change your Paris ticket for an (air) ticket to New York. If you need more money, feel free to ask me for what you need. Because with the money the Institute is going to give you you will be able to pay back anyone. You also need a visa (but let's wait for that because that has to be something very very special.). – no doubt a series of twelve visas.

Goodbye for now
John.

P.S. Vermont is a bit closer to the North Pole than N.Y.C.
I shall guide you as much as you like from the plane to –

---

[1] The following addresses are given in the margin: "Goldbeck: 12 rue Emile Duchaux" and "de Schloezer: 5 rue de l'Assomption".

16

Letter from Pierre Boulez to John Cage
late June / early July 1950

Dear John

I have just received your two letters in Montevideo. They have enjoyed me very, very, much. But, ... für the Institute of International Education, I think that "my ability to understand spoken English" and my "ability to speak English (conversation)" are too little. And never a professor of English will sign the certificate of proficiency in English. It is too hard to learn the conversation during a month. My ability is very, very poor. For the conférence, it is very good. The three titles you have given are the best: 1/Ravel – Schönberg – Stravinsky – 2/Webern 3/Rhythm and dodecaphony – 4/Second sonate and generally, my ideas on the composition. But I must speak in French, I hope! It is possible to change the return to Paris in a travel to New-York. Perhaps, it is necessary to have much money. With your permission, I shall ask you, if I need it. Actually, I have only 80 dollars. It is few. But, perhaps, at the end of our performances at Buenos Aires, I can have 120–$130.

I wait for your letter to send the Application Blanks. But I would rather like send that to you, because if I write mistakes, you can take all right! The names of Souvtchinsky, Schloezer and Goldbeck were the best; I thank you for that. Some blanks are very difficult to answer, specially State who will pay for your transportation in the blank entitled "Financial Statutes". If you can write all these applications for me, in New York, it would be better. I could send to you the photos and the certificate of Heath. The most difficult being to "describe in detail the work I should prefer to do if I receive a grant". I hope your answer for ligth [sic: enlighten?] me!

In all cases, Middlebury is good. And I wait for the second part of this "bouleversant" travel.

In few days, your answer. Yours.

PB

My new addresses:

Either: Compagnie Renaud-Barrault – Teatro Odeon. 367 Esmeralda. Buenos Aires

Or: Hotel Lafayette. 546 Reconquista – Buenos Aires.

Do you prefer Esmeralda or Reconquista?! (Perhaps the second, because Lafayette!!)

17

Letter from John Cage to Pierre Boulez

M.P.B.
c/o Compagnie Mad. Renaud – J.L. Barrault
Theâtre Odéon
Buenos-Ayres, Argentine

2 July 1950

Dear Pierre,

I have just got back from New Orleans. *Mr. Alan Carter (Director, Composers' Conference, Middlebury College, Middlebury Vermont)* will be delighted to have you present this summer. The conference dates are 19 August to 2 September. You can do what you like for it, discussions, anything, but they want you to play some of your music.

I haven't yet had a letter from *Mr. Leslie Brady (Cultural Officer, American Embassy in Paris)*; but I still think that all that will take care of itself. I am trying to get a reduction in the air fare for you. I hope to be successful.

How are you?

Souvtchinsky has sent me a poster for your concert on 18 July.[1] It's great. My god, how I would love to hear it!

Yours as ever,

John

---

[1] The first performance of *Le soleil des eaux*.

18

Letter from John Cage to Pierre Boulez
26 July 1950

M. P. B.
Hotel Lafayette
546 Reconquista
Buenos Aires
Argentina

My dear friend

News of your Paris success gave me great joy comparable to the regret at not having heard the work.[1] But one day and here, no doubt.

I am afraid that the *"Grant"* may not come through for you. Anyway, if it does, it will be unexpected. First of all, I wrote to the Embassy in Paris. No one replied. Secondly, I was told that over there, in Paris, the officials were furious that I had had the audacity to "go over their heads". Thirdly, knowing that, I spoke to Copland, and he telegraphed Paris, supporting your name for a *"Grant"*. Today I was asked if Paris has had an Application from you; I said it has not, because I am still waiting for a reply from Paris.

However, the impossible is still near and possible. We shall see.

If you are coming for the Conference at Middlebury (nevertheless), we can see to the necessary "financial details".

You already know the dates for that: 19 August to 2 September. The name and address of the Conference Director is *Mr. Alan Carter, Middlebury College, Middlebury, Vermont*. But you will have to come here to New York first. If you give me your arrival time, I shall meet you. If not, you will have to telephone me: SPring 7-2864.

<u>Fantastic news:</u> they just phoned me from the Institute office and we spoke about the problem of the *"Grant"*. I mentioned Middlebury, and they said that if you are going to come for that, they can make special arrangements for the Grant without the Paris Embassy! What you must do now is telegraph at

---

[1] This refers again to *Le soleil des eaux*. The success of the concert was reported in the U.S.A. at least by a short review by Frédéric Goldberg in *The Musical Quarterly*, 36/4 (October 1950), p. 598:

> Pierre Boulez's very concise Soleil des Eaux for voices and small orchestra is probably the most significant piece of music written in France for several years. In this case technical complexity and sophistication is found rooted in imagination – in the necessity of inventing (12-tone row or no 12-tone row) new bottles of fantastic design for a new and highly intoxicating wine of tragic flavor. The listener is thrilled and does not feel safe at all.

my expense (I shall pay for it here) (326 Monroe St.) saying that you will be here for Middlebury. I can hand the telegram to the Office as a document. And the miracle will happen!

Have you got a Visa? Get any old Visa; we can change it here at the Institute. See you soon and with best wishes always,

John

I enclose some letters which can help you to obtain a Visa.

19

Letter from John Cage to Pierre Souvtchinsky
after 18 July 1950

My dear friend,

Many thanks for all the material on Pierre's concert.[1] I am very pleased that it was a success. But I was saddened not to have heard the work. We must get it put on here.

At last, Pierre has got a "Grant" from the International Institute of Education! And, moreover, he has been invited to Middlebury College, (Middlebury, Vermont) where he is to give some lectures. But it is a complete mystery to me where Pierre is. Is he on his way here or to Paris? All I know is that he has left Buenos Aires. I 'phoned him there, but he wasn't there any more. If you can give me any information, I should be grateful. In any case, I hope he accepts all these invitations. It would be a great pleasure to see him again.

Also, the Second Sonata will be given in a "League of Composers" concert (in November). And if I were sure that he was coming, I could try to arrange more concerts, lectures, etc. – in order to make his visit here interesting.

If Pierre arrives in Paris and doesn't have enough money to travel here, telegraph me and I shall find the money.

The "Grant" will give him all the money he needs to live here (from September 15th to December 15th).

I am currently working on a piece for prepared piano and orchestra.[2]

Best wishes to you and Mme Souvtchinsky.

John

---

[1] The first performance of *Le soleil des eaux* on 18 July 1950.
[2] The Concerto for prepared piano and chamber orchestra.

20

Letter from Pierre Boulez to John Cage
July or August 1950

My dear John

This letter is going to be a disappointment to you. For I am already on the boat back to Paris. I waited until the last moment with a faint hope of being able to come to New York, but nothing came from the Consulate. This is exactly what happened: I went to the United States Consulate in Buenos Aires, supported by the French Embassy, to make my request for a visa. They made me fill in excessively detailed forms, and took my fingerprints sixteen times. But after that the officials had to make enquiries of the United States Embassy in Paris concerning my civilian status. So I supplied the cost of a reply-paid telegram which takes less than twenty-four hours. And after all that, I stood firm waiting for my visa, the precious visa which ought to allow me to go to the United States. I am still waiting ... officials in every country resemble each other strangely. So I can only hope for one thing, which is to go and see you next year. From now on, I shall know you have to act goodness knows how far in advance to get a visa.

Therefore, at the moment, I am going straight back to Paris to work. I have a month or two ahead of me to work quietly in the Rue Beautreillis. That will be an antivoyage!

Please tell Middlebury that it really isn't my fault if I can't come, but the idiocy on the part of a Consulate.

Apart from that, there is nothing very new. You have had news of the 18 July concert in the Champs-Elysées. Désormière conducted, Irène Joachim sang. The next morning I got a telegram from Souvtchinsky who organized everything wonderfully. Just think that when I went away from Paris, the orchestral score was not copied out, nor the equipment prepared. He and Yvette Grimaud took care of everything and I am greatly in their debt.

I hope that I shall hear the recording when I get back.

As for you, did your trip to New Orleans go well? What are you working on at the moment? With me, it's the same as ever. I am in a hurry to start something new.

I shall be pleased to get back to Paris and the crowd there. You have to console yourself a lot for fouling up a trip.

I am writing to you in haste. For we are breaking the voyage at Rio and I shall take the opportunity to post this letter so that you will know of my disappointment as soon as possible.

I shall send more news soon. Write to me in Paris from now on.

Please forgive me for causing you this useless inconvenience.
Your friend as ever,

PB

21

Letter from John Cage to Pierre Boulez
probably August 1950

My dear friend,

I have just got your letter from the boat. Undoubtedly you have not seen the letter I wrote to you in Buenos Aires with the news of the *"Grant"* which you have just got from the International Education Institute. The story of the fingerprints in Buenos Aires is the story of consulates everywhere. I enclose some letters which may be able to help you now.

The *"Grant"* will give you 175 dollars a month for the three months between the 15th of September and the 15th of December, and an additional 175 dollars for travel within the United States. The thing not paid for is the journey from Paris to here and back. You can pay for the return with the 175 dollars for travel here, – but we still have the problem of the journey here from Paris. If you can arrive here before the 19th of August (Middlebury), it will have to be by plane, and it is a question of 370 dollars. If you go to the Int. Ed. Institute at 173 Boulevard St Germain, Paris, they might be able to help you. Sometimes Air France or the French Government will pay the cost of the journey, since it is a cultural matter. Also you could go to see Mr Leslie Brady, cultural officer at the United States Embassy (he knows the whole story about the *"Grant"* and he is going to arrange the "Visa"); he might be able to help you with Air France or the French Government by finding the means for paying the air fare.

Assuming that none of that works, I've got another idea: I spoke today to a dancer (who is both talented and rich – a curious combination) who can pay in advance for some music which you can write later. She has the idea of doing an interpretation of King Lear (by Shakespeare) and you might be interested in writing some incidental music (instead of playing it as you have just been doing in South America). If you don't like that idea, here is another: I shall look for some more lectures that you could give that would give you more money. In any case we can certainly find the money needed for the air travel.

I have told the whole story to Mr Carter (Middlebury), telling him that we still have hopes that you will arrive here for the Conference.

If you don't get here for Middlesbury, you can travel by boat to arrive here on 15 September; it is cheaper than the plane. Mr Brady and the Institute may even help you by reducing the cost of the boat.

In any case, telegraph me (at my expense) about the 18th of August so that I can know whether or not you are coming. If you need money for the plane (and don't get it by way of Institute-Brady-Air France) telegraph me as well and I will find it. You can always give lectures or write music here to repay the money given (*My French is so bad: I mean that you can always make money here which you can use to repay any money advanced.*)

Wonderful news of your concert at the Champs-Elysées about which Souvtchinsky wrote to me. Bring the recordings here. The Second Sonata is going to be played here in November.

Write or telegraph soon. Your friend as ever,

John

22

Letter from John Cage to Pierre Souvtchinsky
probably August 1950

My dear Pierre,

Boulez has written to me. He is on his way back to Paris by ship. He asked for a Visa in Buenos Aires, but they stupidly would not give him one. Now he needs the money for the plane fare (370 dollars) in order to arrive here in time to give the Middlebury lectures. I told you that he has got the *"Grant"*. I have written to him at Rue Beautreillis telling him to go to Mr Brady at the Embassy, the Institute (170 Blvd St Germain) and Air France and the French Government. Perhaps they will pay the travel costs. If not, I will seek the money here; and I am writing to you now with the thought that you could ask Mme Tézenas (etc.) in looking for money as well. Feel free to telegraph me at my expense at any time if Pierre needs anything. For the Middlebury conferences, he must be here by 19 August. Middlebury will give him $85; the *"Grant"* will give him $700. I can also try to find more lectures for him and in that way he will be able to repay the money people are giving to him at present for the flight.

Pierre told me that it was Yvette Grimaud and yourself who looked after all the arrangements for the concert on the 18th. Bravo!

Your friend as ever,

John

Tell Yvette to send me manuscripts; I can get them published here.

Another idea: perhaps you could speak to Philippe Heugel and he could get involved in finding the money for the flight.

23

Letter from John Cage to Pierre Boulez
1 September 1950

Dear Pierre:

Your telegram just came; I, too, am 'désolé'.[1] The thing I worry about is that I very clearly took for granted that you would come if the arrangements were found here. I even found indirectly a Lady whom I don't know personally who was going to pay the airplane fare if necessary. Forgive me. What you must know is that the whole idea appears to me now as having been inspired by selfishness, – for what our musical world here has to offer you is nothing compared with what you would have given (and still give not even being here). So, in a sense, it would have been a waste of time for you, though not for us.

I am writing a new work for orchestra and prepared piano,[2] and the piano preparation has many microtonal pitch relations, brought about by an object, the height of which can be controlled, that rests on the sounding board and becomes a bridge (making the strings other & similar lengths). Percussion sounds in the orchestra are integral parts of the gamuts which are made up of accidentally chosen complexes. When it is finished I will send you a copy.

How is the printing of your other works, especially the Quartet,[3] coming along? Please don't forget to send me one.

As ever, John

---

[1] Boulez's telegram to Cage is in the Archive at Northwestern University. It is dated 1 September 1950, and reads: "Impossible de venir désolé amicalement Boulez." (JP)
[2] The Concerto for prepared piano and chamber orchestra.
[3] The *Livre pour quatuor*.

24

Letter from Pierre Boulez to John Cage
Autumn 1950

My dear John,

There is nothing to be said; you are a much faster letter-writer than I am. I am ashamed to have delayed so long in replying to you and to have sent only a short telegram.

I am going to recount a little of the history of my return to you. Having arrived at Marseille and disembarked, I dawdled on the way back to Paris, and I didn't discover the mail that was waiting for me until very late. That is why I sent you the telegram so late. As for explanations, here they are: J. L. Barrault had agreed to release me, if I obtained the visa in Buenos Aires, given that there was to be no production with music at Marigny until the beginning of December. I discussed it with him at length. Since the visa didn't arrive, I promised and assured Barrault that I would be there for the beginning of the season to take up my "activities" again as Stage Music Director!! It was agreed verbally. But, in order to exonerate you in the eyes of the Institut International, to whom I shall write in any case, you can say that I was contractually tied to Marigny during the hesitation over the visa application. If it could be set up again for next season?! But I no longer dare ask you for anything after this default.

Excuse me for this whole episode which has caused you so much useless fussing around. And please understand that I am most disappointed to miss this three-month stay in New York. I would really like to have seen you again and to have got to know the people and the feel of where you live. Let's hope that we won't have to wait too long (let's hope that Korea ...)

P. Souvtchinsky has told you about the Soleil des Eaux concert. It seems that Désormière was fantastic. I am still the only one not to have heard my music. I have heard a lot about it. Yvette told me that the orchestral sonorities were most curious. I hope so. It has been recorded on film.[1] Heugel has had it transferred to discs. I think I shall have one that I shall be able to send to you. That way you will be able to judge "de auditu". I shall have to sort that out either with Heugel or with Yvette Grimaud's husband, who works for the radio. In any case, I am determined to send you a copy somehow. You know, as well, that Heugel is going to publish the orchestral pocket score. And, naturally, you will be one of the first recipients.

---

[1] This refers to an audio recording of the work on celluloid, which was used as a medium for sound recording before the discovery of magnetic tape. (RS)

For the time being, I have dived into the orchestra for le Visage Nuptial,[2] on poems by Char; orchestration which is giving me a lot of trouble, because I want it to be very refined. And that only comes by successive small advances. I am very particular about that. The result in le Soleil des Eaux encouraged me in this respect. As for the new piece, the *"Work in Progress"*!,[3] it is too early to speak for as long about it. Silence is more prudent and I shall not break it until much later. I can in any case tell you that it won't be easy to get to grips with it.

I can see that you are currently having a most productive period. I hope that you will send me some of the results sometime. I am thinking a lot at the moment about the phenomena of scales which are continuous or discontinuous, superimposable or not. One can always harbour illusions.

What's new in your far-off, inaccessible New York? Here, Horenstein is soon to put on Wozzeck by Berg, a work which seems to me more and more remarkable for its occasionally inextricable complexity, which has about it something of the Labyrinth without Ariadne's thread. He is going to have fifteen orchestral rehearsals; and can you believe that I am going to do my utmost not to miss a single one. It is going to be a great event, and I am quite overjoyed by it.

Apart from that, I can't tell you anything, even approximately, for this season. You will thank William Masselos for being willing to work on my Sonata. I am relying expressly on you to give him advice on producing the right tempos, expression and tone quality. Tell Morton Feldman as well that I have not forgotten him and that I shall send him a letter soon concerning his quintet.[4]

What a shame for me still not to have seen New York! How idiotic for us not to see each other again this year, when it is possible, because of that stupid business over the missing visa in Buenos Aires. Which of us is going to make the return visit now? Aren't you thinking of coming back to Paris one day? Hoping to hear from you soon, I remain your faithful friend.

PB

---

[2] Cf. no. 3, note 7.

[3] This probably refers to the abortive *Coup de dés* project. In a very early publication of extracts from this correspondence, in which the chronology is not reliable, Deborah Campana reports an interview with Boulez in which he states that the work in question is Oubli signal lapidé. This is most unlikely, since Boulez first mentions this work only in no. 36 (May 1952), nearly two years later. (See the *Bucknell Review*, 32/2 (1989), p. 247, note 2.)

[4] Cf. no. 11, note 4.

25

Letter from John Cage to Pierre Boulez
18 December 1950

My dear Pierre

Yesterday evening, we heard your Sonata; David Tudor played it (magnificently, too) instead of Masselos.[1] Tudor is going to make a recording for you, and, if you like it, we could press for a public recording. (Many thanks for the disc of "Soleil des Eaux"; Heugel and you both sent me a copy. I have given one of them to Tudor. David Tudor is twenty-five, like you, and he is a friend of Morton Feldman.) Before Masselos had begun work on the Sonata, Feldman told me that Tudor had already devoted three months of study to the work (this was in spring/summer). From that it was obvious to choose Tudor *(my French is too bad; forgive me if I continue in English). Tudor had spontaneously devoted himself to the labor of understanding and playing the Sonata; I loaned him the original which you had given me with the sketches.[2] He studied French in order to read your articles in* Contrepoint *and* Polyphonie *(by the way, they never send me these, – although I subscribed) and he has made a collection and study of Artaud. He is an extraordinary person and at the concert (as I was turning pages for him) I had feelings of an exaltation equal to that you had introduced me to 4 rue Beautreillis. Naturally the audience was divided (for the various reasons audiences are), but I can tell you with joy that you have here a*

---

[1] Cage wrote the following programme note for this American première:
   In the Second Sonata, which is being performed at this concert, one finds two rows. One (D, A, D sharp, G sharp, B, E, F sharp. C, C sharp, F, G) is used in the first and third movements. The other (G, F, G sharp, F sharp, C sharp, C, B flat, B. D. E. flat, A, E) relate to the second and fourth movements. In his preface to the work, Boulez remarks: "All the counterpoints are equally important: there are no principal parts, no secondary parts." In this respect as in many others Boulez's dodecaphony bears more relation to that of Webern than to that of Berg or Schoenberg. ... With regard to the rhythmic complexity of his music, Boulez wrote in *Polyphonie*: "Why search for such complexity? In order to find a rhythmic element which corresponds so perfectly to the twelve-tone means that it also is 'atonal'."
   David Tudor kept the Second Sonata in his American concert repertoire. Notably, he played it on 5 July 1951 at Colorado University, on 19 August at Black Mountain College, on 1 January 1952 at the Living Theatre in New York, and on 22 March 1953 at the University of Illinois (according to Tudor's concert programmes preserved in his archives and communicated by John Holzaepfel).

[2] The autograph and sketches of the Second Sonata are found with Boulez's letters to Cage, in the archives of Northwestern University. These documents show that the third movement, entitled "Variations-Rondeau", was finished in May 1946 and that it was originally dedicated to Mme Vaurabourg-Honegger. The manuscript package bears the following dedication: "For John Cage, in memory of our meeting in Paris which was so interesting for us both. With very best wishes." The autograph contains a passage – in regular semiquavers – omitted from the published version.

strong and devoted following. Your music gives to those who love it an arousing and breathtaking enlightenment. I am still always trembling afterwards. After the concert Tudor, Feldman and I with 20 others celebrated and then finally at 4 A.M. the three of us were alone walking through the streets still talking of you and music. The evening before Tudor had played in my apartment and there were many who came to hear, including Varèse, Maro Ajemian, Mrs E. E. Cummings,[3] etc. etc. etc. I enclose some critical notices (which are not studies), programme, etc. *Now we want to prepare a performance of the String Quartet, when can the score & parts be available? We have a real hunger.*

[In the margin, attached by an arrow to the foregoing phrase:]

I would love to arrange a second Invitation here for you on the occasion of the Quartet (*performance*). As you see, I know nothing about the war.[4]

It was a great joy to hear many times all 4 mvts. of the Sonata (a pleasure you had not given me); the entire work is marvelous but the 4th mvt among them is transcendent.

If you could take the time to write to Tudor (perhaps after he sends you a recording) he would be very happy I know. His address is 69 E. 4th St., N.Y.C.

Feldman's music is extremely beautiful now. It changes with each piece, I find him my closest friend now among the composers here.

My music too is changing. I am writing now an entire evening of music for Merce to be done January 17 (flute, trumpet, 4 percussion players, piano (not prepared, violin and cello).[5] I still have one mvt of the Concerto for prepared piano and orchestra to complete; it may be performed in March in Hartford, Connecticut. My string quartet will also be done in March both in Hartford and here in New York. For the Concerto and the ballet I use charts giving in the form of a checker board pre-orchestrated combinations of sound; it is evident that moves may be made on this 'board' followed by corresponding or non-corresponding moves. In the Concerto there are 2 such charts (one for the orchestra & one for the piano) bringing about the possibility of "given" relationships. In the dance music the idea of a gradual metamorphosis of the chart into a new chart is employed. Two other ideas are in my mind now: that each square of the chart be taken as the [added above the line by a spike:] *(at that moment) visible member of a large family of sounds; and the other idea that 4 charts, each one referring to one only characteristic of sound, could be used in stead of one. All this brings me closer to a 'chance' or if you like to an un-aesthetic choice. I keep, of course, the means of rhythmic structure feeling that that is the 'espace sonore' in which [each] of these sounds may exist and change. Composition becomes 'throwing sound into silence' and rhythm which in my Sonatas had been one of breathing becomes now one of a flow of sound and silence. I will send you soon some results.*

[3] The wife of the poet on whose text Boulez was to write *Cummings ist der Dichter* for choir and chamber orchestra (1968–70).

[4] This refers to the Korean War. At the date of this letter, China had just entered the war in support of North Korea, opposing the UN forces under General MacArthur. Boulez had mentioned Korea in no. 24. (RS)

[5] This is the Sixteen Dances, for the forces that Cage indicates.

Thank you again for the recording of your orchestral work (which, seems to me, must be an earlier work);[6] *the parts that interest me the most are those at the beginning and at the end. I admire the separation of voice and orchestra at the beginning. The entire continuity is marvelously poetic and changing and suggests an opera. But I have the feeling that this is an earlier work than those of yours I am attached to through having heard or seen more often. In other words you have walked on to use your metaphor of one foot in front of the other.*[7] *Tell me, if what I say is wrong.*

Your Sonata is still in our ears, and gratitude will never cease. Those who had no courage to directly listen are troubled; you have increased the danger their apathy brings them to. But now I am no longer one of a few Americans who are devoted to you, but one of many.

Very affectionately

John

I would still love to publish one of Yvette G.'s works.

[in the left margin:]

How are friends! Gatti, Stephane and Souvtchinsky.

The feminine principle.

[above:] Merry Xmas! Happy New Year!

[in the right margin:]

How are you? I am unwell occasionally.

---

[6] This still refers to *Le soleil des eaux*. The recording of this première (mentioned in no. 24) was re-issued in October 1986 in a semi-private collection (INA-Caisse des dépots et consignations, Concerts des Champs-Elysées). In the next letter, Boulez replies to Cage concerning this, and clarifies the chronology of *Le soleil des eaux*, the *Livre pour quatuor*, and the Second Sonata.

[7] This isn't exactly Boulez's metaphor, even if he uses it in conversation with his friend. It is taken from a popular French boy-scouts' song: *La meilleure façon d'marcher, c'est encore la nôtre, c'est de mettre un pied d'vant l'autre, et d'se casser le nez!* ("The best way to walk, is the way we walk along, one foot in front of the other, and get your face smashed in!") Cage must be alluding to the conversations in Paris, since this phrase doesn't appear in Boulez's letters until the following one (no. 26, p. 86), where he takes up Cage's comment here.

26

Letter from Pierre Boulez to John Cage
30 December 1950

Dear John,

I awaited your letter anxiously. Rachel Rosenthal brought it to me at last and I was completely absorbed in it. I am replying at once, and because of that – my haste – I am also writing in French. (It reminds you of the old schoolboy maxim: versions are easier than proses!).

The goodwill and dedication with which that Sonata has been treated have pleased me greatly. I hope one day to get to know David Tudor, but even now I owe him a great debt of gratitude, and I'm going to write to him by the same post to thank him for his magnificent performance. You ask me for the quartet?[1] Picture me to yourself, completely paralyzed by copying, on account of that damned quartet. And here is why. I have to copy out two scores in full. One with bar-lines for performance – for the parts –, bar-lines that are in any case no more than a quantification of the values of rhythmic units between two bar-lines; and on the other hand a score to be read – a study score – without a single bar-line, but with the real rhythmic markings, which is to say purely horizontal ones according to cell. That makes about 200 pages (yes, 200!!) to copy out again. So taking into account the engraving, I don't see the quartet coming out before June. For I am not giving all my time to it. I have started, in addition to the Mallarmé Coup de Dés,[2] a new piece of chamber music.[3] Saby came out with the magnificent reaction, when I told him the number of instrumentalists (49): it is "musique de grande chambre". Really, it will be a collection of 14 or 21 polyphonies[4] (maybe more), I don't know yet, very long in duration. But one will be able to select what one likes.[5]

[6][There are 7 groups of 7 instruments: 2 groups of woodwind, 1 group of

---

[1] The *Livre pour quatuor*.

[2] See no. 13, note 1.

[3] This refers to *Polyphonie X*. The Paul Sacher Stiftung possesses the draft score (seventeen pages) of a first version for forty-nine instruments. Its second version calls for only eighteen, which the article "Possibly ..." records by taking from this work, without naming it, the list of instruments (see *Stocktakings*, pp. 130–1). The work was completed in 1951; it was first performed, conducted by Hans Rosbaud, on 6 October of that year (and not 1961, as an error in Jameux's book suggests).

[4] A "polyphony" here refers to an autonomous section of music, made up of several groups of instruments, the groups playing against each other polyphonically. (RS)

[5] Paul Griffiths points out that this is the first mention by Boulez in this correspondence of recourse to some form of chance operation. (personal communication)

[6] The two sections between square brackets (pp. 80–6 and 86–8) were first published in *Orientations*, pp. 129–37.

brass, 2 groups of percussion: 1st group, pitched percussion (piano, xylo-phone, harp, timpani), 2nd group: unpitched (skin-metal-wood). Lastly 2 groups of strings. All of that is based on the transformations of a single series, which works as follows:

1) Series of twenty-four ¼ tones:

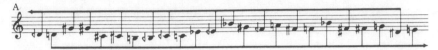

which divides into 2 series of ½ tones:

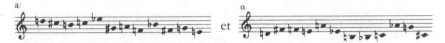

From series a, I narrow the intervals by ¼ tones:

which gives me a ¼-tone series missing twelve notes and which can only be used on transpositions of its own notes. I then restore this series to semitones by translating the ¼-tone notes, which gives me:

I put series α through the same process, giving me Cc and γ.

Then I enlarge the intervals of series a by 1¼ times, which gives:

which, restored to semitones, gives:

The same for series α which gives me Ee and ε.

I then construct an ideogram by taking the common notes from the 4 series in semitones, β γ δ ε:

With this series fφ, I reconstitute 2 series in ¼ tones with fφ→ and fφ← ± ¼ tone and observing the alternation of semitones and ¼ tones implied in my series A, i.e.:

which therefore gives 2 forms: F and Φ which complete the cycle.

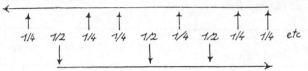

Thus I have 3 complete series of 24 ¼ tones; and 4 series missing 12 quarter tones

A, F, Φ   Bb, Cc, Dd, Ee,

2 series of semitones;	4 derived semitone series;	their ideogram
a and α (components of A)	β, γ, δ, ε	fφ (component of F and Φ).

The general structure of these polyphonies is thus organized by the deduction of their series.

Rhythmically, I make use of 7 organizations, based on a single cell:[7]

3 component, or simple rhythms:

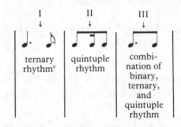

[7] Boulez used these examples again in his article "Possibly ..." (*Stocktakings*, p. 121).

[8] It is not clear, here and in the following table and discussion, whether Boulez regards the basic form of this motive as being dotted or undotted. The essential feature throughout is the 2:1 ratio between the notes (see below). (RS)

4 compound, or combinatory rhythms:

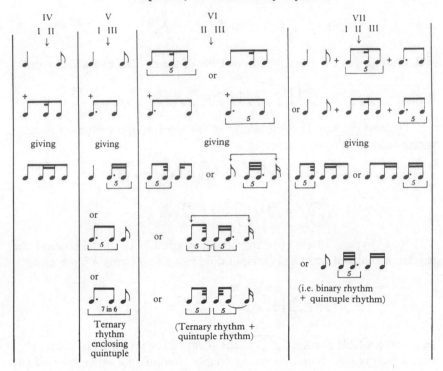

I put each of these simple rhythms through 7 series of transformations.

For example, I take rhythm I.

a) <u>Simple transformation:</u> by adding a dot; reducing the note value. Augmentation; regular or irregular diminution. Irrational transformation:

b) <u>Written-out rhythm.</u> By the smallest note value or its derivatives, the attack point of the initial rhythm included or not included: which gives:

c) <u>Hollowed-out rhythm.</u> Introduction of the syncope, but with only a single attack.

or with the attack and the rests inverted:

d) <u>Geared-down rhythm.</u> Multiplication of the rhythm by its own ratio:

e) <u>Derived rhythm.</u> Decomposition of the rhythm into written-out values taking account of its own ratio:

f) <u>Rest-rhythm.</u> In a non-retrogradable rhythm,[9] one of the poles of the rhythm is replaced with the corresponding rest, in all forms. Which gives:

In a retrogradable rhythm ( ) the pivot cell or symmetrical cells.

g) <u>Rest-rhythm.</u> In a non-retrogradable rhythm, the other pole of the rhythm is replaced with the corresponding rest. Which gives:

In a retrogradable rhythm, the pivot cell and a symmetrical cell; or 1 symmetrical cell.

<u>Next.</u> The non-retrogradable rhythms I make retrogradable by adding on one of their own note-values, which gives:

α) or . Then from α, I go through the whole cycle β/γ/δ/ε

applying the same transformations.

I make retrogradable rhythms non-retrogradable:
thus: becomes or

Then I obtain further:
α) from retrogradable, non-retrogradable:

---

[9] Rather confusingly, Boulez uses "retrogradable" here and in the following explanations to mean rhythms that do *not* change when retrograded, i.e. palindromic rhythms. (RS)

from non-retrogradable, retrogradable: ins 22 here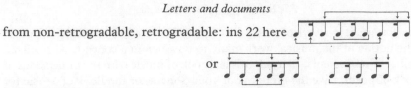

or

etc. . . . with symmetrical or asymmetrical augmentation.
For a cell that is fairly complicated to begin with, such as:

VI)[10]

this gives very complex results of the type:

development
of VI: d)   or:

As for the actual composition, I want to broaden the scope of Polyphony itself
to include what has been done for Counterpoint. In other words, polyphony
will serve as counterpoint. Unequal polyphony, moreover; in other words,
answers will be able to take place between 3 voice and 5 voice polyphonies, or
between 4, 6, and 7 voice, etc. . . . In addition, the instrumental group will
vary with each new Polyphony.

For example the first will be for all 49 Instruments. 7 times 7.

The second will be for only 12, grouped 3 times 4: 4 Violins, 4 Violas, 4
Cellos.

The third for brass and percussion divided into 4. {2 pianos}, {Harp,
Timpani, Xylophone, Celesta, Vibraphone}, Brass, {Percussion I,
Percussion II etc. . . . etc . . .}

In certain polyphonies, I shall also make use, as you do in the music you are
in the process of writing, of sampled sonorities [*sonorités échantillonées*], i.e.
sound aggregates, linked by a constant but movable within the scale of
sonorities. Like you, too, and as in my Quartet, I can build the construction
with all the possibilities afforded by the material, in other words a construction where the combinations create the form, and thus where the form does
not stem from an aesthetic choice.

For example, the first polyphony is constructed like this at the start:

WOODWIND I: Series a with rhythm III. WOODWIND II: Inversion of series a
with rhythm II. Brass: Series α with rhythm I. Pitched percussion: Inversion
of series a with rhythm IV. Unpitched percussion: Rhythm VII. STRINGS:
Series A with rhythm V. Strings II: Inversion of series A with rhythm VI.

As you can see, the rhythmic complexity is a function of the complexity of
the series or the instrumental formation. The architecture of this piece will be
based on the exchanges between series and rhythms and the possible transformations of monoseries and polyrhythms or polyseries and monorhythms.

---

[10] In fact, this rhythm occurs in column VII, not VI, of Boulez's table. (RS)

As you see, it is a work of pretty vast scope. Above all, I would like to get rid of the notion of the musical work made to be given in a concert, with a fixed number of movements. Instead, this is a book of music with the dimensions of a book of poems (like the grouping of your Sonatas or the Book of Music for Two Pianos.[11]

Still one step at a time. I hope I won't smash my face in by walking on the edge of the sidewalk![12]]

As for the "Soleil des Eaux", that was a step in the wrong direction, or at least a hop on the spot. The work was written straight after the Second Sonata and before the Quartet, for the Radio; and since the poetry was very simple, so was the music. (Nevertheless it is completely athematic). I gave it this preface taken from a book by René Char himself which I offer for your consideration so that you won't have it in for me too much over this easy work:

"Warning:

We have within us, on our temperate side, a suite of *chansons* which flank us, communicating wings between our breathing in repose and our highest fevers. These are almost banal pieces, mild in shade, old-fashioned in outline, whose tissue however carries a tiny wound. Everyone is allowed to attach an origin and term to this questionable reddening".[13]

Yesterday (29 December), at the Avenue de Messine Cinema, I saw Burgess Meredith's film on Calder, for which you did the music.[14] It was marvellous, the synthesis of music and image quite perfect. It is the first time that I have felt the music to be necessary to a film. I was with Gatti and Joffroy and we liked the film very much. Calder's objects are very beautiful, two sculptures in particular. The photos and montages are extraordinary achievements. I particularly liked the silence coming with the fixed-frame shots after the music with the moving camera, and also a rhythmic diminution on several sonorities. I should like to know how you managed, technically, for example in the scene where Calder is shown using machine-tools in turn, where the soundtrack makes use of these factory noises.

[When I read your letter, you cannot imagine how happy I was to see how we are progressing in making discoveries, and in the same rhythm. I won't construct a theory about this, but Saby and I have both greatly pondered all these questions of the organization of sound material. And I am thinking of writing a little book based on the principle that sound material can only be organized serially, but widening the principle to extreme conclusions, i.e.:

---

[11] The *Sonatas and Interludes* for prepared piano (1946–8) and *A Book of Music* for two prepared pianos (1944).

[12] See no. 25, note 7.

[13] This "Warning" is the first text of the series of poems "La sieste blanche", from the René Char collection *Les matinaux*, published by Gallimard on 20 January 1950. The phrase "within us" is an addition by Boulez, and in the original the word "reddening" [*rougeur*] is underlined. Cf. René Char, *Oeuvres complètes* (Paris: Gallimard, 1983), p. 291.

[14] See no. 4, note 3.

that within the entire scale of sounds from vibration 16 to vibration 20,000[15] you can take a series of notes such as: A (a^1 b^2 c^3 d^4 e^5 f^6 g^7 ... n); that the sound space will be defined by the transposition of A onto all the degrees that make up A, i.e.: B (b^1 b'^2 c'^3 d'^4 e'^5 f'^6 ... n'), C (c^1 b''^2 c''^3 d''^4 e''^5 ... n'') up to N (n^1 b_n^2 c_n^3 d_n^4 e_n^5 f_n^6 ... n_n^7) so that by the inversion of A, where A is (a, b = a + x, c = a + y, d = a + z, etc....) one has A (a, b = a − x, c = a − y, d = a − z etc ...) taking a as a pivot, and all the transpositions based on A.

Graphically this could give:

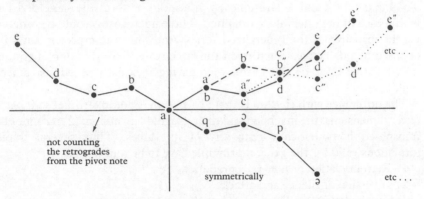

Another inversional space is defined if you take b (or c or d) and not a as the pivot note. (which would not change the transpositions of the original). Thus you have a space defined by a constant and a variable.

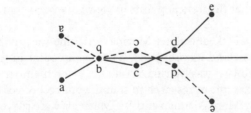

Thus one can organise the whole of the sound material, whatever it may be.

In this way, the notions of modality, tonality and the series are closely combined so that they now become a single idea. The same applies to the notions of continuity and discontinuity in the sound material; since it is the choice of the discontinuous within the continuous. This is what I am aiming at with my ¼ tones. In two or three years, they will be 1/12 and 1/24 tones.

Moreover, I have also found a graphic formula to cover absolutely the whole scale of sounds with 1/4 and 1/3 tones, and you shall see how: taking the smallest common denominator (a simple property of the fractions 1/3 and 1/4).

---

[15] Boulez refers to the audible frequency spectrum of 16 Hz (vibrations per second) to 20,000 Hz. (RS)

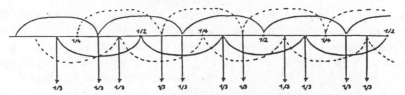

You start off your division in 1/3 tones, then go to 1/2 and 1/4 tones, and each division, by successive superpositions, gives intervals of twelfth-tones. To obtain 1/18th and 1/24th tones, you have to perform the same division within each of the intervals so obtained. These microcosms could be ordered via the principle of the generalized series. And thus a microcosm could be opposed to a defective structure on the large scale. I am thinking of ending my Mallarmé Coup de Dés in this way (having a specially tuned instrument built).

The difference with rhythm is that (1) rhythm is not invertible, so it has 2 fewer dimensions: the inversion and the retrograde inversion; (2) it cannot be transposed homothetically onto any of its values. Thus several transformations valid for the general principle have to be found: i.e.:

1) Retrogradation or non-retrogradation.
2) Inversion of silence and attacks.
3) Augmentation or diminution, regular or irregular.
4) Rhythm written out or not written out in single-unit notes or their derivatives.
5) Introduction of the syncope within the rhythm.

So you can see that theoretical points of view have been confirmed since we last met.]

I must tell you a little anecdote. Marina Scriabine was giving a lecture on contemporary music and its problems. There is no point in telling you how the lecture went, since it was Marina Scriabine (you remember our visit?) – At that point, as an example of research in sound, your records of dances for two pianos recorded by Maro Ajemian and W. Masselos were played. All well and good! But afterwards a gentleman got up – for it was a lecture-debate – and said, "What do you think about be-bop?" – in all seriousness. (I hope, by the way, that you have heard of be-bop, which is the new style of jazz implanted in Paris by Dizzy Gillespie – i.e. "Dis-y Ineptie" ["What Rubbish"], "alla Joyce" – and which is causing a storm in St-Germain des Prés.) The gentleman in question was a *poète lettriste*[16] who was making out that your music was be-bop, and that there was no solution in music for be-bop. By this point, I was crimson with rage, and I threw the worst insults I could think of at them. I was with Souvtchinsky; we were finally overwhelmed in front of such stupidity. In the end I replied to them that, faced by such bullshit, you don't discuss, you just insult. Which I did not refrain from doing.

---

[16] *Lettrisme* was an avant-garde literary school of the time sometimes called *poésie concrète* in English-speaking countries. It advocated the use of onomatopoeia in poems without meaning.

But let's get back to the Sonata. I eagerly await Tudor's recording. Saby as well is burning to have it. For I too would like to hear that fourth movement! – It is so good to think of such dedicated and intelligent friends. I should love to get to know both of them, Tudor and Morton Feldman. For here, I am completely cut off from musical company: Leibowitz, Nigg or Martinet!! I have to say as well that it is unbearable. As for the others, it can't even be contemplated. We live here among nonentities. Luckily there is the little circle of friends whom you know well and we are becoming more and more inseparable, Gatti, Saby, Joffroy and me. We are trying not to think of the war too much, and to live each day as it comes, going as far as we can with our investigations.[17]

As for Souvtchinsky, he is Providence itself. He is a model of tireless friendship, devotion, comradeship and efficiency. Why are we not all together in the same 'geometrical locus', whose abstraction would be our guarantee?

Your walks with Tudor and Feldman make me think of our own with Gatti, Saby and Joffroy, where we are perpetually trying to shine better light on all the problems that crowd in on such an un-self-disciplined imagination.

On the subject, you are amazed not to have received Polyphonie and Contrepoint. Be amazed no longer; the publisher has gone bust and I don't think the second edition of Contrepoint will ever appear. It was centred on the 200th anniversary of Bach's death. It will come out – if it ever does – slightly after that holy feast![18]

On the subject (again), have I already told you that I've got to write a long article – to appear in a little collection of essays on Russian music that Souvtchinsky is publishing[19] – on the Rite of Spring? I've got to hurry up, I haven't begun it yet.

I will let you know again that R. Leibowitz's credit is at a low ebb and nobody, here, any longer believes in that false prophet. He has had his day, and justice is being done.

It is a long time since writing a letter gave me such great pleasure.

Your dear friend as ever.

PB

---

17 This last sentence is quoted by Cage in his "Lecture on something" (1951), *Silence*, p. 145. (JP)

18 In fact, Boulez's article, "Bach's moment" appears in *Contrepoints* no. 7 (and not no. 2) in 1951 (pp. 71–86). The journal had indeed run into difficulties: the first five issues appeared in 1946, no. 6 in 1949; it passed from the Éditions de Minuit to Richard-Masse and finished with the eighth issue in 1951. The special number devoted to Bach, and only one year late, included articles by R. Schwab, B. and M. Benson, A. Coeuroy, F. Goldbeck (the general editor), M. Pincherle, H. L. de la Grange, J. Liaud-Sabiel and G. Brelet, as well as a drawing by Dufy and a composition on the name B-A-C-H by Charles Koechlin.

19 "Strawinsky demeure" in P. Souvtchinsky (ed.), *Musique Russe* (Paris: Presses Universitaires de France, 1953), vol. 1, pp. 151–224; reprinted as "Stravinsky remains" in *Stocktakings*, pp. 55–110.

Bonne Année, Bonne santé (that's the ritual formula here) –

Hello to Merce and all the New York friends.

I almost forgot one thing. Could I possibly have the equipment and score of Varèse's Ionisation. F. Passerone, who is Professor of Percussion at the Conservatoire, would like to have it played for his students at the end of the season. Ask Varèse if it is possible. Also, would you have any of your spare scores, of those which we have heard on record here; Passerone would be agreable to getting them played.

Gatti wrote to you yesterday.

Tell Morton Feldman that I am going to write to him in a day or two. This time it's true. I have already got paper and envelope ready.

When shall we meet again?

27

Letter from Pierre Boulez to John Cage
between 7 and 21 May 1951

Dear John,

What has become of you? No news. Complete silence reigns over the Hamlet of Brooklyn.[1] It has to be said that I have not been prolix either. I have not even thanked you for the Ezra Pound *Contes*[2] which I have only glanced through so far, not having the opportunity to take my time over them – and I have to take my time, my knowledge of English being so rudimentary.

I have had a visit from Seymour Barab, who gave me your group letter, two months or more ago now.[3] I haven't seen him again since and I am not sure what has become of him, although I did meet him very briefly at midnight one evening near St Germain des Prés.

Thank you for that last letter. I do hope not to disappoint those who have faith in me. I am still working on the same piece I told you about in my last letter.[4] But I have undertaken a new series of works (currently for two pianos, but it might require three or four). In this series of works,[5] I have attempted to realize the serial organization at all levels: arrangement of the pitches, the

---

[1] Armand Gatti's nickname for Cage.
[2] This refers to Pound's *Cantos*, written between 1919 and 1959; the first complete edition of the cantos then written had been published in New York in 1948.
[3] Missing from the collection of Cage's letters to Boulez.
[4] This refers to *Polyphonie X*. See no. 26, note 3.
[5] The first book of *Structures* for two pianos (1951–2; Jameux no. 14). The second book was written between 1956 and 1961 (Jameux no. 25). Boulez had in fact planned a further two books which were never written.

dynamics, the attacks, and the durations. The pitch organization being able to be transmuted into the organization of the durations or dynamics or attacks. To such an extent that all the structures are interchangeable. There are two possible methods of organization: "mechanical" organization, which means that the combined units are used here only in single dimensions: horizontal, vertical, diagonal. Then there will be "directed" organization or organization of combined units. I've taken over your chess-board system for my own purposes, by making it serve on dissociated, antagonistic, and parallel or anti-parallel levels. If only we could discuss all that face to face. Why don't you come to Paris?

Here, paralysis rules! Menotti's "Consul" is a triumph.[6] On the radio I heard, "1902, Debussy, Pelléas et Mélisande; 1951, Menotti, le Consul." This is to show you what a paroxysm of noise-making we are in.

I have been having a slanging match with Ansermet yesterday and today. He needs the whole of phenomenology – taken backwards, moreover, since he starts off from the essence of a privileged interval, the fifth, in order to arrive at the existence of intervals in general – in order to cover his reactionary position against contemporary music.[7] This notion of aberation or impasse comes up over and over. I replied that the accusation could be reversible. And when he accuses others of absurdity, those others could return the compliment with just as much rigour.

Apart from that, I am writing two articles: one on the rhythmic structure of the Rite of Spring[8] – the second: on dodecaphony, in which Mr Leibowitz and his academicism will be taken vigorously to task.[9]

We have had the first hearing, by Munch in rehearsal, of a Fifth Symphony by Honegger.[10] Disastrous. At the same time we had something – I don't know what – by Copland. Even worse.

I have written to Feldman. But I'm afraid that I wasn't too keen in the end on the works he sent me. I'm sorry if he has taken it badly. I hope he hasn't got it in for me. The same goes for your pupil Christian Wolff. But I am getting worse and worse at expressing myself concerning other people.

Dear John, I am impatient to get your news. It would give me courage. And courage is needed to carry on constantly the struggle of honesty with oneself and to remain combative in the face of idiocy and bad faith. I feel that fortunately we are people who can have a certain solidarity in this matter.

6 For once, France was not behind the times: *Le consul* by Gian Carlo Menotti had just been premièred on 1 March 1950 in Philadelphia.
7 Ernest Ansermet, principal conductor of the Orchestre de la Suisse Romande, set out his phenomenological conception of music in his book *Les fondements de la musique dans la conscience humaine* (*Foundations of Music in Human Thought*) (Neuchâtel: La Baconnière, 1961) and in his *Ecrits sur la musique* (*Writings on Music*) (Neuchâtel: La Baconnière, 1971).
8 See no. 26, note 19.
9 "Possibly ...", *Stocktakings* pp. 111–40.
10 The première took place in Boston on 9 March 1951, conducted by Charles Münch, and the French première was on 7 May 1951, for French radio with the Orchestre National under the same conductor.

Nicole Henriot was very sorry not to see you when she passed through New York. She phoned you several times but could not get a reply.

As ever from Beautreillis,

PB

28

Letter from John Cage to Pierre Boulez
22 May 1951

Dear Pierre:

Your second letter arrived[1] and I hasten to reply, for it has been, naturally, on my mind to write to you for many months. The long letter you sent with the details about your work was magnificent, but I think that it is at least partly due to it that I have not written sooner, for I was concerned to write a letter worthy to be read by you, and I didn't feel able. All this year (in particular) my way of working has been changing, and together with that changing I was involved in many practical commitments (performances, etc.), and when your first letter came,[2] it caught me in the midst of activity and at a point where my way of working was still unformed (and needing to be formed). This seems now to have happened; at least I am writing a long piano work[3] (unprepared) which will carry me through October or November, and I doubt whether anything radically new will enter my technique until I finish this particular piece, so that I feel free now to tell you what I have been doing, and what it was that led to this new work.

In Paris I began the String Quartet, and interrupted the writing of it to do the Calder film which you heard. The Quartet uses a gamut of sounds, some single and some aggregates, but all of them immobile, that is staying always not only in the same register where they originally appear but on the same strings and bowed or produced in the same manner on the same instruments. There are no superpositions, the entire work being a single line. Even the tempo never changes. The continuity (what I call method)[4] is uncontrolled and spontaneous in all except the 3rd movement, where it is strictly canonic, even though there is only one 'voice'. Such ideas as the following occur; direct duration limitation with retrograde or inverse use of the gamut or vice versa. This gives some interesting results since the gamut to begin with is asymmetrical. The sound of the work is special due to the

---

[1] In fact, Cage had not replied to the letter of 30 December 1950 (no. 26), and the following one (no. 27) began with a reminder of this.
[2] I.e. no. 26.
[3] This refers to *Music of Changes* (1951).
[4] Cf. Cage's terminology presented in no. 5.

aggregates and to using no vibrato. It has been performed twice and is being recorded by Columbia, and next Friday will be done again on a program with your 2eme Sonata and some music of Feldman.

You ask for details about the Calder music,[5] particularly the section of noises. What I did was very simple, to record on tape noises actually produced in Calder's studio in the course of his work. The sounds which have the regular accelerandos are produced by large flat rectangles of metal bringing themselves to balance on narrow metallic supports. With about "two hours" of tape I satisfied myself and then proceeded to choose those noises I wished and cut and scotch-tape them together. No synchronizing was attempted and what the final result is is rather due to a chance that was admired. Unfortunately I did this at the last minute (after the music for prep. pn. had been recorded); had I done it at the beginning, I rather imagine I would have made the entire film in this way (using also sounds recorded from nature).

After finishing the Quartet I wrote Six Melodies for Vn. & Pn which are simply a postscript to the Quartet and use the same gamut of sounds (but, naturally, with different timbres). Then I began to write the Concerto for prep. pn and chamber orchestra (25 players). A new idea entered which is this: to arrange the aggregates not in a gamut (linearly) but rather in a chart formation. In this case the size of the chart was 14 by 16. That is to say: 14 different sounds produced by any number of instruments (sometimes only one) (and often including percussion integrally) constitute the top row of the chart and favor (quantitatively speaking) the flute. The second row in the chart favors the oboe and so on. Four rows favor the percussion divided: metal, wood, friction, & miscellaneous (characterized by mechanical means, e.g., the radio). The last four favor the strings. Each sound is minutely described in the chart: e.g. a particular tone, sul pont on the 2nd string of the first vn. with a particular flute tone and, for example a wood block.

I then made moves on this chart of a "thematic nature" but, as you may easily see, with an "athematic" result. This entire first movement uses only 2 moves, e.g. down 2, over 3, up 4, etc. This move can be varied from a given spot on the chart by going in any of the directions. The orchestra (in the first mvt.) was thus rigorously treated, while the piano remained free, having no chart, only its preparation, which, by the way is the most complicated I have ever effected and has as a special characteristic a bridge which is elevated from the sounding board of the piano to the strings and so positioned as to produce very small microtones. In the 2nd movement the piano has a chart provided for it having the same number of elements as that for the orchestra (which latter remains the same). This movement is nothing but an actually drawn series of circles (diminishing in size) on these charts, sometimes using the sounds of the orchestra, sometimes using the sounds of the piano. (In all of this work the rhythmic structure with which you are familiar in my work, remains as the basis of activity.)

---

[5] Here Cage is replying to the first letter received, no. 26.

In the 3rd and last part of the Concerto (the entire work is in one tempo) the two charts metamorphose into a single chart upon which moves are made. This metamorphosis is brought about by use of a method identical with that used by the Chinese in the I Ching, their ancient book of oracles. Three coins are tossed: if 3 heads appear it is a 6 (⊖) (female moving towards male); if 2 heads & a tail, it is a 7 (——) (male, not moving); if 2 tails & a head, it is an 8 (—— ——) (female, not moving); if 3 tails (⊝) it is a 9, (male moving towards the female []). I then established that the piano was male, the orch. female and proceeding by tossing coins found what sounds (7s & 8s) remained from the charts of the 2nd mvt. and which ones (6s & 9s) had to be freshly invented (a 6 became a piano sound taking the place of an orch. sound & a 9 vice versa[)], or an actual aggregate in time came about, that is to say a series of sounds, some orchestral, some piano, taken as a single element in the chart. This is an extension of the aggregate idea and was suggested by the manner in which Chinese characters are indexed, that is, according to the number of brush-strokes required to write them, so that a character with 8 brush strokes is, of course, not 8 characters but only a single one. By making moves on the charts I freed myself from what I had thought to be freedom, and which actually was only the accretion of habits and tastes. But in the Concerto the moves brought about the new freedom only in so far as concerned the sounds. For the rhythmic structure was expressed by means of ieti-control (3 sounds in 2 measures, 5 in 4 etc.) and the idea underlying this is distant from the idea underlying the moves. Another characteristic of the Concerto which disturbed me was the fact that although movement is suggested in the metamorphosis-idea underlying it, each part is like a still-picture rather than like a movie. And another point I must mention is that the orchestra moves almost always in half-notes.

This work was not finished until last February because I interrupted it to write Sixteen Dances for Merce Cunningham. I used the chart ideas but for a combination of pn, vn, flute, cello, trumpet & about 100 percussion instruments played by 4 players. The chart now became 8 × 8 (having 64 elements) disposed Fl, Tpt, perc., perc., pn., pn, Vn, Cello. The size of this chart is precisely that of the chart associated with the I-Ching, but rather than using it in the I-Ching manner I continued to make moves on it as on a magic-square. When it was necessary to write a piece with specific expressivity, e.g. a 'blues' (because of Merce's intention) I simply eliminated all those sounds that didn't apply to a scale suggesting blues (having chromatic tetrachords): After each pair of the dances, 8 elements disappear and 8 new ones take their place, so that the sounds at the end of the evening are entirely different than those at the beginning. At each point, however, the situation presented is a static one.

At this point my primary concern became: how to become mobile in my thought rather than immobile always. And then I saw one day that there was no incompatibility between mobility & immobility and life contains both. This is at the basis of the manner of using the I-Ching for the obtaining of oracles. That is, having tossed the coins, one tosses five times more, obtaining a hexagram, e.g. 6, 9, 8, 7, 7, 7 becomes

which on recourse to the chart, gives the number 6 moving towards the number 25.
If a hexagram appears which is without 6s or 9s only one number is obtained. I
then devised the following ways of working. Having established a rhythmic
structure, I provide myself with the following charts:

1 for tempi (64 elements; 32 active, 32 inactive)
1 for superpositions (in the case of the present piano piece from 1 to 8)
8 for durations (64 elements)
8 for aggregates (32 sounds, 32 silences)
8 for amplitudes (16, the other 16 keep preceding loudness)

Of these last three classes of charts 4 are immobile & 4 are mobile (immobile =
remains & is capable of repetition, mobile = disappears once it has been used,
bringing a new sound to its position in the chart[)]. This relation of mobile-
immobile changes whenever a mobile number (odd) is tossed at the beginning of an
intermediate rhythmic structure point.

With regard to durations I had become conscious (through having settled so
consistently in the Concerto on half-notes) that every note is a half-note but
travelling as it were at a different speed. To bring about greater distinctions of
speed I have changed the notation so that I now use, for instance:

as a simple duration and measure it out on the space of the mss. with a ruler. For
the present piano work I also control the sound-aggregate charts in the following
way: 4 in any direction (vertical or horizontal) give all 12 tones & in the case of
mobility, 4 in time bring all 12 tones (repetitions allowed & no series present).

I interrupted the writing of this piece to write my Imaginary Landscape No IV
for 12 radios[6] using exactly the same ideas. Every element is the result of tossing
coins, producing hexagrams which give numbers in the I-Ching chart: 6 tosses for
a sound, 6 for its duration, 6 for its amplitude. The toss for tempo gives also the
number of charts to be superimposed in that particular division of the rhythmic
structure. The rhythmic structure is now magnificent because it allows for different tempi: accelerandos, ritards etc. The radio-piece is not only tossing of coins
but accepts as its sounds those that happen to be in the air at the moment of
performance. The chart for sounds in this case aggregate tunings: e.g.

---

[6] *Imaginary Landscape No. 4 (March No. 2)* for twelve radios (twenty-four players and
conductor), 1951.

$$72 \longrightarrow 100$$

$$64;$$

$$55n \longrightarrow 65.$$

I have some recordings of this and will send you one; you will also shortly receive your recording by Tudor. He has been very busy and on tour and then finally ill in a hospital. & so has not yet sent you a record. He was moved by your letter to him but he has a curious inability to write letters; if you ever receive one from him it will be something of a miracle.

I miss you terribly and should love to come to Paris; but I have no money to do so and am only living from day to day. How I hope that we will soon see each other again! Tudor speaks of coming to Paris next Spring. You would enjoy each other profoundly, I am sure. One day your father wrote to me from Ohio, & I have always regretted that we failed to meet.

You can see from my present activity how interested I was when you wrote of the Coup de Des of Mallarmé.[7]

And I have been reading a great deal of Artaud. (This because of you and through Tudor who read Artaud because of you.)

I hope I have made a little clear to you what I am doing. I have the feeling of just beginning to compose for the first time. I will soon send you a copy of the first part of the piano piece. The essential underlying idea is that each thing is itself, that its relations with other things spring up naturally rather than being imposed by any abstraction on an 'artist's' part. (see Artaud on an objective synthesis) This is all written in a great hurry, & forgive me; I have to leave to give a concert of music in the Colgate University, up north. Will write soon again. Very affectionately, John.

P.S.

I asked Varèse (many months ago) about the Ionization, as you asked me to do. He says that there is only one set of parts and that he has to keep it here. However, one could get the score easily from New Music Edition 250 W. 57th St. N.Y.C.

Maro & Anahid Ajemian will be in Europe next fall and winter playing recitals and Křenek's Double Concerto[8] *he wrote for them (with orchestra). Perhaps Désormière wd. like to do it. (Although I don't personally like the piece).*

I have not been very well and am still not; there are so many things wrong that I wdn't know where to ask the Doctor to begin.

Merce and I went on another concert tour last month to San Francisco, Denver, Seattle, etc. I always take your music with me (spreading the gospel).

Please don't forget to send me the Quartet as soon as it is available. My devotion to your work does not diminish but rather grows. David says his playing

---

[7] See no. 13, note 1.
[8] This refers to the Concerto for two pianos of 1951.

of your Sonate is improving and that it will be better than ever. He is a magnificent pianist.

We all wish either that you were here in New York or we were all with you in Paris. It would be a marvelous life.

Always yours,

John

29

Letter from Pierre Boulez to John Cage
between 22 May and 17 July 1951[1]

Dear John,

I have just seen Christian Wolff. We talked a long time, and he got me to see the latest dispatches from New York. It was all very exciting and made me regret all the more that we don't see [each other] more often. I must write you a long letter soon on the subject of your last letter.[2] I found it incredibly interesting. We are at the same stage of research. I hardly have any time at the moment, since I am in the middle of work. I will write at the beginning of August.[3] A bientôt – and your as always.

> PB
> *Dear John*
> *Just a minute to say hello,*
> *I'll write later in detail*
> *about what happens or whatever*
> *Christian [Wolff]*

---

[1] This letter was probably written in July, to judge from Cage's reply (no. 30).

[2] This is the letter of 22 May (no. 28), in which Cage gave many details concerning his works.

[3] Boulez indeed wrote in August, but in reply to Cage's request for an article (no. 30).

30

Letter from John Cage to Pierre Boulez
17 July 1951

Dear Pierre,

Thank you for your letter. This is just a note to say that Henry Cowell wants to write an article[1] about current research in music for the Musical Quarterly, and would like to have (as soon as possible) a statement from you about the nature of your research.

How I wish I were there in Paris to see you!

Always yours,

John

31

Letter from Pierre Boulez to John Cage
August 1951

Dear John –

A thousand pardons for the delay in replying to you. But Christian Wolff must have explained the reason to you. I am in the middle of correcting my Polyphonies material. And it is no joke. I am wandering through galaxies of *mistakes.*

First of all, thank you for sending me the letter from Craft which contained

---

[1] This refers to a long account of New York musical life which was published in the *Musical Quarterly* 38 1 (January 1952), pp. 123–36. The article talks first about Cage, then Feldman and Boulez (and finally Busoni). From Boulez's letter which follows (no. 31) Cowell drew several general ideas about athematicism and rhythm, and the seven examples of possible rhythmic groupings (pp. 133–4). The article states (p. 132):

Cage says, "Boulez influenced me with his concept of mobility; my influence on him is that he accepts my idea of aggregates." [Cf. no. 37: "I [Boulez] owe to Cage the idea of sound complexes."] An aggregate in Cage's thinking is the relationship of miscellaneous and apparently disparate objects established by their juxtaposition in space, as furniture and other objects in a room are related by their simultaneous presence there. Similarly, different sorts of musical media may be conceived as constituting an aggregate, and so used as a unit of building material for the creation of musical forms.

a plan for performing my Polyphonie in New York. You might now hear it for yourself next Spring.[1]

I have been wanting for so long to reply at length to your June letter.[2] I enjoyed it so much that I have put off replying each time I have started – so that the response might be worthy of your letter. So excuse me once again. I am only replying between two correction sessions and two sessions at the Folies-Bergère[3] (because for a month, up to 14 September, I am in that appalling dump.)

I am writing to you now especially for the "statement" that you requested for Henry Cowell. Excuse my writing in French, but if I had to translate it! – That way I would not reply to anything ever again, neither accurately, nor in the time available to send it. I ought to have given it to Christian Wolff, but I did not have the time to write it before he left here.

So here is a little essay which I deliver to you before you pass it on to H. Cowell.

[4][This year, my whole attention is focussed on the expansion and homogeneity of the field of serialism. Thinking that music has entered a new stage of activity, the serial form, I have attempted to generalise the notion of the series itself.

A series is a sequence of n sounds, in which none is the same as any other, as far as frequency is concerned, forming a series of n-1 intervals. The derivation of series from this initial series is made by the transpositions b, c, ... n of the whole series, starting with each of the initial series' frequencies. Which therefore gives n series. The inverse series also produces n transposed series. Thus a total of 2n series arise.

If one takes a series between the frequency band F and the frequency band of double the frequency, 2F, then serial transposition may be achieved by multiplying or dividing the frequencies by 2, 4, etc., up to the limits of the audible frequency range.

This is the case – reduced to the number 12 – of the dodecaphonic series. In this case, all the transpositions occur between one band of frequencies

---

1 On the date of the first performance of *Polyphonie X*, see no. 26, note 3. This project never came to pass. After hearing the Südwestfunk recording, Boulez decided to withdraw the work (cf. Jameux p. 66).
2 This refers to the letter of 22 May (no. 28), which no doubt reached Paris in June.
3 At this time, he was employed playing the Ondes Martenot.
4 Cage published the following section in brackets in English in *Transformations: arts, communication, environment*, 1 3 (1952), pp. 168–70, together with similar statements solicited from Morton Feldman and Christian Wolff, and one of his own, under the title, "Four musicians at work" (pp. 168–72). These latter three texts are republished below (no. 32). Cage's article may be compared with the various descriptions of his works given in his letters to Boulez. Boulez's statement was published in *Orientations*, pp. 137–42. As Boulez indicates further on, the examples are taken from both *Polyphonie X* and *Structures*. More precisely, the pitch, dynamics, attacks, and durational series are those of *Structures*. By contrast, the examples of rhythmic possibilities are taken from *Polyphonie X*. These may be compared with no. 26 above and with "Possibly ... " (*Stocktakings*, pp. 111–40). Unlike the article, this letter gives the complete transpositional table of the series in *Structures* (compare the article's Ex. 3).

and the band of twice the frequency: $F, - 2F_1, F_2 - 2F_2$, etc ...
This may be represented graphically as:

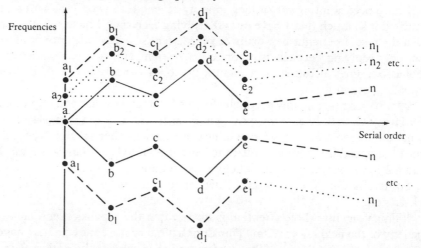

Given this, we may now turn to the dodecaphonic series in more detail. If we transpose it, as suggested, in the order of its component pitches, we obtain a square which reads the same horizontally as vertically. We now number the pitches according to the order of their appearance in the original series. Thus:

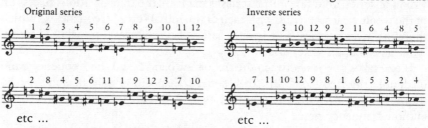

Original series

1 2 3 4 5 6 7 8 9 10 11 12

2 8 4 5 6 11 1 9 12 3 7 10

etc ...

Inverse series

1 7 3 10 12 9 2 11 6 4 8 5

7 11 10 12 9 8 1 6 5 3 2 4

etc ...

Which <u>in figures</u> gives the following double serial organisation:

A

1	2	3	4	5	6	7	8	9	10	11	12
2	8	4	5	6	11	1	9	12	3	7	10
3	4	1	2	8	9	10	5	6	7	12	11
4	5	2	8	9	12	3	6	11	1	10	7
5	6	8	9	12	10	4	11	7	2	3	1
6	11	9	12	10	3	5	7	1	8	4	2
7	1	10	3	4	5	11	2	8	12	6	9
8	9	5	6	11	7	2	12	10	4	1	3
9	12	6	11	7	1	8	10	3	5	2	4
10	3	7	1	2	8	12	4	5	11	9	6
11	7	12	10	3	4	6	1	2	9	5	8
12	10	11	7	1	2	9	3	4	6	8	5

B

1	7	3	10	12	9	2	11	6	4	8	5
7	11	10	12	9	8	1	6	5	3	2	4
3	10	1	7	11	6	4	12	9	2	5	8
10	12	7	11	6	5	3	9	8	1	4	2
12	9	11	6	5	4	10	8	2	7	3	1
9	8	6	5	4	3	12	2	1	11	10	7
2	1	4	3	10	12	8	7	11	5	9	6
11	6	12	9	8	2	7	5	4	10	1	3
6	5	9	8	2	1	11	4	3	12	7	10
4	3	2	1	7	11	5	10	12	8	6	9
8	2	5	4	3	10	9	1	7	6	12	11
5	4	8	2	1	7	6	3	10	9	11	12

In this table, figures may therefore be used, either to stand for the notes themselves with this number in the series, or to stand for the transposed series having this number of transposition. On the other hand, if one has a figure as the serial origin, one is not obliged to begin with an initial serial note, but can begin with whichever note: provided that a logical process of serial derivation is used in this way to define a structure. Without which, there would not be sufficient justification of the process. Obviously one may move from one table to the other; for example, if in table B, I take the horizontal line beginning with 4, I have 4/3/2/1/7/11/5/10/12/8/6/9. I can transfer to table A and have the serial sequences: 4/5/2/8/9/12/3/6/11/1/10/7; 3/4/1/2/8/9/10/5/6/7/12/11, etc. ...

If in this initial series, I define each note according to an intensity, an attack and a duration, it is clear that this will give me other serial definitions. Thus for the intensities, I take:

1	2	3	4	5	6	7	8	9	10	11	12
pppp	*ppp*	*pp*	*p*	*meno p / quasi p*	*mp*	*mf*	*più f / quasi f*	*f*	*ff*	*fff*	*ffff*

for attacks:

(See the piece entitled: Modes de valeurs et d'intensités, by Messiaen.) for durations:

So I have the possibility of relating the 3 structures to the serial structure proper.

These structures are not parallel. So one can have levels of interchangeable structures, or counterpoints or structures. Thus the serial structure defines completely its own universe; even in terms of timbre, if one wishes to proceed in an analagous manner.

It is obvious that in terms of rhythm, one can use rhythmic <u>possibilities.</u> For example, if I use the rhythms:

with serial variants of the same number:

a) ♪♪♪♪♪ ♪.♪. | etc. simple transformation –   which may react with all the others

b) ♪ ♪ ♪ ♪ ♪♪ | etc. written-out values.

c) ♪♪♪ ♪ ♪♪ ♪ | etc. hollowing-out   governed by the

d) ♪♪♪ ♪ ♪♪ ♪ | etc. self-deriving   others

e) ♪ ♪ ♪♪ ♪ ♪♪ | decomposition into elements

f) 𝄽   ♪   the long element silent – which may react with all the others

g) ♩   ♪   the short element silent – which may react with all the others

I can also make a serial table with 7 rows which will be different from the serial table for the notes. I can consider the cells to be the possibilities. In the sense that I can make use of them by augmentation or diminution, regular or irregular.

The same goes for intensities; you can have variable schemes of intensities under the denomination of a single figure. The same goes for attacks.

The tempo itself can have a serial structure. For example, if one plays in 4 tempos, one will have a serial table of 4 rows.

It is obvious that up to this point we have envisaged the series as being defined arbitrarily. It is possible to consider that a series, <u>in general</u>, may be defined as a function of frequency f(F), acting on the functions of duration f(t), intensity f(i) etc. ... where only the variable changes, the function remains constant. Overall, a serial structure may be globally defined as Ψ {f(F), f(t), f(i), f(a)}.

Algebraic symbols are used as a concise way of making the different phenomena concrete, and not with a view to a truly algebraic theory of musical parameters.

If the function may be transferred from durations to intensities, the serial structure may be termed homogeneous. If the functions are not transferable (the serial structure of the durations different from the serial structure of the intensities, etc ...) then the global serial structure is heterogeneous.

Thus the global serial structure may be seen from a double point of view: on the one hand the activity of serial combination, with structures produced by the automatism of numerical relations; on the other hand, directed and interchangeable combination, where arbitrary choice plays a much bigger role. The two ways of regarding the musical structure can obviously provide an extremely effective dialectic of musical development.

On the other hand, the serial pitch structure dissolves the horizontal-vertical duality, given that composing returns to following 2 coordinates in arranging materials: frequency and duration, which are acoustic phenomena.

Thus one is relieved of all melody, harmony and counterpoint, until further information is available, since the serial structure has made these three essentially modal and tonal notions disappear.

I think that with mechanical means of reproduction – the tape recorder in particular – structures will be made possible that no longer depend on instrumental difficulties and in which one will be able to work with given frequencies, with serial derivations. And in this way each work will have its own universe, its own structure and its own methods of derivation on each level.

In this way, one may multiply the series by itself within the serial space. So that if one may reproduce, between a and b of an initial series, the series in a reduced form, this will give ranges of proliferation of the musical material, to be realised by relation to the other serial functions.]

So there you are, dear John, that's what I have written, all too hurriedly, to let you see where I've got to. You can present it to H. Cowell, after reading it yourself, and you can extract what you think are the best bits.

The examples are taken from my Polyphonies and some pieces for two pianos that I am writing at the moment, entitled: (I do apologize to Feldman, but I thought of it first!) Structures.[5]

Very soon I am going to write you a long letter concerning the one you sent me.[6]

I can tell you straight away, that I didn't think much of Feldman's attempts with white squares.[7] Much too <u>imprecise</u> and too <u>simple</u>. Maybe Christian Wolff has spoken to you about them anyway. But I shall say so myself in a letter to him. I was always suspicious of Mondrian, I prefer Klee and how! –

Send me a little note to let me know you've received this paper.

Best wishes as always.

PB

---

[5] Feldman had written a string quartet in 1951 entitled *Structures*. Cf. no. 27 and no. 35 on Boulez's attitude to Feldman and Wolff.

[6] Boulez develops the ideas of the following paragraph at length in no. 35.

[7] See the example from *Projection Four* published in Feldman's statement below (no. 32).

32

Statements by Morton Feldman, John Cage and Christian Wolff collected by John Cage[1]
1951–2

---

morton feldman

What determines the initial conception of my *Projections* and *Intersections* is a weight either reminiscent or discovered. Weight for me does not have its source in the manipulation of dynamics or tensions but rather resulting from a visual-aural response to sound as an image gone inward creating a general synthesis. The notation is presented graphically where each box is a clock-time duration.

Projection: The player is allowed to choose any sound designated for either High, Middle or Low. Duration and pitch are given and entrance is exact. Dynamically it is low throughout.

Intersection: The player is allowed to choose any sound designated either High, Middle or Low. The player may make any entrance within a given clock time duration but must hold until end of given duration. The player is free to choose any dynamic at any entrance but must maintain sameness of volume. What is desired in both the *Projections* and *Intersections* is a pure (non-vibrating) tone.

---

[1] These statements were published, with the bracketed section of no. 31, in *Transformation: arts, communication, environment*, 1/3 (1952), pp. 168–72, under the title, "Four musicians at work" (see no. 31, note 4). They were preceded by the following introduction:
John Cage, when asked to report on current musical activities told us, "At the present moment, several kinds of music are appearing that give the impression of being new. The following statements by four composers report what is happening!' Recorded works of Cage are: Amores I and IV and Three Dances (Disc), Sonatas and Interludes (Dial), String Quartet in Four Parts (Columbia). A recent work is Imaginary Landscape No. IV for 12 Radios. Morton Feldman and Christian Wolff live in New York City, and have works published by the New Music Edition. Pierre Boulez lives in Paris, is published by Amphion and Heugel & Co.; he has written articles in Polyphonie and Contrepoints.
Cage's contribution was republished in *Silence*, pp. 57–9, with none of the music examples reproduced here.

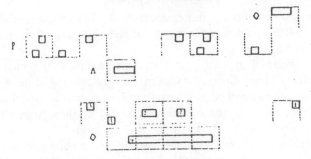

Morton Feldman. *Projection 4* (for violin and piano). MS p. 1.
◆ = harmonic. P = pizzicato. A = arco. Numbers inside boxes refer to number of tones played at once.

john cage

My recent work (*Imaginary Landscape No. IV* for 12 radios and the *Music of Changes* for piano) is structurally similar to my earlier work: based on a number of measures having a square root, so that the large lengths have the same relation within the whole that the small lengths have within a unit of it. Formerly, however, these lengths were time-lengths, whereas in the recent work the lengths exist only in space, the speed of travel through this space being unpredictable.

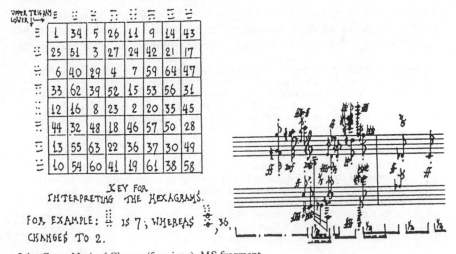

John Cage. *Music of Changes* (for piano). MS fragment.

What brings about this unpredictability is the use of the method established in the I-Ching (Book of Changes) for the obtaining of oracles, that of tossing 3 coins 6 times.[2])

Charts are made of an equal number of elements (64) which refer to Superpositions (1 chart) (how many events are happening at once during a given structural space); Tempi (1 chart); Durations (n, the number of possible superpositions, in these works, 8 charts); Sounds (8 charts); Dynamics (8 charts).

Where there are 8 charts, 4 at any instant are mobile and 4 immobile (mobile means an element passes into history once used giving place to a new one; immobile means an element, though used, remains to be used again.) Which charts are which is determined by the first toss at a large unit structural point, an odd number bringing about a change, an even number maintaining the previous status.

The Tempi and Superpositions charts, however, remain unchanged through the entire work.

In the charts for sounds, 32 of the elements (the even numbers) are silences. The sounds themselves are single, aggregates (cf. the accord sometimes obtained on a prepared piano when only one key is depressed), or complex situations (constellations) in time (cf. the Chinese characters made with several strokes). Sounds of indefinite pitch (noises) are free to be used without any restriction. Those of definite pitch are taken as being 12 in number. In any chart for sounds (there being 32 sounds) two squares (4 times 4) exist, one above the other. Reading horizontally or vertically one reads all 12 tones. In the case of the mobility of sounds (disappearance into history) 4 in succession also produce the 12 tones, with or without noises and repetitions. In the case of "interference" (the appearance of a sound having characteristics in common with the characteristics of the previously sounded situation) the characteristics that produce the interference are omitted from the newly appearing sound or cut short in the situation that has previously sounded. In the radio piece, numbers on a tuning dial are

---

[2] In the version published in *Silence*, the rest of this column and the music example from *Music of Changes* are omitted and replaced by the following paragraph:

Three coins tossed once yield four lines: three heads, broken with a circle; two tails and a head, straight; two heads and a tail, broken; three tails, straight with a cricle. Three coins tossed thrice yield eight trigrams (written from the base up); *chien*, three straight; *chen* straight, broken, broken; *kan*, broken, straight, broken; *ken* broken, broken, straight; *kun*, three broken; *sun*, broken, straight, straight; *li*, straight, broken, straight; *tui*, straight, straight, broken. Three coins tossed six times yield sixty-four hexagrams (two trigrams, the second written above the first) read in reference to a chart of the numbers 1 to 64 in a traditional arrangement having eight divisions horizontally corresponding to the eight lower trigrams and eight divisions vertically corresponding to the eight upper trigrams. A hexagram having lines with circles is read twice, first as written, then as changed. Thus, *chien-chien*, straight lines with circles, is read first as 1, then as *kun-kun*, 2; whereas *chien-chien*, straight lines without circles, is read only as 1. (*Silence*, pp. 57–8)

written instead of sounds, whatever happens being acceptable (station, static, silence).

In the charts for dynamics only 16 numbers produce changes (1, 5, 9, etc.); the others maintain the previous status. "These are either dynamic levels or accents (in the piano piece), levels, diminuendi and crescendi in the radio piece. In the piano piece, combinations of dynamic levels (e.g. p) indicate accents; in the case of a sound complex in time this may become a diminuendo or (by retrograde interpretation) a crescendo, or derived complex.

In the charts for durations there are 64 elements (since silence also has length). Through use of fractions (e.g. 1/3; 1/3 + 3/5 + 1/2) which are measured following a standard scale (e.g. 2 1/2 cm. equals ♩), these durations are, for the purposes of musical composition, practically infinite in number. The note stem appears in space at a point corresponding to the appearance of the sound in time, that is if one reads at the tempo, or changing tempo indicated. Given fractions of a quarter, half, dotted half and whole note up to 1/8, simple addition of fractions is the method employed for the generating of durations. Because addition is the generating means employed, the durations may be said to be 'segmented' (e.g. ♩♪♫♪).

These segments may be permuted and/or divided by 2 or 3 (simple nodes). A sound may then express the duration by beginning at any one of these several points.

A way of relating durations to sounds has been thought of in the course of this work but not in it utilized: to let 4 durations equal a specified length (on the chart, horizontally or vertically and in mobility four in succession) – this specified length being subject to change.

The chart for Tempi has 32 elements, the blanks maintaining the previous tempo.

Each one of the events (1 to 8) is worked from the beginning to the end of the composition. For instance, the 8th one is present from beginning to end but may sound only during a structural space that has been defined by a toss (for Superpositions) of 57 to 64. It is then not only present but possibly audible. It becomes actually audible if a sound is tossed (rather than a silence) and if the duration tossed is of a length that does not carry the sound beyond the structural space open to it.

It is thus possible to make a musical composition the continuity of which is free of individual taste and memory (psychology) and also of the literature and 'traditions' of the art. The sounds enter the time-space centered within themselves, unimpeded by service to any abstraction, their 360 degrees of circumference free for an infinite play of interpretation.

Value judgements are not in the nature of this work either as regards composition, performance or listening. The idea of relation (the idea: 2) being absent anything (the idea 1) may happen. A "mistake" is beside the point, for once anything happens it authentically is.

christian wolff

I Making music within small areas of pitches (3, 4, 5, 8 or 7 pitches have been used for individual pieces): The idea that simultaneous combinations of pitches, likewise overlapping combinations of pitches result in one "sound."

For instance 1 ♩ (a combination of 2 pitches) – a sound, ♩♩ (overlapping pitches) – a sound. Sounds of greater complexity are also possible.

e.g. ♩♩♩ ♩♩♩

A piece is then made with a gamut of these sounds, both simple and complex. Duration, timbre, and amplitude are free.

II Making music in a structure which fixes sounds in a preconceived space without regard for linear continuity. (The nature of the sounds: simple and complex as in previous situation; amplitude, timbre and duration are static or fixed however.) A structure is made with a number of measures having a square root. The structure is then planned within a square of these measures. A pattern or series of patterns is superimposed on the square, e.g.

1	2	3	4	5
6	7	8	9	10
11	12	13	14	15
16	17	18	19	20
21	22	23	24	25

In the above this pattern is a smaller square of 9 measures. Four of these patterns overlapping at the edges fill up the area of this particular piece. The individual structures are then filled in with sounds. The order in which the measures are composed may vary.

III Making music with combined gamuts of timbre, pitch, amplitude, and duration. Structure as described in II. Pitch gamuts as described in I. Gamuts of timbre are made with combinations of varying numbers of instruments (e.g. flute, violin; flute, violin, cello; cello). Gamuts of amplitude are made with varying numbers and combinations of dynamics, e.g.

Gamuts of duration are made in the same way

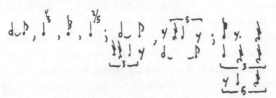

These gamuts are combined by choice and necessity. (E.g. if the choice is first made from the timbre gamut and calls for a flute, the choices of pitch, duration and amplitude are necessarily confined. If the duration gamut is used and a combination of three durations is chosen, a timbre combination of three instruments must be chosen. However, the number of pitches or amplitudes in a combination can vary from one to three, though the particular pitches are confined by the ranges of the instruments chosen.)

Christian Wolff. *Serenade* (for flute, clarinet, violin). MS fragment.

33

Letter from John Cage to Pierre Boulez
summer 1951

Dear Pierre:
Thank you for sending the 'statement'[1]; Henry Cowell's article will be published in January and I hope (for that and also for a possible performance by Fizdale and Gold in December) you can send me a photostat of the 2 piano work you are

[1] I.e. the information contained in no. 31.

writing (which you will play in England).[2] *Even if Fizdale and G. don't decide to play it, Tudor and some one else here could do it; in fact, the latter plan is better. In any event we are anxious to see and hear.*

When I finish my "Music of Changes" (sometime around Christmas) I shall send you a copy; and also I want to send you a copy of the piece for radios[3] *and a recording of it. Feldman, who has great difficulty imagining that you do not like his work, will send you a new Intersection on graph for piano.*[4] *He is somewhat mortified knowing that you also do not like Mondrian. The difference of opinion seems to me like one of distance. Close up or far away. (Far away, the entire earth is seen as a single point.) If, also, you talk to Feldman, I am sure you will recognize his quality. His work is scarcely to be admired for its intellectual characteristics, but rather for his letting the sounds be and act. I admired your critics (via Christian) of his rhythm in the Intersections, that the endings of the sounds should also be free (at the discretion of the player) as are the beginnings. But then I also admire Feldman's answer when he heard your criticism: "That would be another piece".*

I have not seen David Tudor since the beginning of the Summer. He may return in a week or so. When he does we shall try to get him to record your 2ᵉᵐᵉ Sonate. He hopes to go to Europe next Spring for the purpose of meeting you. Then you will discover that his silence as regards letter-writing and record-making is quite the opposite of his friendliness and piano-playing. I realize (and am impatiently looking forward) that you may be coming here with J. L. Barrault; please let us know when any such plans mature, because it would be nonsensical for me to be off on a tour in California or David on a boat to Europe with you here among the skyscrapers.

I am delighted with your charts; when I send you the Changes I shall also send you the charts I used. As I see it, the problem is to understand thoroughly all the qualities that act to produce multiplicity. These one will understand most nicely (fine differences) when aided technologically. I am enthusiastic about your project with Schaeffer & the radio,[5] *and anxious to be working on a similar project here. I am 'pulling as many strings' as I can.*

My present way of writing is very painstaking (measuring the distances); it took me six weeks to copy the second part of the Changes. Now I compose two pages and then copy them, then compose two more, etc.

I have also tried charts of words based on a gamut of vowels and then made poems by tossing. (Which means that I can extend the method to include vocal works).

Forgive this short hurried note; it only means to say thank you for sending the

---

[2] This information was probably given to Cage by Wolff on his return to New York. The BBC was to turn down *Structures* (see no. 35).

[3] This refers to *Imaginary Landscape No. 4*, mentioned above (see no. 28, note 6).

[4] *Intersection II*, for piano (1951).

[5] Boulez gives an account of this in no. 35.

statement. When Christian told me of being with you and all the friends I became more 'homesick' than ever. Please say hello for me to everyone.

Always yours,

John

34

Letter from John Cage to Pierre Boulez
after 6 October 1951

Dear Pierre:

I have been hoping for a letter from you, but no doubt you are very busy. Also hoping that you will send a photostat of your 2 piano piece which I should like to have performed here in February. I am still working on the "Music of Changes" but since writing to you I have heard Tudor play 2 parts of it and I think it is something that will interest you. Tudor is again away in New York until Xmas and so nothing has been done about recordings but when he returns I shall get to the work of urging him to record your 2eme Sonate. My Changes, some pieces of Christian's and Feldman's Intersection 2, which records we would send on to you, with scores. Do you have a record of the Polyphonie that was done in Germany?

The Cowell article will be published in January[1] and another one in which I used your statement will appear sooner in a magazine called Transformations.[2] Shall send these to you as they appear.

As the time grows longer since those months in Paris, I miss you more.

Should you want to come here on one of those International Education arrangements (such as was planned before and didn't work out) now is the time for you to go to the Embassy & apply. I am not on the Committee this year but I have friends on it who could be influential. This year they pay travelling expenses to N.Y. and expenses while here. I realize this might be an unwelcome interruption to your work. But naturally I think of nothing more desirable than to see you again.

Is anything happening in the project with Schaeffer?

Very affectionately,

John

---

[1] Cf. no. 30, note 1.
[2] Cf. no. 32, note 1.

35

Letter from Pierre Boulez to John Cage[1]
December 1951

Dear John,

I do apologize for not writing more often. But I prefer to "meditate" over my letters. For here is the long missive I have been promising you since I got yours in May[2] – where you were explaining your *"work in progress"*.

That letter gave me an extraordinary amount of pleasure. Everything you say about the tables of sounds, durations, amplitudes, used in your Music of Changes is, as you will see, along exactly the same lines as I am working at the moment. Which is to say that, beyond the "Vast Ocean" . . . The only thing, forgive me, which I am not happy with, is the method of absolute chance (*by tossing the coins*). On the contrary, I believe that chance must be extremely controlled: by using tables in general, or series of tables, I believe that it would be possible to direct the phenomenon of the automatism of chance, whether written down or not, which I mistrust as a facility that is not absolutely necessary. For after all, in the interpolations and interferences of different series (when one of them passes from durations to pitches, at the

---

[1] This letter has a curious history. It does not appear in the collection at Northwestern Library, but a facsimile of page 5 was published by Peyser (opp. p. 87). At Cage's request, she provided a photocopy of page 3, which was written on the back of page 1. Robert Piencikowski did the work of transcribing not only pages 3 and 5, but also of reconstructing important parts of page 1, visible through the page, with the help of a fragment translated by Cage in *Silence* (cf. the Introduction of the present volume, pp. 21–2 and notes 67 and 68). In this form it was published in the Paul Sacher Foundation edition (pp. 182–9). This sufficed to show, by its chronological position in the correspondence, that it was not, as Peyser maintains, the earliest description of Boulez's serial method. Subsequently, a translation of the letter made by John Cage for David Tudor was discovered in the Tudor archive by John Holzaepfel. Possibly, as Holzaepfel suggests, Cage intended to publish the letter as he had no. 31. Holzaepfel kindly provided this letter, which was published in full in the French edition of this correspondence (Paris: Christian Bourgois éditeur, 1990, pp. 181–91) with the unknown passages retranslated into French from Cage's English. John Holzaepfel's critical edition of the letter will appear in a later volume of the *Publications of the Paul Sacher Foundation*. This critical edition will provide a full inventory of orthographical errors and other material details of Cage's translation, which are not given here. In the following notes, the initials (JH), (JJN), and (RS) identify those by John Holzaepfel, Jean-Jacques Nattiez and Robert Samuels respectively. (JJN)

This translation combines the extant French text with Cage's translation, which is indicated by the use of bold type. Cage's manuscript shows signs of haste and occasionally over-literal translation; he frequently indicates his uncertainty over a word or phrase by the use of brackets and question marks. These have all been retained, and the most easily identifiable errors noted. (RS)

[2] I.e. the letter of 22 May 1951 (no. 28). (JJN)

same moment as another passes from intensities to attacks, etc . . .), there is already quite enough of the unknown. – I am a little afraid of what is called 'automatic writing', for most of the time it is chiefly a lack of control. The idea that I find most interesting in all that you have explained to me is the opposition between mobility and immobility of the constitutive elements of a table, on the one hand; on the other, the tables of varying tempi which themselves define the durations. The only inconvenience in the case of a performance by a human executant is the exactitude which must be very difficult to obtain. But, after an appropriate education, despair is not necessary. (As for music measured with a ruler, there again we meet, for for my experiments at the Radio with Schaeffer, I do the same thing, but that I shall presently describe.) I wait with great impatience for this 'Music of Changes', if you cannot send all of it, at least some parts. Especially since it could be played here by Yvonne Loriod.

I have not heard your Imaginary Landscape.[3] But I have already defended it on the Radio here, for a program called 'Young Music', which takes place the first Sundays of each month. Here is how it happened. This program was demanded of me in October to make 2 lectures on Rhythm in Contemporary Music (now I am considered a specialist in the subject,[4] in the same way they might have required of me directives on reproduction among protozoa.) The first has already taken place. I had as objects Stravinsky and Messiaen. But on the program preceding that one, there had been an interview with [M——] on his sojourn in America. He spoke of his activity in the U.S. And he saved for the last the June concert where Imaginary Landscape was given at the end of the concert.[5] He said it was stupid, typically "american" etc. (In revenge, he made one listen to his Melodies for Voice and Clarinet (dodecaphonism genre, – muted with sordino)). That made my ears very hot. And I required that, to give the promised lectures on rhythm, I be allowed to make a point on your account. For I have forgotten this again, that at the end of the program a 'reconstitution' of your piece for radios was made which

---

[3] This refers to *Imaginary Landscape No. 4 (March No. 2)*. See note 5 below and no. 28, note 6. (JJN)

[4] Because of the article "Propositions", published in *Polyphonie* II (1948) and reprinted as "Proposals" in *Stocktakings*, pp. 47–54 (JJN)

[5] *Imaginary Landscape No. 4* was in fact first performed on Thursday, 10 May 1951, in the MacMillin Theater of Columbia University (programme in the David Tudor archive). Calvin Tomkins writes that "over Cage's objections, the *Imaginary Landscape* was placed last on the program as the *pièce de résistance*" (*The Bride and the Bachelors* (New York: Viking Press, 1968), p. 113). This decision proved unwise since the programme began at 8.30 in the evening and consisted of a total of twelve works. By the time the performance of *Imaginary Landscape* began, it was so late that most of the radio stations within receiving range had gone off the air, resulting in a sparsely textured performance at a very low dynamic level. See also Henry Cowell's account of the concert in "Current Chronicle", *Musical Quarterly* 38 (1952), pp. 123–35. (JH)

was of a rather heavy humor. I titled my text: "The establishments of Mr. Prudhomme in the U.S.A." (I said in my sense it was an anglo-saxon quality.) And I didn't mince matters.

(In order to give you an example of the 'connerie' of this poor [M——], he had printed typewritten lists of all his activities in the U.S.A. with his <u>creations</u> (?!)[6] of Webern, his recordings (foul) of Berg, his activity as a conductor and finally his creations as a composer. And there, I am not lying, for the pieces for voice and clarinet, he had mentioned: 1st performance at X … 2nd performance at Y and so on up to the <u>6th</u> performance. Look out for him, for I know he has gone back to N.Y. He is a —— pedant, a blockhead and malicious.)

This parenthesis closed I proceed with my second lecture on rhythm which is on Webern and you. I quote long extracts from your article which appeared in Contrepoints 6[7]. And I also took elements from the presentation of the Sonatas at Mme. Tezenas' house[8] (what you told me at the time of the little interrogation in my house.) Finally I spoke of your latest works following your letter of May. As illustrations, I played an extract from the Construction in Metal, and an extract from the 3rd of the Three Dances for 2 pianos.[9] After having spoken of the tables for tempi, durations and the integration of silences in the table of aggregates, I concluded thus: "One conceives the extraordinary diversity and the astonishing flexibility of such a distribution of musical time. Thus this dialectic of sound-silence established (*instaurée*)[10] by duration springing from an ascetic rigidity in the act of leading to a hierarchy in the unitary differentiation governing an opposition between permanence and renewing of the durations. One can only give extreme approval to a project of so rich a potential." this lecture, I will record Thursday 13 and it will go on the Radio Sunday 16.

I am very sorry not to have very much liked Morton Feldman's Intersections.[11] But I am anxious to give my thoughts precisely about

---

[6] Presumably, Boulez meant "first performances", here and in the following sentence (*créations* in French). The "(?!)" may have been added by Cage. (RS)

[7] Cage's article is reprinted here as no. 5. (JJN)

[8] Cf. no. 1. (JJN)

[9] For the recordings of these two works, see no. 1, note 16, and no. 6, note 5. (JJN)

[10] The typescript reads *instaurie*. (RS, JH)

[11] Cf. Feldman's comments on *Intersection* in no. 32. In nos. 11 and 27 Boulez alludes to Feldman's manuscripts that he has received; these are probably *Illusions* (1949) and *Projection II* (1951). See no. 11, notes 3 and 4. (JJN)

Apparently Boulez had also previously received, either directly from Feldman or through Cage, *Intersection I* for orchestra, the score of which is inscribed "Feb. 1951", and *Intersection II* for piano solo, inscribed "August 1951", since he refers here to "Intersections" in the plural. It seems likely that Boulez is referring to *Intersection I* and *Projection II* when he writes "I can tell you straight away, that I didn't think much of Feldman's attempts with white squares. Much too *imprecise* and too *simple*" (in no. 31). Feldman responded to this criticism via Cage: "Feldman, who has great difficulty

them. I am sure Christian Wolff has told you faithfully what I had to say, but I prefer to write it. Since I've lost his address, you will transmit to him this little passage. When I read these Intersections, it was not the direction in which these works go that I question. On the contrary, I find the direction excellent. But the realization seems to me much less. For it indicates a <u>regression</u> from all that has been done up to the present. Far from being a progress, an enrichment, it lacks a stock (provisioning) of the techniques previously acquired. In the first place the fact of tempo indicated by a scale in seconds signifies a constant metric unity which is 60, and this for all the works. I am willing that one have metric unities which may be multiples or divisions of 60. But I do not see why one would have only that. To take the ?[12] coordinates of real time, is to refuse all the fractional values by relation to 60 (a simple metronome is then perfect for him); and to refuse again all the irrationals of the divers kinds. Between an indication placing ? notes between the second ? and the second quarter; and the quite simple notation of a triplet of 8ths with the quarter $= 140$ for example, it is certain that the 2nd notation has all the advantages. First, because one has irrational unity by relation to the second $140/60 = 7/3$; secondly, because at the interior of this unity, there are still irrational divisions. It is then certain at that moment that classic notation is more <u>efficacious</u> in the case than[13] the graphic notation with the seconds as abscissae.[14] It is not that I am against the notation of time in abscissae (you will see farther on that I use it for my electro-acoustic experiments), but that I am against the inefficacious use of it. For one obtains a music more <u>summary</u> than before. That I do not tolerate at any price. When one changes methodology, it is because the new that one takes is capable of rendering an account of phenomena – here rhythmic phenomena – for which the old is no longer capable. Here this is not truly the case. It was (?) certainly at the beginning. The endeavour of a greater rigor, but the result is contrary. There is following this the fact of a

imagining that you do not like his work, will send you a new Intersection on graph for piano" (In no. 33); i.e. *Intersection II*. (JH)

[12] Here and subsequently Cage has been unable to decipher Boulez's handwriting. (JJN)

[13] The typescript reads "that". (RS, JH)

[14] It is not clear from the foregoing discussion to which of Feldman's compositions Boulez is referring. The tempo indications of both *Intersections I* and *II* are given in metronome markings ("72 or thereabouts" – the same as in *Projection 2* – and "158" respectively). Furthermore, both scores are written in graphic notation, as is *Projection II*, using numbers or letters: there are no quarter notes or eighth-note triplets. And Boulez had already written approvingly of *Illusions* (see no. 11). Moreover, the *Illusions* are written in standard notation, but their tempo indications are "very fast" and "slow and tranquil", respectively, and the quarter notes and eighth note triplets in these pieces occur within clearly metered bar lines. (JH)

In this passage, Cage seems to have translated the French *unité* (unit, here a unit of time) as "unity" (RS)

total lack of control in the frequencies. To write a band of frequencies is clearly non-definition of sound, but against the grain of the mathematical method of successive approximations: it is there an inverse method, of successive non-definitions! It is very evident that I cannot admit a role so vague (given) to range (tessiture). I easily admit and found very remarkable with you, this method of complex sounds, or of complexes of sounds. That is to say that I do not admit sound under the single aspect of a pure frequency, but also as a relation of frequencies. But I pretend very simply that these frequencies ought to be the object of a rigorous control in the construction, and if one cannot establish the absolute value of each one of them, one ought not to establish the relative value of their interdependence. Or, if one wishes to leave thus pavements[15] of available frequencies, it requires an improbable virtuosity of writing. And again these pavements would be very restricted, conditioned by the very strict relations of the divers unfoldings and of their values relative to each time of unfolding. This would be nearly comparable – in a classic counterpoint – to that which one might replace each contrapuntal line by its inversion, its retrograde and its retrograde inversion! If it were a question of a counterpoint of 3 voices, it would already be: $4 \times 4 \times 4 = 64$ possible eventualities for each note! Here we have nearly the best relation! I do not believe that the use of pavements of frequencies, in the Intersections, corresponds to as rigorous a control. And since one can obtain a unique sound repeated at 4 octaves, a perfect accord[16] or the 12 tones, that bothers me enormously. Moreover supposing that interpreters are imaginative, they would then be composers.... Vicious circle. And then I have not nostalgia of the instant at that point. Finally, the fact that it is at the interior of a (unit) of time that one can (start) the sound – parallel to the band of frequencies – I think that that also requires a very rigorous control. Summing up, I think of these Intersections that they are certainly in a path which is exact, but that they let themselves go dangerously to the <u>seduction of graphism alone</u>. Now, we are musicians and not painters, and pictures are not made to be performed. willingly I would ask Feldman – and it is with great friendship that I permit himself this remark – to be more hard to please with myself, and not to satisfy himself with a seductive exterior aspect. As to Mondrian, no, I love him truly not at all. For his pictures are the most denuded of mystery that have ever been in the world. Let us distinguish all the same this false science from a true science which is less easy to decipher. It is against the <u>facility</u> of

---

[15] This translation is obscure. Cage may be translating the word *rues* or *routes*, i.e. "pathways" or "avenues"; or, more likely, *pavés*, which can mean "tomes" (RS)

[16] The French phrase *accord parfait* means "triad" here. (RS)

a Mondrian that I rise up. Such simple solutions are not to my taste. (Personally the <u>abstract</u> pictures of Klee, – and even the others – are infinitely closer to me and I find them much more probing, even in pictorial technique). For the rest, genuine works are those in which one can never come to an end ("infinite nucleus of the night")[17]; and when all is said, one has still said nothing, and one will never say anything.

Excuse my having gone into this so lengthily. But I think it was necessary to do it in order to avoid all (misunderstanding?). You said: "This difference of opinion seems to me like one of distance. Close up or far away."[18] I think even so that it is 'close up'. For I do not hold essentially "to see the entire earth as a single point." that would give me the dizziness of 'infinite spaces' and would have as result only interstellar silence. (And absolute zero from the point of view of temperature understands itself!)

Since we are theorizing, have you received Contrepoints 7? I spoke to you about it a long time ago.[19] It was a number on Bach. And I spoke there of the obsession with classicism that (arose) in the pre-ceding generation (Schoenberg, Stravinsky etc.). Elsewhere, I wrote recently for an English review "The Score", special number on Schoenberg, an article entitled "Schoenberg is dead".[20] Essentially this is what I say: "The essential cause of the Schoenberg checkmate resides in the profound misappreciation of the serial FUNCTIONS properly so-called brought about by the very principle of the series. – Otherwise they turn into a state more embryonic than efficacious. We mean also that the row intervenes with Schoenberg as the small-est common denominator in order to assure the semantic unity of the work; but that the elements of the language thus obtained are organised by a pre-existent non-serial rhetoric. It is there, we feel able to affirm, that the provoking INEVIDENCE of a work without intrinsic unity resides." Farther along, I also say: "If the Schoenberg checkmate exists, it is not by juggling it away that one undertakes to find a worthwhile solution to the problems posed by the manifes-tation (epiphany) of a contemporary language." And I conclude, "Continuing, let us keep from considering Schoenberg as a sort of Moses who died in view of the Promised Land, after having brought

[17] This translates the phrase *Le noyau infracassable de nuit*, which Boulez often quotes at this period, but the derivation of which he can no longer remember. Although perfectly comprehensible in French, *infracassable* is a neologism (from *fracasser*), which explains Cage's difficulty in translating this word; "infrangible" might be an adequate rendering. Here the phrase expresses the idea that a work should be of a complexity such that the creative process that gave rise to it cannot be entirely laid bare. (JJN, RS)

[18] Cf. no. 33. (RS)

[19] Cf. no. 6, note 7. (JJN)

[20] "Schoenberg is dead", *The Score*, no. 6 (May 1952), pp. 18–22; reprinted, with some changes embodied in the later French version, in *Stocktakings*, pp. 209–14. (JJN)

the Tables of the Law from a Sinai that many would wish obstinately to confuse with Walhalla. (During this time, the dance around the Golden Calf is in full swing[21]). We owe to him in all truth Pierrot Lunaire ...; and some other works which are more than enviable. With all due deference to the surrounding mediocrity which very speciously would like to limit the damages to "Central Europe". – It becomes however indispensable to suppress in oneself a misunderstanding full of ambiguities and contradictions; it is time that the check-mate be neutralised. A gratuitous boasting, (or) more a foolish falsity does not take part in this placing to the point, but a rigour which exempts itself from weakness and compromise. Also (if indeed?) – not to write it without any desire for stupid scandal, but without chaste hypocrisy as without useless melancholy, SCHOENBERG IS DEAD."

I believe that this putting things clearly was indispensable in order to be able to separate me from the dodecaphonic academicians.[22]

As far as concerts go, we have heard very few things up to the present. Simply, the first concerto of Bartók for piano and orchestra, that had not yet been heard here. Aside from that – nothing. I played in a concert with 4 pianos some quarter-tone works of Wyschnegradsky. It is very bad, and the sounds themselves become (heavy). – Melodies of Marina Scriabine in imaginary landscale (Souvtchinsky pretends that this is only an assemblage of the most obscene Russian syllables! ...) Have you heard Rake's progress?[23] What ugliness! They just have announced Britten's Billy Budd[24] in London; to be transmitted by the Radio here. I have not had the courage to listen.

As for my Polyphonie[25] played in Germany, I have not yet been able to hear it. The German Radio does not let its recordings go out. Heugel has tried to have them personally. But it is very difficult; rights etc. Souvtchinsky, Joffroy and Goldbeck all went there – for at the moment I was in London with Barrault. Messiaen was also there. They all told me that Rosbaud, the director, was admirable. 12 rehearsals. The performance went very well. As you saw in the

---

[21] Cage had considerable trouble deciphering and translating this sentence, which reads in the typescript, "Continuing, let us keep from considering Schoenberg as a sort of Moses who died in view of the Promised land, after having brought the Tables of the Law from a Sinai that ? would wish obstinately to confuse with Walhalla. (During this time, the dance around the Golden Calf ? its full)". The version here follows that of *Stocktakings*, p. 214. The metaphor of Moses and the Golden Calf is a reference to Schoenberg's last opera, *Moses und Aron*. (JH, RS)

[22] This remark confirms that "Schoenberg is dead" was written essentially as an attack on Leibowitz. (JJN)

[23] The opera by Stravinsky. It was first performed in Venice on Tuesday, 11 September 1951. Apparently Boulez heard a radio broadcast of the work. (JH)

[24] *Billy Budd* by Benjamin Britten (Op. 50) was first performed on 1 December 1951 at Covent Garden. (JH, JJN)

[25] *Polyponie X*. See no. 26, note 3. (JJN)

article you sent me, the reactions were diverse. The protests presented to the German Radio were numerous. What do you expect! So much the worse! I continue my way; none of this preoccupies me. I have not yet written the last movements which I am going to get to soon. The Quartet is not yet copied; thus not yet edited.[26] It is necessary for me to find the time to do it. As for the piano pieces, I did not play them in London. The B.B.C. did not accept them, for fear of scandal, I think. As for the others, they are far from being finished.[27] I shall keep you informed. But for the time being they are more or less dead, not having had the time to work on them. Tell D. Tudor not to record my Second Sonata, for I have made some modifications of details (suppressing annoying chromaticisms, controlling certain vertical coincidences, etc. . . .).[28] I will send them to you soon and you can pass them on. My First Piano Sonata has just been published by Amphion. I shall send that on to you too, as to C. Wolff and M. Feldman. It's a "souvenir of youth". You know it and will forgive it!

Now I want to talk to you about the research that we are carrying out at the moment at the Radio under Schaeffer's patronage.[29] – . . . As instruments to work with, we have: microphones for recording, disc cutters; two tape recorders for ordinary recording. A variable speed tape recorder: 12 speeds in the proportions of the tempered scale. Ordinary and double speed. Which already gives 24 speeds. Lastly a three-track tape recorder, which allows you to mix three tapes at once. There are filters, for modifying sonorities.

We have devoted ourselves to theoretical work on the categorisation of sound in order – as one does with normal instruments – to work more clearly from clearly defined functions of sound. And here is how:

A/ Pure dynamic. (Pure attack: impact). At its most pure, this sound is

[26] This is the *Livre pour quatuor* (JJN). "Edited" here is Cage's translation of *édité*, i.e. "published". (RS)

[27] This refers to *Structures* for two pianos. Cage's preceding letter (no. 33) shows that a performance of *Structures* was planned for England. Since none of Boulez's letters mentions this, the news may have come from Christian Wolff. Evidently, the BBC refused the project. Boulez planned at this stage to write two further books of *Structures* (see no. 27, note 5). (JJN)

[28] Cage had written, "I have not seen David Tudor since the beginning of September. He may return in a week or so. When he does we shall try to get him to record your 2nd Sonata" (no. 33). The attempt was unsuccessful due to lack of underwriting (David Tudor in conversation with JH, Stony Point, New York, 25 July 1990). Much later, when Earle Brown produced a series of recordings of new music for Time/Mainstream records, he tried to persuade Tudor to record the sonata, along with *Music of Changes* and Ives's *Concord Sonata*. This attempt was also unsuccessful, but for different reasons: by this time (c. 1952), Tudor had played neither the Boulez nor the Cage work for several years, had never played the *Concord Sonata*, and was already moving away from piano performance altogether in favour of live electronic music. (Earle Brown in conversation with JH, Rye, New York, 13 June 1989) Tudor never recorded the Boulez Second Piano Sonata. (JH)

[29] Boulez told Cage of this in no. 6 (see no. 6, note 4). He attended a course in *musique concrète* between 19 October and 13 December 1951. (JJN)

symmetrical, or in other words not retrogradable (it cannot be played back-words). It has only one axis of symmetry.

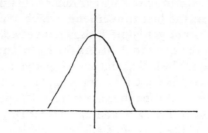

B/ Dynamic maintained by variable and functional stabilisation.

a/ Dynamic actively maintained. The attack has to be maintained by some constant mechanical means (comparable to a bow exciting a string).

b/ Dynamic passively maintained. In other words a phenomenon of reso-nance either natural or produced with artificial reverberation (echo chamber).

In any case these sounds are retrogradable, that is, non-symmetrical.

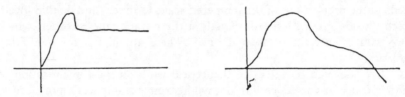

c/ Pure static. At its most pure, this is not retrogradable (comparable to organ notes.)

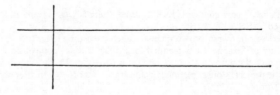

it permits all axes of symmetry.

In each category, the three[30] following distinctions may be applied.

α/ <u>Frequency</u>. (1) The sound is situated in a range of frequencies or is made up of a superimposition, a complex of frequencies, frequencies with irrational relationships between them.

(2) Or you can have a pure frequency, or frequencies in multiples of two, both of them (simple harmonics) reinforcing the first frequency.

β/ <u>Timbre</u>. (1) This can be <u>heterogeneous</u> in which case it will have either <u>fixed</u> or <u>variable</u> components. Their index is established.

[30] There are actually not three, but four, parameters taken over by the general series. (JJN)

(2) It may be <u>homogeneous</u>. In this case its characterizing index must be established.

γ/ <u>Intensity</u>. The intensity of a sound-complex or of a sound may be (1) Multiple. Here one can play with the stability or variability of the respective intensities and also play with their relationships.

or else (2) Single. And in this case, if the intensity is stable, its index is established; if it is variable, its coefficient of variability.

δ/ <u>Duration</u>. In order to work with durations, given a sound to begin with of some duration (– some length of magnetic tape), the relations between frequency and duration must be established, which is to say the index of transposition.

As you can see, there are a number of parameters which allow a strict calibration to be established.

At present I am working on an étude on *a single sound*.[31] The sound of an African sanza[32], amplified, recorded very close to the microphone and reverberated artificially using a timp. This gives a very rich sound with a strong attack and long decay.

I established 72 transpositions of this sound using the variable speeds. Which is to say that the tape is made into a loop on the tape recorder, and the speed is changed. Which gives three loops in the sounds:

	1, 2, 3, 4, 5, 6 . . . 12	
4N	t_1 t_2 etc.	
2N	$2t$, $2t_2$	
N	$4t$, . . .	hence the 72 sounds
M	$8t$, . . .	
M/2	$16t$, . . .	
M/4	$32t$, etc.	

Given sound 1 at the given time t_1 (measured on the tape loop), the half sound will give $2t_1$, the sounds underneath $4t_1$, etc. . . . up to $32t_1$; then sound 2 gives me t_2, t_2, etc. . . .

This étude is based solely on the transformations [*interversions*] of the time series and the pitch series. For I have two serial tables to organize these. I have not yet used the timbres, intensities or modes of attack. You can see the richness already. For to make the structures evident, I use the sound right way round and wrong way round. In order to write the score, I have the lengths in magnetic tape in units of time; (t_1 = 8cm, 1). And I represent them in scale on a graph with the pitches

[31] *Etude sur un son* (Jameux no. 13a). See no. 6, note 4. (JJN)
[32] Cf. Boulez's interest in the sanza in his lecture on Cage (no. 1). (JJN)

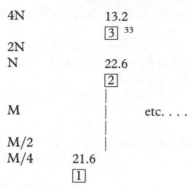

The distances are indicated according to an exact scale: 2mm for 1cm (though not here, obviously!)

This means that sound 1 is at pitch M/4 with a time corresponding to 21.6cm, sound 2 at pitch N follows on directly from it, and is superimposed on sound 3 at pitch 4N with 22.6cm and 13.2cm respectively. (You have to know that 77cm = 1″[34] to have an order of size). Thus you can see, one works better on the work without being preoccupied with the question of the second.[35] Moreover the relations t_1, t_2 are very complex: since they obey the law 9/8, 81/64, 4/3 etc....

Finally if one uses for example the abstract series of notes:

1   7   4   5   2   etc.

and the abstract series of times

8   6   3   7   9   etc.

one can make a registration of rhythm like a registration of notes.

That is to say to pass from the pitch 1–N[36] to the pitch 7–4N then to the pitch 4 M/2 etc., and to pass respectively from the time $8t_8$ to the time $32t_6$ then to the time $2t_3$ etc. so well that the registration of the time can be parallel or in this case <u>inverse</u> to that of the sounds, which introduces the cuttings and the silences.

For if one uses sound 4–M/2, which has a real time of $16t_4$, with the time $2t_3$, one will have a truncated sound.

If on the contrary one uses the sound 7–4N, which has a real time of r_7, with the time $32t_6$, one will have a silence which follows the sound of: $32t_6$–t_7. (If one plays the sound on the wrong side,[37] the

---

[33] The figures in the boxes are difficult to decipher; however, Boulez clearly explains the table in the following paragraph, allowing them to be reconstructed. (RS)

[34] Boulez means that the tape recorder has a speed of 77cm to one second. This is extremely fast for a machine at this date; possibly it is an error for '7.7cm'. (RS)

[35] An allusion to the earlier comments on Feldman. (JJN)

[36] The references to Boulez's earlier table have been standardized from Cage's manuscript for clarity. Boulez here means "sound 1 at speed N", "sound 7 at speed 4n", etc. (RS)

[37] I.e. reversing the direction of the tape; Cage may well have mistranslated "*à l'envers*" (upside-down), which can also refer to musical inversion. (RS)

silence precedes the sound; but one may also invert the proceeding.)

One may also at the interior of a sound establish relations of turning upside down for a 3rd series. That is to say, if one uses sound 5–M/4, which is very long, then the sound 7–M/2 etc.

One may have at the same time a series 6 4 3 etc. and establish the relations of 6 to 6/4 = 3/2, then 4/3. Thus in the sound 5–M/4:

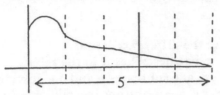

One may divide it in 2 parts of which the relation = 3/2 starting from the attack. To play the 2/5 before the 3/5. To put the 3/5 wrong way, or the 2/5. to put both wrong way. Which gives graphically:

one introduces thus the irrationals at the interior, even of the sound.

You see all the richness which it is possible to exploit! That will require time and is a question of montage (like cinematic montage).

Nevertheless I beg (still!) from Schaeffer a tape recorder with variable speed, being able to give the micro-distances, or speeds that one can <u>prepare</u> and which will not necessarily be in relation to the tempered scale.

In order to play these results in a hall, one uses stereophonic projection with very large loudspeakers in the 4 directions of the room with a control desk being able to direct the sound in the 4 directions and an intensity potentiometer. That gives completely unheard-of results.

I have worked on this subject on the generalisation of the rows to n intervals of which I spoke to you nearly a year ago.[38]

Let there be n sounds which are situated at the interior of a band of frequencies from single to double, no sound repeating itself. One then has: a b c d . . . n.

How to establish a transposition: (see also my last letter[39] and the tables.)

[38] In no. 28, 30 December 1950. (JJN)
[39] No. 31, August 1951. (JJN)

One has:

$$
\begin{array}{llcl}
a & b & c & \cdots & n \\
b & b+(b-a) & c+(b-a) & & n+(b-a) \\
c & b+(c-a) & c+(c-a) & & n+(c-a) \\
\cdots \\
n & n+(n-a) & c+(n-a) & & n+(n-a)
\end{array}
$$

1) If $b > a$. One takes the difference $b - a$.

   I) If $b + (b - a) < n$, one describes it in the table.

   II) If $b + (b - a) > n$, one subtracts n and one inscribes.

2) If $b < a$. One takes $b + n - a$, and one inscribes $b + (b + n - a)$. One falls back in the preceding case. By this method, one falls always back to the interior of a to n. One then has afterwards to multiply by all the multiples in order to cover the entire sonorous space.

$$
\begin{array}{llcl}
a & b & c & \cdots & n \\
a & a-(b-a) & a-(c-a) & & n-(n-a)
\end{array}
$$

1) If $b > a$ take $b - a$.

   I) If $a - (b - a) < n$, inscribe it.

   II) If $a - (b - a) > n$ take $a + n - (b - a)$.

2) If $b < a$ take $b + n - a$.

   I) If $a - \{(b + n) - a\} < n$, inscribe it.

To transpose these inverse series, one will be in the preceding case. That, you may easily verify with the series of 12 sounds. E.g.

$$
\begin{array}{lcccc}
& 1 & 8 & 11 & 10 \text{ etc.} \\
\text{Transpositions} & 8 & 3 & 6 & 5 \\
& 11 & 6 & 9 & 8
\end{array}
$$

From the 1st to the 2: $8 - 1 = 7$

In the row 2: $8 + 7 = 15 - 12 = 3$

In the row 3: $11 + 7 = 18 - 12 = 6$

From the 3 to the 4: $10 + 12 = 22 - 11 = 11$

    $6 + 11 = 17 - 12 = 5$

    $9 + 11 = 20 - 12 = 8$

For the inversion:

1	8	11	10
1	6	3	4	etc.

From the 1st to the 2nd sound:

$$8 - 1 = 7$$
$$1 + 12 = 13 - 7 = 6$$

From the 1st to the 3rd: $11 - 1 = 10$

$$1 + 12 = 13 - 10 = 3$$

What is interesting is to generalize for all series.

If you want only seven tempos in relation to fifteen sounds, it is possible.

in a series	3	4	7	2	etc . . .
of seven	4	5	①	3	etc . . .
sounds	7	①	④	6	etc. . .
etc. . . .					

in a series	3	4	7	2	etc.
of fifteen	4	5	⑧	3	etc.
sounds	7	⑧	⑪	6	etc.
etc. . . .					

Depending on whether you have seven or fifteen, the transpositions differ by certain sounds which are here [illegible]. Thus one can create interferences between the two. Hence <u>series of series</u> can be created from this, varying according to the structure. This gives infinite possibilities. For instance, between a large interval: as for example between 4 and 7, I can introduce another series f reducing the intervals of the first in the proportion

$$\frac{7 - 4}{15 - 1}$$

Graphically it looks like

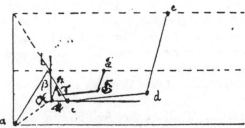

[Caption:] If you consider b to c. As you can see, all the intervals would be reduced by analogy with the large intervals and in the proportion:

$$\frac{|c - b|}{|e - a|}$$

Thus a whole series of series can be envisaged in the proportion:

$$\frac{|b - a|}{|e - a|} \frac{|b - c|}{|e - a|} \text{ etc. . . .}$$

There is more to come before having exhausted the solutions in practice!!

My dear John, I shall finish my letter here. For you must have had enough of figures and graphs. But as soon as I have a beard and no hair any more (which will make me want to practise these exercises) I shall write a great big book on the series![41]

We still have to find the means of realizing these projects. But find them we will.

Concerning the Schaeffer group, we are organizing a series of broadcasts on the Experiments in Musique Concrète. About Electronic Music in general. We should like to have editorials, sorts of explanations, about five minutes long, which give a point of view on the necessity of electronic music. We should like to have an editorial from you. And also from Varèse. If you could give me his address, I shall write to him to ask if he would accept.

We are also going to have an International Chronicle in which we would like to publicize abroad everything that is going on in the electronic field. We are relying on you in short to be our New York correspondant.

Moreover, at the end of the year we are planning to bring together our researches in a little resumé which we shall certainly let you know about.[41] Write back to let me know if you like the idea of this Editorial. Write it in English, I shall translate it (I have some dictionaries here now!!). But before writing anything, wait until I give you confirmation. It's not worth working for nothing, and in any case I will talk to you about the whole thing in more detail.

You know that Messiaen is developing wonderfully. I spoke to you about his Mode de valeurs et d'intensités. He has just written some organ pieces on 64 durations, with registration modes.[42] He is going to let a little committee of us hear them soon. I recently received music from a young Belgian musician from Liège – 22 years old –, whom I met at Royaumont in June.[43] This is some sacred songs for voice and string trio.[44] It is very interesting and remarkably well written. I haven't replied to him yet, but they were a pleasant surprise.

That is all my news, dear John. You can see that we're not completely inactive.

Say hello to Christian Wolff for me. And give my very best wishes once again to Morton Feldman, despite the disagreement we have on certain matters. Also say hello to David Tudor, the silent hermit.

On the subject, my projects for the next year are as follows: I am leaving

---

[40] An explanation of Boulez's compositional technique, and then not a treatise, only appeared in *Penser la musique aujourd'hui* (Mayence: Schott's Söhne, 1963; translated by S. Bradshaw and R. R. Bennett as *Boulez on Music Today*, London, 1971). (JJN)

[41] This project seems to have come to nothing. In any case, Boulez was shortly to quarrel with Schaeffer (see no. 44). (JJN)

[42] This refers to *Soixante-quatre durées*, no. 7 of the *Livre d'orgue* first performed by Messiaen in 1952 in Milan and in which Messiaen has acknowledged Boulez's influence (in an interview with Georges Nicholson on Radio-Canada, 1987). (JJN, JH)

[43] This is Henri Pousseur. The letter that accompanied this package is dated 27 November 1951 (communication from Robert Piencikowski). (JJN)

[44] *Trois chants sacrés*, for soprano, violin, viola and cello, first performed in Salzburg in 1952. (JJN)

for Egypt and Italy – with Barrault – from 28 February until about mid-May.[45] I shall be back in Paris certainly by the end of May. If D. Tudor is coming to Paris then, he must come and see me without fail.

When shall we meet again? A trip to the U.S.A. (Canada – U.S.A. – Mexico) with Barrault is planned starting next October.[46] How marvellous it will be if it comes off! I think I would find Bartholdi's statue[47] the greatest human artistic achievement! (On second thoughts, it's still crap.)

I hope you will have the patience to read this twaddle to the end. Your friend as always.

PB

36

Letter from Pierre Boulez to John Cage
before 21 May 1952

Dear John

I have just received Transformation[1] – And many thanks for sending it. I am going to give a copy to Gatti, Saby, Joffroy and Souvtchinsky.

What a wonderful journal! It gave me so much of your news.

I met a friend of yours here – a painter, but I no longer recall his name – and we talked a lot about you.

I am going to send you an issue of the Revue Musicale (I've already requested it, but I don't know if they have done it) in which I have written a fairly long article where I mention your work.[2] I hope to do one soon for a journal called "Les Carnets Critiques".[3]

How are you?

Some good news for you. It is now almost certain that we will go to New York for six weeks from 12 or 15 November. With J. L. Barrault. I am overjoyed at the thought of this journey and of being able to meet you all.

We played one piece from "Structures" with Messiaen on first piano and

---

[45] This explains the gap between this letter and the following one (no. 36). (JJN)

[46] This was indeed to happen. Boulez met Cage again in New York on 11 November 1952 (see no. 39). (JJN)

[47] Boulez refers to the Statue of Liberty, the work of the sculptor F. A. Bartholdi (1834–1904). (JJN)

[1] See no. 32.

[2] "Possibly ...". See also no. 26, note 7. The passage concerning Cage is reprinted here as no. 37.

[3] This project seems to have come to nothing.

myself on second. There was some rumpus and a little irritation.[4] We should play the three that are written in Darmstadt, Germany in July and on Cologne Radio.[5]

I am also preparing something for 12 voices a cappella which should be put on in Berlin in September. On a poem by Gatti.[6]

You can see that I am working hard at the moment.

There is a concert of "musique concrète" (Schaeffer) on 21 May with *Messiaen,* who has written something specially, myself, P. Henry and Schaeffer.[7]

I hope to write to you at greater length soon. But at the moment I haven't much time. Do forgive me. I just wanted to make my presence known to you. To let you know how much you are always present [with] us.

On that, I shall be taking your records to Germany (percussion-prepared piano, electronic music). The director of Cologne Radio is very interested and wants [to hear them].

I am writing in a hurry, but you can supply all the missing words. A bientôt for a long letter. And a thousand thanks for the journal.

Best wishes.

PB

37

Pierre Boulez on John Cage in "Possibly..."[1]

1951–2

... As for John Cage, he has given us proof that it is possible to create nontempered sound spaces, even using only existing instruments. This is to say that his use of the *prepared piano* is not merely an unusual area of percussive piano technique in which the sounding-board is to be invaded by a

---

[4] To be exact, on 4 May 1952.

[5] The whole of the first book of *Structures* was played on 13 November 1953 in Cologne, but by Yvette Grimaud and Yvonne Loriod.

[6] This refers to *Oubli signal lapidé,* first performed by the Marcel Couraud vocal ensemble on 3 October 1952, but in Cologne (according to Jameux).

[7] This concert, given in the hall of the Ancien Conservatoire, included the following works: André Hodeir, *Jazz et Jazz;* Pierre Boulez, *Étude sérielle sur un son* and *Étude sérielle sur sept sons;* Pierre Henry, *Vocalises;* Olivier Messiaen, *Timbres-durées;* Michel Philippot, *Le joueur de bruits;* Rollin, *Étude vocale.*

[1] This article was first published in *La Revue musicale,* no. 212 (April 1952). The article was reprinted as "Possibly ..." in *Stocktakings,* pp. 111–40. See also no. 26, note 7. The translation printed here has been produced for this volume from the original *Revue musicale* version.

strange, metallicizing vegetation. It has much more to do with calling into question acoustic ideas which have gradually become fixed in the course of Western musical evolution; for this prepared piano becomes, by way of a do-it-yourself tuning system, an instrument capable of producing frequency complexes. John Cage thinks indeed that the instruments created for the needs of tonal language no longer correspond to the new necessities of music, which refuses to regard the octave as the privileged interval on the basis of which different scales are reproduced. From this arises the wish to give each sound, from the beginning, a prominent individuality. If this individuality is unvarying for the whole of an extended work, then because of their repetition over time, a global and hierarchical neutrality results in the scale of frequencies. In other words, a unique mode arises made up of multiple sounds which cover the entire tessitura; and one might fall into the trap that was to be avoided at all costs. Notice at once, however, that if the tablatures were more numerous, the polarization would be much richer, given the interference patterns that would then be created between them. By contrast, if each sound is treated as absolutely neutral *a priori* – as is the case in serial technique – the context causes a different individuality of a sound to come forth on each of its appearances. This sort of reversability of cause and effect is a phenomenon notable because of its curiosity.

We also owe to John Cage the idea of sound complexes; for he has written works in which, instead of using pure sounds, he employs chords which have no harmonic function, being essentially a sort of amalgam of sounds linked to timbres, durations and intensities, each of which characteristics may differ according to the different components of this amalgam.

Again his method of conceiving rhythmic construction should be noted; this has to do with the idea of real time, evidenced by the numerical relations where the personal coefficient is not involved; further, a given number of measure units gives rise to an equal number of units of development. This method leads *a priori* to a numerical structure, which John Cage labels prismatic, and which we would rather term 'crystallized'.

More recently, John Cage has been concerned with creating structural relations between the diverse components of a sound, and to this end he employs tables which organize each component according to parallel but autonomous divisions.

The direction pursued by John Cage's research is too close to our own for us to fail to mention it . . .

38

Letter from John Cage to Pierre Boulez
summer 1952

Dear Pierre:

Forgive me for not having written sooner; by rights I should offer you countless apologies but that would just take your time. I have been busy. Your last long letter was marvelous and gave much pleasure.[1] I am very anxious to hear your Etude for a single sound and also the more recent one for seven. Can't you get the Radio to send copies over here? I am hoping to arrange a concert next season either wholly or in part electronic; if wholly, we would have to draw heavily on "musique concrète", because our work proceeds quite slowly. So far we have 3 movements of a work by Christian Wolff,[2] an inconsequential work of mine for 43 phonograph records (Imaginary Landscape No. 5) and 17 seconds of a more interesting piece to which I have not yet given a title.[3]

After the Music of Changes (which I trust you have received;) I wrote two Pastorales for prepared piano.[4] The pianist also blows whistles. And in another piece which changes its title according to where it is performed (e.g. 66 W. 12th)[5] bowls of water, whistles and a radio are used in addition to the piano. Both pieces, are composed in the same way as the Changes but have fewer superpositions and so the density is slight. The 66 W. 12 piece is notated according to actual time and the performer uses a stop watch to determine his entrances.

The phonograph piece was done in 18 hrs. because it was needed for a dance program. And since it is on tape it brought about my present connection with Louis and Bebe Barron who are sound engineers. David Tudor helped make this first piece and so enjoyed the work that he said he would prefer to do such work to teaching, as far as making a living was concerned. So shortly after that I raised $5,000. (given by Paul Williams) which we divide 4 ways and then each month tax each member of the project to pay for the materials. We use the machines owned by the Barrons and at present have no funds for additions. The $5,000 will carry us through Nov. 15 and assures us of 2 full days per wk in the studio. We have 2 tape recorders. Louis Barron has an arrangement for variable speed but it is

---

[1] This must refer to no. 35, to which Cage had not yet replied, and not to no. 36, which is relatively short.

[2] This refers to *For Magnetic Tape* (1952).

[3] This refers to *Williams Mix* (see No. 43).

[4] Dated 1951.

[5] This piece later had its title fixed as *Water Music*. It was first performed on 2 May 1952 at the New School for Social Research in New York, which is situated at 66 West 12th Street; whence its title here. See D. Campana in the *Bucknell Review*, 32/2 (1989).

rather makeshift. The sound is in the middle of the tape and the tape travels at 15 or 7½ inches per second. (I envy you your 77cm.)[6]

For the piece we are now making I use the same method again as in the Music of Changes, but there are a few modifications: the sounds are classified in six groups which are overlapping: A = city sounds; B = country sounds; C = electronic sounds; D = music, especially manually produced "musical" sounds; E = vocally produced sounds and vocal music; F = small sounds which require amplification to be useful. These capital letters which refer to source are followed by three letters, c or v, meaning, roughly controlled or variable. The first refers to frequency, the second to overtone structure, the third to amplitude. A line drawn underneath the capital letter indicates a duration control, rhythmic pattern easily achieved by making a "loop", – an endless tape. Avvv might then be a straight recording of traffic whereas Dvvv could be jazz or Beethoven. Avcv will be traffic (e.g.) having suffered a control of its overtone structure, through filters or reverberation.

This is a very free way of permitting action and I allow the engineers making the sounds total freedom. I simply give a list of the sounds needed, e.g. Evcv F̲vvv (double source). If a source is ccc by nature, then v means a control. I do not specify how a sound shall be interpreted (in this regard) but leave it to the engineers.

The charts for the composition involve these sounds, durations, attacks and decays, superpositions, and "n", a fraction which is a factor in the structure and in 32 out of 64 durations. (This corresponds to flexibility of tempo.) The attacks and decays are specific cuts of the tape plus or minus from a duration point. They are also "cross-grain" use of the tape (which affects the overtone structure as well[)]. I have organized single and double cuts (to a central pt.) and then use a "t" to indicate more complicated cuts or curves which are invented at the moment of cutting. The entire score is made like a dress-maker's pattern – to size. A single-page = 1 1/3 seconds. 8 individual tapes are made and then super-imposed if one wishes a single tape or disc in the end but naturally more tapes are preferable with many loudspeakers. The composition however uses 16 charts and so the durations are segmented (as in the Changes) to make possible otherwise impossible situations. It often happens that, with plus and minus operations, a sound "ends" before it "begins" or even that the sound that "follows" it happens first. In general superpositions 1 to 8 increase density and those from 9 to 16 increase fragmentation. I have not dealt in this piece with the possibility of running the tape backwards except in the case of the "cross-grain" cuts e.g.:*

The number of sounds used is large. I begin with 1024 cards to make the 16 charts. A totally variable sound will have a frequency of 32 out of 1024 whereas Cccc (e.g.) will have a frequency of 2.[7] The cards are dealt after being carefully shuffled (in one of the classical Tarot ways) into the charts. Each chart has a fund of cards available to it as the "mobility" principle (from the Changes) operates. These are refreshed as necessary. This whole thing is cumbersome in the extreme and I now realize that as I go on I must involve computation rather than the cards with their character of uniqueness. I discovered this from the attacks and decays, where, because there are 2 factors infinite unpredictability comes about through their interaction. However we are working, but the work is very slow. I go this week to North Carolina to teach for 3 weeks and I think I shall simply put the students to work composing and cutting the tape. The piece as planned is 20 minutes, but 4 minutes alone (the first "movement") will be 192 pages! And by the time that is finished I will surely have new ideas.

As you see I have increased rather than decreased the element of chance in this work. Another thing characterizing it is the fact of many people working on it in all of its aspects. So that it is not "my" work. David Tudor has been composing superpositions 7–11. A student from Illinois worked etc.

I am anxious to have a copy of Schaeffer's book on Music Concrète.[8] Would you ask him to send me one?

I am also anxious to know your plans; it is very exciting to be looking forward to seeing you again soon and here. Naturally I can hardly wait. News of your work always pleases me and more and more one hears of it here (in the newspapers, etc.)

Merce choreographed part of the Symphonie pour un Homme Seul[9] (a terrible piece) for a Festival at Brandeis University. There I met again Bernard Blin whom you probably know (was connected with Schaeffer).

This last Spring I organized concerts and also gave lectures and that kept me busy too. I lectured at the University of Illinois and they were so interested that I might conceivably go there to continue the work with magnetic tape. All my interest is now in this field and I doubt whether I will be writing any more "concert" music. On the other hand the public here is just beginning to be aware of the "prepared piano", so that I shall hear a performance in October of my concerto for prepared piano and orchestra, paid for by the Musician's Union! David Broeckman, the conductor would also like to play a work by you. Can a score be sent? We are hoping to hear your Polyphonie.

David is going to play your first Sonata on programs this summer and in the Fall.[10]

---

[7] Cage refers here to the frequency of *occurrence* of the sound, not its acoustic frequency. (RS)

[8] Pierre Schaeffer, *A la recherche d'une musique concrète* (Paris: Seuil, 1952).

[9] *Symphonie pour un homme seul*, by Pierre Henry and Pierre Schaeffer, first performed at the École Normale de Musique in Paris on 18 March 1950.

[10] The work was in fact played by David Tudor on 12 August 1952 at Black Mountain College and on 29 August at the Maverick Concert Hall. Eventually Tudor incorporated

Please keep us informed about when you will be here so that we can arrange a concert while you are here. Lectures etc.

I have the sad news that the building in which I live will be torn down in a year; but you will be here before that happens. It is a delight and now, as I write, many birds are outside on the fire-escape where I put food for them. They will put up a new 20 story building to house more people. New York is beginning to look like a prison.

Whenever you want an article for a magazine on electronic music, let me know; and if anything is written besides Schaeffer's book I am anxious to see it.

I am full of admiration for the way in which you are working and especially for the way in which you have generalized the concept of the series, and in your Etude for a single sound[11] made the correspondance between frequency and duration. I am fascinated by the correspondances between rows of different numbers.

I am afraid this is a very sketchy letter and scarcely worth sending to you. However, you must realize that I spend a great deal of time tossing coins and the emptiness of head that that induces begins to penetrate the rest of my time as well. The best, I keep thinking, is that we shall meet again soon.

Please greet all the friends for me. I miss you all.

Always yours,

John

39

Letter from Pierre Boulez to John Cage
1 October 1952

My dear John.

Lots of things to tell you. And then you know how letters get put off from one day to the next. Now we are about to leave – in a week. And it still has to be done.

Firstly – Thank you for the Music of Changes. Which I <u>liked a lot</u>, and which I was so pleased to get. I was absolutely charmed by this development in your style. And I am with you all the way. It is certainly my favourite amongst everything you have done. And I have lent it here to all my young composer friends. Now comes the problem of playing it here, either by Y. Loriod or by Y. Grimaud. We are going to arrange it with P. Souvtch-

---

it into the programme of several recitals: on 28 April 1954 at the Fisher Concert Hall, New York, and on 28 November 1955 at Portland State College (according to programmes kept in the David Tudor archive and communicated by John Holzaepfel).

[11] Cf. the discussion of this process in no. 35.

insky. In any case you cannot know how much I agree with you – I can tell you this enthusiastically.

2nd) Your long letter told me all about what you are doing at the moment, and you know how interested I am. Everything you tell me about music on magnetic tape I find extremely interesting. We will have the chance to talk about it at length. Especially since this research is going on now in Germany too.[1] And I shall fill you in about everything I have seen over there.

3rd) Cologne Radio must have written to you (NDWR-Köln); for I spoke to them about you, and passed on your records, which they copied. They want to put on a two-hour broadcast about your music and would like some recent recordings and some explanatory notes or things you have written. I have passed on the issue of the Transformation journal as well as an item about you in a festival brochure; and the text by L. Harrison on the prepared piano which appears in the 2 piano record set. If you could send them a recording of your "Music of Changes", they would be overjoyed. I think it was Stockhausen who wrote to you. He is a young German composer, most remarkable.[2]

4th) From Belgium, you should have had a letter from Froidebise. In Liège they are putting on a journal "of shock" which will involve only people with the best intentions! Say yes to them and we are expecting an article from you.[3]

5th) I arrive in New York on 11 November. And thank you for the suggestions about the apartment. We are staying in N.Y. until 7 December; but if there are extensions, until 21 December. I wouldn't want to put you out. But if you could find me a bedroom where I can work in quiet I would like that solution best. Above all I don't want to inconvenience you. If there is someone amongst your friends or acquaintants, who could rent me a room, that would suit me perfectly.

Meanwhile, they (the Co.) have reserved a room as for the actors, at the Great Northern Hotel (– where Milhaud stays, it seems!!).

I shall bring my Structures and the musique Concrète with me.

I am happy to think that at last we are going to see each other again, to go on and on nattering. After three years, we have something to talk about. I will have my latest things to show you: Structures for 2 pianos; and some a capella choral pieces, written for 12 voices (12 soloists), which Marcel Couraud is going to sing here.[4] These choral pieces are on poems by Gatti, which I shall also get you to read. I hope to have quite a bit of time in New York, so we can see each other very often; I think that won't inconvenience you and won't be a

---

[1] This is a reference to the electronic studio of the West-Deutscher Rundfunk in Cologne, founded in 1951 by Herbert Eimert and where Stockhausen also worked.

[2] This is the first mention of Stockhausen by Boulez. His enthusiasm for Stockhausen's work in this correspondence is noteworthy in view of their later divergence of practice. (RS)

[3] This journal was to be called *Variation*, after the name of a contemporary music performance group. The editorial board included Souris, Philippot, Fano, Deliège and others. The project was abandoned.

[4] This refers to *Oubli signal lapidé* (see no. 36, note 6).

waste of your time. I have asked some young colleagues here to send you their music. For I would also like to show you all that.

I will have something to talk to you about concerning techniques for subdividing and multiplying a variable unitary value, with two superimposed rhythmic series. Which would correspond to a rhythmic complex – of the same sort as a harmonic and tessitura complex – I will have something to show you concerning how I make use of non-directional sound complexes.

As for you, you will explain to me everything you are doing, your recent experiments with magnetic tape. Perhaps I shall arrive in time to hear your Concerto for Prepared Piano and Orchestra. I very much hope so, or else to hear a recording.

On the subject, has Schaeffer sent you his book?[5] And have you received the issue of the Revue Musicale with my article in it?[6] I am seeing Schaeffer the day after tomorrow and I shall ask him.

Otherwise, I shall write to you on board ship – where I shall spend seven quiet days, except maybe for seasickness, if the storm carries on as violently as at present. Let's hope in any case that I face that eventual trial gallantly.

Marianne Souvtchinsky passed on to me the Harper's Bazaar for July in which you could not be photographed better, as with the "Boza Mansion". That is a foretaste of what I shall see. In this way, I won't be at all displaced. –

I am posting my letter and I don't think you will have time to reply before I leave. We are leaving here on 6 October (i.e. in precisely five days). So I think you would do better to reply directly to Montreal (Canada) where I shall be from 14 October.

Here is the address: P.B.
                                 Cie Madeleine Renaud – J.L. Barrault
                                 Theátre His Majesty's –
                                 Montréal

There is also another address, (for I don't know the address of the theatre, but it appears that it is very well-known):
                                 c/o Canadian Concerts & Artists
                                 817/818 – Castle Building – Montréal
You can choose according to which you prefer to write to.

Please excuse this disjointed and hasty letter. But I absolutely must post it immediately.

So, I expect a note from you; I shall write to you from the boat; in any case, rendez-vous on 11 November.

And long live us!

                                              PB
                                              (still: 4 Rue Beautreillis)

[5] See no. 38, note 8.
[6] "Possibly ...".

40

Letter from Pierre Boulez to John Cage
Montreal, end of October 1952

My dear John.

Thanks for your excellent letter[1] which I had not so long ago, since we only arrived here two days ago. I am very happy to accept your offer to put me up in your apartment. And for me the advantages of the view, the piano – without mentioning the attraction of staying in a house destined soon to disappear (the romantic melancholy of future ruins!) – incomparably outweigh the inconvenience of a 40-minute journey. I much prefer to be some distance away from the theatre. But I accept on the condition that it won't put you out. Like you I hope that this way there will be several good evenings beneath the sign of Monroe.[2]

I am annoyed that your Concerto wasn't played well by the orchestra, and it's a great pity that it wasn't recorded.[3] I still have the option of reading the score at your apartment. I am pleased for you that the work on magnetic tape is coming along. But who do you talk to about such work! I too had to take weeks to put together three minutes of music. It's a workman's job: sticking the sounds end to end, making montages, tracking down errors; we will soon be able to set about the most delicate tasks – for example, the Arab engravers on copper (if there's a 3rd World War).

Anyway, we will have plenty of time to talk; for there are two shows without any music (la Répétition, and Occupe-toi d'Amélie[4]). So that makes about a week or ten days when I shall have the evenings free.

On the subject, I wanted to write to you from the boat. But you know what boats are. You stroll about, you have a look at everything that is going on and you don't have the slightest inclination to write even the shortest letter (At least, that's what happens as far as I'm concerned[)]. So I shall explain everything that I am doing at the moment face to face with you; I think that will be better. Moreover, I hope that after the stay in New York my English will be considerably improved, and that I will be able to talk if not easily, at least correctly.

I leave you the task of doing something about my music.

I would indeed like to play my pieces for two pianos with D. Tudor. They

---

[1] This letter is missing from the collection kept by Boulez.

[2] A reference to Cage's address, 326 Monroe Street. (RS)

[3] This refers to the Concerto for prepared piano and orchestra.

[4] *La répétition, ou l'amour puni*, by Jean Anouilh: world première by the Compagnie Renaud-Barrault at the Marigny theatre on 27 October 1950; and *Occupe-toi d'Amélie*, by Georges Feydeau, in repertory from 4 March 1948.

are very difficult; and we would have to have time to work on them together. In any case, even if we can't play them properly, we could read through them between us.

I hope he will play me your "Music of Changes", which, I think, he must know to perfection by now.

I am bringing with me the "musique concrète" on records.[5] They will send me the tapes from Paris, if necessary. I have all of the "Symphonie pour un Homme seul;" by Schaeffer[6] in this form, with which I hope you will regale yourself. And a "vocalise" by Pierre Henry which will delight you no less. I put them in (these two things) out of impartiality, but not without irony. They (I mean the two authors) saw the impartiality in this, but not the irony. Which is a pity for them; but we shall have a good laugh. I have also brought an extract from Messiaen's étude.[7]

You mentioned that I should meet Claude Jutras here. But you didn't give me his address. I consulted the telephone directory. There are lots of Jutras, but not one Claude; (only Charles and Camille, under the letter C.) – As for doctors called Jutras, which I found, there isn't a first name corresponding to the one you gave me. There is one called Albert who – according to the directory – has to do with X-rays at the Hôtel Dieu; and another called Fernand, who works in odontology. But maybe he isn't on the phone. So if you have his address, send it to me. We leave here on 2 November – (How good to think that in [?] weeks we shall meet in New York.)

I meant to go and see McLaren.[8] But when I found out that he lives in

---

[5] On 22 December 1952, Boulez put on a concert of *musique concrète* works at the McMillin Theater of the University of Columbia, with a programme slightly different from that of the Paris concert of 21 May 1952 (see No. 36, note 7), and from that which Boulez gives here: Pierre Schaeffer, *Étude noire*; Pierre Henry, *Tam-Tam IV* and *Batterie fugace*; Pierre Schaeffer and Pierre Henry, *Symphonie pour un homme seul* (extracts); Pierre Henry, *Antiphonie*; Pierre Boulez, *Étude sur un son*; Olivier Messiaen, *Timbres-durées*; Pierre Boulez, *Étude II*. Boulez's two *musique concrète* études, separated by dance sequences without musical accompaniment, continued to be performed in North America under the title *Fragments* as part of the Merce Cunningham dance company's repertoire: on 30 December 1953 at the Theater de Lys in New York, on 20 January and 8 December 1954 at the Brooklyn Academy of Music, on 15 November 1955 in San Francisco, on 21 November 1955 at Portland Civic Center, on 25 November 1955 at Tacoma, and on 18 May 1956 at Washington Hall (programmes from David Tudor archive communicated by John Holzaepfel). For another American performance, see no. 43 below.

[6] This piece was written jointly by Schaeffer and Henry in 1950. (RS)

[7] Presumably Messiaen's *Timbres-durées* for tape. (RS)

[8] Cage's comments on Norman Maclaren are worth reprinting here for their connection with his preoccupation with the structuration of time during this period. They were omitted from the version of his article published in *Contrepoints*:

Just as art as sand painting (art for the now-movement rather than for posterity's museum of civilisation) becomes a held point of view, adventurous workers in the field of synthetic music (e.g. Norman McLaren) find that for practical and economic reasons work with magnetic wires (any music so made can quickly and easily be erased, rubbed off) is preferable to that with film. (*Silence*, p. 65)

He adds in a note:

Twenty-four or *n* frames per second is the 'canvas' upon which this music is written; thus, in a very obvious way, the material itself demonstrates the necessity for time

Vancouver, I cooled off a bit (so to speak); and I gave up altogether when I was told how far apart Vancouver and Montreal are.

This is a city, here, which I still haven't had time to see. I went to the big park right in the centre of the city. The autumn shades of the trees, the city at my feet, the night lights, lots of little squirrels not wild at all: a fine subject for a primary-school essay. I won't give you the pleasure of a longer description.

Apart from that, I don't think there's much to see. No museum; no old piles (as the enlightened amateur archaeologists say). We are going to try to take a trip[9] to the Great North. That may seem a fine exaggeration to you (and you would be right). But to the Laurentian forest which is only 50km from here. We are going to hire a 5- or 6-seater car. And we shall go on our adventure discreetly and modestly.

Our ears are ringing here with Cartier and Champlain, with religion and censure, with family and puritanism. As for the rustic accent, it is quite notice-able – (You have to take the distractions of travelling where you find them).

Anyway, we shall soon be living in the same time zone; it's a great step towards meeting up.

I have got to know here the Russian-American impressario of the Co. M. R. JL B.[10] in New York. A certain Mr Hurok whom you must know. He looked to me like a wild slum landlord. I had a ¼-hour discussion with him, because he thought that 14 musicians for Amphitryon[11] (*incidental music by F. Poulenc*) was much too much. Out of a spirit of contradiction, I took Poulenc's side and said that that score was orchestrated for 14 instruments, and would sound very bad any other way. You can picture it! (In my opinion, it would still sound pretty good for two ocarinas and whistle).

That's the latest on the start of this tour. I am working at home in the evenings, after the show.

I am greatly looking forward to making the acquaintance of 326 Monroe Street soon, and to being around whilst I am in residence. You can't know how much I think you for that. Anyway, I shall thank you even more warmly in person. We can organize meals, as well, and get-togethers – for I have a daily allowance ($15) for my vital needs. That will be our common vital needs; and it will be much nicer like that.

I am crossing off the days to go before we meet.

Say hello to everyone for me. And long live Christopher Columbus.

PB

(rhythmic) structure. With magnetic means, freedom from the frame of film means exists, but the principle of rhythmic structure should hold over as, in geometry, a more elementary theorem remains as a premise to make possible the obtaining of those more advanced.

9 Here a word has been torn off.

10 I.e. Madeleine Renaud and Jean-Louis Barrault.

11 Molière's play was performed by the Compagnie Renaud-Barrault at the theatre Marigny from 5 December 1947.

41

Letter from Pierre Boulez to John Cage

The Lord Elgin Hotel
Ottawa Canada

2 Nov.[1] [1952]

My dear John.

More than a week before we meet again. One week exactly, since we arrive in New York on 11 September,[2] as planned. We leave Quebec on the 10th in the afternoon, and we arrive in New York on the 11th (Tuesday) at eight o'clock in the morning at Central Station. If anything is changed, you will get an emergency note.

I shall be so pleased to see you! I won't give you a complete run-down on what I've been doing either, since we are going to be able to do it in person so soon.

Thank you for your letter[3] in which you gave me Claude Jutras' address. As you said, he is indeed a young doctor – at 22, he has just finished his medical studies – the son of a doctor. But he isn't a musician particularly; he is more interested in the cinema; and especially now, having finished his studies – for he does not want to be a doctor – he is going to devote himself almost entirely to that: cinema and dramatic art. He told me about some experiments he did with magnetic tape, but he himself doesn't think them very interesting. Now the tapes have completely deteriorated (the sticky-tape didn't hold, and so his whole montage has come away on all sides); so he couldn't let me hear them. But I don't think there's anything to regret, since, even according to him, it was very rudimentary. He showed me two films, an "avant-garde" one with flesh and bone characters, which isn't wonderful. But he made it two years ago. He also showed me a film entitled "Abstractions", animated abstract painting, in which the best things are due to the chance movement of ink on wet paper. For from a pictorial point of view proper, it is still fairly weak.

But he's a good lad, with common sense. Nevertheless, I think he is terribly lacking in contacts and models in this fair city of Montreal, where there isn't the slightest thing to be proud of.

On the same occasion – and for the first time – I saw a large number of McLaren's films. I have to say I was most disappointed. There was a disarming naivety and lack of taste. (Especially of the Fiddle de Dee sort,

---

[1] Boulez first wrote "Sept.", which was struck through and corrected.
[2] This is a slip for 11 November.
[3] This letter from Cage is missing from the collection.

etc. . .)[4] the music, in particular, even his synthesized music, which is never-theless indeed good, hasn't a clue about what the music of today is. As for the animations themselves, I don't find them all that far from Walt Disney (Fantasia – sur Bach).[5]

That's the lowdown on those meetings.

Today a performance with Sauguet's music (charming!) and, afterwards, an official reception at the French Embassy (charming again!).

But soon Monroe Street will see and hear us. Say hello to David Tudor, whom I am very keen to know. Tell him to get several doses of aspirin ready – I will do the same – for "Structures" really isn't easy. But since he has worked on your "Music of Changes",[6] I think he is seriously prepared! Could I hear it? – I hope that Maro Ajemian isn't angry because I didn't want to write anything for her and her sister.

I can't wait to see you again. And when I think that after three years apart, there is only a week left, I am like a horse coming out of the stables, and I want – Joshua in reverse – to cut the days short.

A bientôt and best wishes.

PB

Have you heard from Belgium recently (about the "Variation" journal?)

42

Pierre Boulez on John Cage in 'Tendencies in recent music'[1]

1953

. . . In the following generation, an American musician, John Cage, was led to

[4] *Fiddle-De-Dee*, a film by N. McLaren made in 1947.

[5] Bach's Toccata and Fugue in D Minor is used in Walt Disney's *Fantasia*.

[6] "Jo ChAnGEs" is written above "of changes", connected by an arrow:

Jo ChAnGEs.
↗
of Changes

[1] This article first appeared as "Vers une musique expérimentale" in *La Revue musicale*, No. 236 (1967), pp. 28–35, edited by Pierre Schaeffer. According to Albert Richard's introductory notes, it was written for the "Première Décade Internationale de Musique Expérimentale", organized by the Groupe de Recherches de Musique Concrète and held in Paris between 8 and 18 June 1953. It was reprinted as "Tendencies in recent music" in *Stocktakings*, pp. 173–80, without the two music examples, which are in Boulez's handwriting. The translation printed here has been produced for this volume. The "pièce pour piano" by Stockhausen is the penultimate system from *Klavierstück IV* (Universal Edition, 1954), p. 12. This was therefore published *after* Boulez had quoted it in this article. Cage had told Boulez in no. 33 that he had sent him a copy of *Music of Changes*. Boulez thanked him for it on 1 October 1952 (in no. 39).

think that, no matter how carefully the clichés of the old tonal language are avoided, the responsibility for them remains, for a large part, with our instruments forged according to the requirements of that tonal language. Therefore he, like Varèse, turned towards percussion; a sound world without definite pitch, where only rhythm is a strong enough architectonic element to allow a valid, non-improvised structure. Without mentioning, obviously, timbre relations and acoustic relations which exist between the different categories of instruments employed (skin, wood or metal) ...

... What remains to be discovered is still non-tempered sound worlds. Why, indeed, should a taboo be made of that decision, which has given immense benefit, but which has henceforth lost its *raison d'être*, given that the tonal organization which demanded this standardization is practically destroyed? Certainly, the instrumental factor is not the least of the things that have prevented the development of musical thought based on non-tempered intervals, drawing instead on the concepts of note complexes or sound complexes. All the acoustic approximations that have gradually accumulated during the evolution of the West must disappear, since they are no longer necessary; but how, for the moment, is the problem of this production of sound to be resolved?

The prepared piano of John Cage, the American musician already mentioned, gives a home-made and embryonic, but nevertheless plausible, solution. In any case, the prepared piano has the immense merit of making concrete here and now the sound worlds which we have to give up provisionally, given the difficulty of realising them. Thus the piano becomes an instrument capable, by means of a do-it-yourself tuning system [*une tablature artisanale*], of giving frequency complexes. A tuning system, when it is realized that in order to prepare the piano, different materials such as metal, wood or rubber are placed between the strings, at certain important points along their length. These materials modify the four characteristics of the sound produced by the string: its duration, amplitude, frequency and timbre. When it is recalled that a single key, for a large part of the piano, corresponds to three strings, and if the diverse materials placed at important points along each of these three strings are imagined, some idea of the variety and complexity of sounds obtained in this manner can be gained. This shows the way to a future evolution of music where instruments can aid in the creation of a new sound system that both needs and calls for them, thanks to the development of progressively more perfect tuning systems . . .

43

Letter from John Cage to Pierre Boulez

Monsieur P.B.
c/o Compagnie Mad. Renaud-J.L. Barrault
Teatro solis
Montevideo, Uruguay

May 1, 1953

Dear Pierre,

My cold has disappeared and the "Williams Mix" is on its way to you.[1] *I have sent 9 tracks: one is all 8 mixed and the others are the single tracks. Before each one there are synchronization marks: (audio frequency oscillator sine waves) 1 kilocycle; 1 second silence; 400 cycles per second; 1 second silence; 1 kilocycle; 1 second silence; 2.5 kilocycles; 4 seconds silence and then the music. We performed it at the University of Illinois with 8 tape recorders and 8 loudspeakers, the former in full view on the stage and the latter situated around the audience (about 800 people). We performed your Etudes, one from two loudspeakers and one from three. The rest of the music was heard from all 8 loudspeakers at once, except the Batterie Fugace*[2] *and the Timbres-Durées,*[3] *both of which we made travel around the audience. I would have liked to experiment further with more complex use of the loudspeakers, but time did not permit. Earle Brown's piece like mine uses 8*

---

[1] *Williams Mix* for magnetic tape (1952). There is an eight-track version by Cage.
[2] *Batterie fugace* by Pierre Henry, first performed in Paris on 29 April 1951.
[3] *Timbres-durées* by Messiaen (see no. 36, note 7).

machines and 8 loudspeakers. The experience of the 8 loudspeakers is extra-ordinary. There is no room for anything but immediate listening. The air was so alive one was simply part of it. This however was our reaction and that of only some of the audience. Most people were alarmed and retreated to the idea of "boundaries of musical action". Let them build whatever walls; someone will always be getting out. (There is, by the way, an increasing conservatism develop-ing here; it is called "consolidation" and means neo-classicists using 12 tone rows and vice-versa: corollaries: technical mastery – expressive power.) We have not yet made a New York hearing of the tape music. I don't know exactly why. For one thing the economic situation for me is extremely bad; I never know from one day to the next where money will be coming from. I had hopes and spent my time trying to get support for the tape music from Foundations and Universities but I have had no success. And the results of my work which please me only serve to produce a strong negative reaction in those I ask for help. I tell you this not to arouse sympathy but to explain why I have not yet organized a performance here. I also think that another architecture than the concert hall will be needed for a hearing that is excellent. The loudspeakers around the audience should also be above the audience. Perhaps no architecture at all: out of doors with the loudspeakers on the tops of buildings. A magnetrillon!

I have done no composing since you were here; I helped Earle make his piece, and from time to time ideas came for my next work which as I see it will be a large work which will always be in progress and will never be finished; at the same time any part of it will be able to be performed once I have begun.[4] *It will include tape and any other time actions, not excluding violins and whatever else I put my attention to. I will of course write other music than this but only if required by some outside situation such as one that has just arisen: a poet here (French), George Guy, has asked me to make music for a reading of Le Coup de Dés. I would like to do this but I told him that you may have already made such music and in that case he should use yours. He will write to you about it. I will not begin anything until I hear from you whether or not I should do it. He is also interested in promoting a recording of Tudor's playing of your 2nd Sonata. This I hope will come about.*[5] *A man named Evar (I believe), at present on his way to Paris, and who is head of a small recording company, will try to see you or Heugel about all this.*

I had a very pleasant letter from Schlee of Universal about the possible publication of my Changes. I will be happy if they decide to do this.

David wants more music from you, from Stockhausen, from Froidebise; please bring all this about and more, more music!

It is my fault you have not yet received the drawings by Philip Gustin[6]. *Shortly you will have them. It is simply a matter of procrastination.*

---

[4] This work became the so-called "time-length" pieces of 1953–6. (JP)
[5] This plan did not come to pass.
[6] This is Cage's mistake for Philip Guston. (JP)

Christian wrote a new piece which uses all 88 tones.[7] *I think it is magnificent and he says it is the result of his conversations with you. David played it at a program at Harvard last Sunday (we drove up in the little Ford). It is about 12 minutes long. Christian will be in Europe this summer, but not in France, because it appears that it is not definite whether he is a Frenchman or an American. If the former he could be inducted into the military, which, naturally, he wishes to avoid. So, he will pass the summer in Italy, Switzerland and Germany. If you will be in Germany, as I imagine, let us know where so that he can get to see you.*

I think that the University of Illinois is considering inviting you there some time next year; I hope that happens; we would see you soon again!

They made a recording of David's concert and so I have been able to have a tape of the Music of changes sent to Eimert in Cologne. They also have a recording of your 2nd Sonata, but David is not satisfied with his performance of it on that occasion.

Merce, David and M.C.[8] *are all going to Black Mountain College this summer. I will stay here. The four of us have organized a "Package Festival", an announcement of which we are currently sending out to Colleges and Universities throughout the country. If we get enough responses we would make enough money to support the tape music ourselves, without outside help. We would give concerts, lectures, discussions, etc. I enclose one of our brochures.*

I think that is all; I have not attempted to tell you about the path of my musical ideas because nothing is very clear yet. What is clear is made more or less pointless by rather crucial obscurities. I need still to spend some days alone.

It was a delight to all of us that you were here, – and "soon again 'twill be". Everyone sends love to you and all the friends.

Always yours,

John

44

Letter from Pierre Boulez to John Cage
after 18 June 1953

Dear John,

This is a small harbinger of news. I am breaching the wall of silence – one must live against the times –

It is useless to make excuses. I am deeply ashamed of never having written since leaving New York, so ashamed that I have been having nightmares! I

---

[7] This refers to *For Piano I* (1952).
[8] This is the poet Mary Caroline Richards. (JP)

see you appear in judgemental or avenging guises that each time reproach me for my laziness in writing.

Even after receiving the *Tape-Music*[1], I was in the middle of preparations for the Bordeaux festival (Ch. Colomb-Milhaud-Claudel).[2] Then there were innumerable proof corrections from which I didn't think I would emerge alive. Then there was a stay in Metz, far from Paris, where I got down to some serious work at last. Then a stay in the South, cut off by the strike; (on the subject, I got a very late letter from Ch. Wolff; I suppose he went back from France without trouble). Now there is a short trip to Venice and the rehearsals of Ch. Colomb. So I was aware that this could not go on much longer without the silence between us becoming intolerable.

Soon I am going to write you a damned long and detailed letter, going over, through and on about everything that has happened this year, about what has gone on here (Stockhausen has become quite remarkable), on several projects I have got on at Marigny – (extremely restrained concerts of contemporary music).[3]

I shall tell you about the rows I have been having with Schaeffer: that would be enough to fill a huge folio! I shall tell you that the experimental studio is more and more crap, and that Schaeffer is a pain in the arse; and that I hope I shall soon be working with Stockhausen at the electronic music studio of Radio-Cologne.

I shall also tell you that I have re-written my 2nd piece for 2 pianos;[4] that, in the middle of all that, I am writing a little something for voice and 6 instruments;[5] and that I have completely re-written the first a cappella choral piece.[6]

I will have a discussion with you about the Tape-Music. For that will revive our conversations, which have already been animated, and seem certain once more to turn on the necessity of chance.

I will tell you too that I have had a row with Nabokov, who is still organizing a festival with a supporting conference and competition; and that I turned down his invitation and sent him a letter in which I put the mercenary lackey in his place.

Apart from that, in concerts here: Nothing. It's desperate. Everything, from that point of view, is going on in Germany.

Scherchen, alone, came to conduct the 1st Paris performance of Webern's

---

[1] This is Cage's *Williams Mix* (1952).

[2] *Christoph Colomb* by Paul Claudel, with incidental music by Darius Milhaud. World première by the Compagnie Renaud-Barrault at the Marigny Theatre on 21 May 1953.

[3] The "Concerts du Petit Marigny", begun in 1953, were to become the famous "Concerts du Domaine musical".

[4] This refers to the revision of *Structure Ib*.

[5] This "little something" was to become *Le marteau sans maître*, written between 1952 and 1955 (Jameux no. 16).

[6] *Oubli signal lapidé* (see no. 36, note 6).

last orchestral variations. That's it for the year. (With also a first performance of Berg's Postcards[7] by Horenstein).

I was forgetting that there was also the première of Rake's Progress[8] which I didn't attend. That's what musical life here is coming to!! Isn't it glorious??

Oh! I almost forgot to tell you that by the same post I am sending you the Pléiade Mallarmé.[9] (I had to wait until I had several shekels for that!) – That will help you to wait patiently for the second letter which will follow very soon.

I hope you haven't got it in for me because of the abominably long silence and that this transoceanic dialogue can get going again. (I also have a photo of you, David and M.C.[10] and of the whole group on the departure quay when I left N.Y.)

A bientôt until the second letter. A thousand good wishes and a thousand over.

Give warmest greetings to everyone from me.

PB

45
Letter from Pierre Boulez to John Cage
July 1954

Claridge Hotel
Tucuman 535
Buenos Aires

Dear John.

I have just got your letter[1] and I hasten to reply.

[?][2] the drawings[3] were sent back to you after an annoying episode.

---

[7] I.e. the *Altenberg Lieder*. (RS)

[8] *The Rake's Progress*, opera by Stravinsky, first performed in Paris on 18 June 1953 at the Opéra-Comique, Paris. (The work was premièred in Venice, on 11 September 1951; see no. 35 and note 23.)

[9] The first complete edition of Mallarmé's works, edited by H. Mondor and G. Jean-Aubry, was published by Gallimard in the Pléiade edition in 1946.

[10] Probably Mary Caroline Richards (see no. 43, note 8).

[1] This letter has been lost. At the time of writing, Boulez was on the second tour by the Compagnie Renaud-Barrault.

[2] A portion of the letter has been torn off.

[3] This concerns the drawings by Philip Guston referred to in no. 43.

I had received an advice that the drawings had arrived, asking me to pay the necessary to get them through customs. Then, as always happens in such circumstances, I lost the note. And the time to leave was already approaching. I received, just as I was about to leave – two or three days beforehand, if I remember right – another summons. At that point, I asked Fano to go to the customs-office to extract at last the great drawings which were still imprisoned by the customs. Then I left with an easy mind. But things could not be sorted out so simply! In São Paulo, I had a letter from Fano, telling me that it was impossible to deal with the formalities of the customs, without a signed authorization legalized by the French Consul of wherever I was. Obviously, I scuttled over to the French Consul who immediately made out a paper legalizing my signature, the authorization, etc. ... etc. ... I went away with an easy mind once more. And then at Montevideo, I got another letter from Fano telling me that the authorization arrived too late, and that when it came into the customs' possession, they informed him that the parcel had gone back to New York. I was most upset firstly and foremostly because of the drawings, and secondly and no less foremostly because of the rudeness. Anyway, we are good enough friends for you not to believe me guilty of a refusal or negligence.

I had heard of your European projects from Phillippe Heugel and Heinrich Strobel (of Südwestfunk in Baden-Baden). And I had myself received from some foundation or other (Carnegie or Guggenheim) a grant to fill out for you, to certify that ... and that ... – you bet I certified, and I sincerely hope that the grant will be useful for something. I heard from Strobel that you may be taking part in the Donaueschingen festival; and Ph. Heugel told me about David's recital at the École Normale. I agree entirely with the date, venue and recital. Very good, more than perfect. I am already greatly looking forward to seeing him again.

My poor John, I haven't had time to write to you much this year and you must think I am the last word in ingratitude. To think that you welcomed me so well when I was in New York and that I haven't written to you since.[4] But if you knew the work I have had this year! Arranging the four Petit Marigny concerts was no small task. For I did absolutely everything from arranging the programmes to hiring the instruments (not to mention such things as contacting artists or taking care of lodgings). Luckily we had Barrault's financial backing. For in order to put on concerts like that properly, there was a fairly considerable deficit. We still don't know whether we can carry on next season. P. Souvtchinsky and Madame Tézenas are organizing themselves to try and form a committee. We need about 1½ million francs (if not 2 million) before we can hope to begin. It is not an easy sum to find. Moreover, we have to find a secretary. For I don't mind telling you that I am not keen to lose all my time as I have done this year. Practically speaking, I have been able to do

---

[4] Boulez is so busy that he has forgotten the preceding letter (no. 44).

absolutely nothing from December to April. At the end of April, we went on tour. You can easily imagine this season's disastrous history as far as my work goes.

As you know, we have published one of the Company's journal issues on Music,[5] which was a great success since now the print run is exhausted. We ran off 4000 copies: a higher figure than one could hope for with such a specialized journal, and one with the leanings you could observe (even if you don't entirely agree, as you showed in the letter you sent me at the time[6] and to which I didn't have time to reply. But we shall come back to that). It has led P. Souvtchinsky and me to found a music journal. It is called "Domaine Musical".[7] I hope you will have got it, since I gave your name and address for the mailing list. As you will see, – or as you have already noticed – it is in the same direction as the other one. A bit wider in scope (section on music ethnology to which I am greatly attached).[8] A little less condensed and "manifesto"-like than the Compagnie Barrault-Renaud journal. Stockhausen's article is most remarkable: a shame that it was translated by steam-power, and that it was published incompletely. P. Souvtchinsky's article was also one of the journal's principal items. You can see from the rest of the contents, the names have hardly changed (It has to be said that apart from permutational possibilities ... it is difficult to change). As none of us wants to write an article every month, and furthermore it is a tricky business anyway to write an interesting article, and especially to receive a collection of them, we have decided that there is no need to publish more than two per season. One in April-May. The other in October-November. All this long preamble is to put you in the picture. I intend – and the letter has brought the request forward – [to ask you] to give me an article on the subject of your choice for the second issue, which will come out in October. As I am the editor of this publication, I absolutely refuse to impose subjects on the contributors to numbers. But in order to give a certain unity to the contents, I have to give some directions so that the same subject is not discussed 3 times; or if it is, that it is in a different manner by each contributor. For you, I should like you to talk to me a bit in advance, to be able to integrate it easily into the contents. I mean: what your latest experiments are, and what subjects

---

5 "La musique et ses problèmes contemporains", *Cahiers de la Compagnie Madeleine Renault – Jean-Louis Barrault*, 2/3, 1954. This issue contains a famous portrait of Boulez by Barrault, Boulez's article "... Auprès et au loin", and articles by Descartes, Barraqué, Fano, Philippot, Artaud, Martenot, Pousseur, Stockhausen, Michaux, Gatti, Schaeffer, Couraud, Souris, Goléa, Char, de Schloezer and Souvtchinsky. It was republished in 1963.

6 This letter is lost.

7 This journal ran for only one issue (Spring 1954, Grasset). In summary, it contained articles by Boulez ("Probabilités critiques du compositeur" and "Hommage à Webern"), Barraqué, Philippot, Hodeir, Joffroy, Fano, Jacobs, Le Roux, Brailoiu, Rouget, Dupin, Souvtchinsky, Stockhausen, Goléa, Vallas and Barrault.

8 The issue contained two ethnomusicological articles: "Élargissement de la sensibilité musicale" by Constantin Brailoiu and "Notes d'ethnographie musicale" by Gilbert Rouget.

have preoccupied you lately. Propose two or three subjects to me; and I w. tell you which would suit the overall contents of the number best – (I thin. perhaps: the Disappearance of the Interpreter?) Write to me quickly. I hope you will accept. Tell me what you think and what you think about! It would have to be sent to Paris before the end of August – the time to translate it! For one has to have a certain leeway.

As for me, I am in South America for another month. The same round trip as last time – Rio, São Paulo (where I met a very interesting group of people). Montevideo (boring!). Now Buenos Aires – after Santiago in Chile. On returning to Paris on 17 August, I leave again for Germany on 19 August: first Darmstadt, (where they are going to put on, or at least so I hope, the Visage Nuptial[9]); then Cologne, where I am going to work with Stockhausen on some electronic music works. I am staying there until the end of September beginning of October. I am coming back for a week or so to start off the season with Barrault, then I leave again for a week in Baden-Baden and Donaueschingen, where they should put on "Le marteau sans maître"[10] on which I am working at the moment. After 16 October I am coming back finally to Paris for the whole season.

What else should I tell you about my current activities: I am Milhauding[11] with all my might (because of Christopher Columbus, who is making me discover America as much as I like). Most of the time I am ending up with amateur choirs, with whom you have to begin by teaching solfège, then French pronunciation. They are very nice, but it is a tricky job! Apart from that, I am keeping as much of my time as possible for writing "Le marteau sans maître", which I mentioned above: which is for Flute in G, Xylorimba, Vibraphone, Percussion, Guitar, Viola and contralto voice. I am trying to go ever further and deeper, and also to widen my outlook. With the two a cappella choral pieces I wrote last year, it is one of the works that has given me the most trouble. I am trying to rid myself of my thumbprints and taboos; I am trying to have an ever more complex vision – less visible and more worked out in depth – I am trying to expand the series, and expand the serial principle to the maximum of its possibilities. Besides, the article I had written for the Cahiers[12] was quite explicit. I had to cut the ending short,[13] because it

[9] *Le visage nuptial*, in the version for chorus and large orchestra, was not performed until 4 December 1957 in Cologne, conducted by Boulez (Jameux no. 7b).
[10] In fact, *Le marteau sans maître* was premièred in an incomplete version on 18 June 1955 in Baden-Baden, conducted by Hans Rosbaud. Its full première took place on 21 March 1956 (communication from Hans Oesch concerning Lev Koblyakov's research).
[11] Milhaud wrote the incidental music for Claudel's *Christoph Colomb*, which the Compagnie Renaud-Barrault were performing (cf. no. 44, note 2).
[12] "... Auprès et au loin" (see note 5 above). Reprinted as "... Near and far" in *Stocktakings*, pp. 141–157.
[13] At the end, Boulez writes:
  Let us view the work as a sequence of refusals in the midst of so many probabilities; a choice must be made, and therein lies the difficulty so easily magicked away by the expressed desire for "objectivity". This choice is precisely what constitutes the work, renewing itself at each instant of the compositional process; the compositional

would have been too long given the page layout, but I shall take it up again soon.[14] Obviously we disagree as far as that goes – I do not admit – and I believe I never will admit – chance as a component of a completed work. I am widening the possibilities of <u>strict</u> or <u>free</u> music (constrained or not). But as for chance, the thought of it is unbearable! I hope that, when you come to Europe,[15] you will be able to hear this "Marteau sans maître", either at Donaueschingen or in the recording that they are certainly going to make at Südwestfunk.[16]

Stockhausen is more and more interesting! He is the best of them all in Europa! Intelligent and gifted! I greatly enjoy discussing with him – even fiercely, if necessary – all the current problems. He is a real conversationalist. And I am looking forward to working with him in Cologne. He has been in the Studio a year now and no longer needs technical help. We are going to work in the studio alone and I am hoping to do some excellent work, even in the short time. I have heard his first electronic work[17] – and despite certain restrictions which are not important anyway – it is the first work of this genre to be successful from the auditory point of view. He is extremely sensitive to sonorous qualities, to the life of sounds; and it is thanks to that that he has been able to succeed at the first attempt. At the same time, it has to be said that he can work very peacefully in Cologne: Eimert, the director of this studio is very liberal and lets him do what he wants, when he wants and how he wants! (Which is not the case with the beloved Schaeffer, with whom my relations are now totally cold!! Moreover I <u>refused</u> to work with him, although he asked me more than once. The concretion studio[18] is now vegetating as well as can be expected, which is not too well! It is hardly talked about.)

That's the news. I await your reply concerning the article. I am in Buenos Aires at the Claridge Hotel until 14 July. –

All best wishes –

PB

act can never be assimilated to the mere juxtaposition of encounters within a huge statistical construct. Let us safeguard this inalienable freedom: the constantly longed-for joy of an irrational element (*Stocktakings*, p. 157)

14 "Soon" is saying rather a lot. "Alea" was to appear in 1957 (*Stocktakings*, pp. 26–38).
15 Cage indeed returned to Europe for a tour with David Tudor, visiting Donaueschingen, Cologne, Paris, Brussels, Stockholm, Zurich, Milan and London in the autumn of 1954. He does not seem to have met Boulez on this occasion. Cage's influence on Stockhausen and the composition of *Klavierstück XI* has been attributed to the concert in Cologne (D. Charles in J. Cage. *For the Birds: John Cage in conversation with David Charles* (London: Boyars, 1981), p. 125). However, Stockhausen had already dedicated the *Klavierstücke V–VIII* to Tudor.
16 Cf. note 10 above.
17 This may refer to *Étude* (one-track, 1952) or to *Elektronische Studien* (1954; the first, dating from 1953, remains unpublished).
18 I.e. the studio of the Groupe de Recherches sur la Musique Concrète, actually headed by Henry at this date. (RS)

46

Letter from Pierre Boulez to John Cage
end of July beginning of August 1954

Hotel Grillon
Santiago de Chile

My dear John,

This is a quick note in reply to you[1] to fix things with you as quickly as possible concerning the article for Domaine Musical 2.

The subject suits fine; if I understand, it is about: the material of music and the actions (schemes)[2] that are produced by its nature? That is, the nature properly called of what is termed the musical material; what qualities it must consist of; what it must exclude from the object to make it susceptible to a dialectic of development *and so on . . .*

So send this article as early as possible in August, to my address in Paris.

I hope to have a fairly international selection for this second issue, and I am looking forward to it.

When do you arrive in Europe? I remember that you told me already, and I think it is early October, but I am not very sure.

Here the journey is continuing, with Milhaud as the most reliable witness to my permanence. I have alas very little – by which I mean none at all – time to work for myself.

The tour ends in ten days or so. Phew! then we return – but we certainly won't have finished with Christopher Columbus! Discovering America gives you no rest.

All best wishes.

PB

[handwritten: letter statement about American wildness]

---

[1] Cage's letter has been lost.
[2] The French word "agissements" (schemes) has been placed above "actions" (actions).

47

Pierre Boulez: article 'Cage' for the *Encyclopédie Fasquelle*[1]

1958

CAGE John. American composer, (Los Angeles 1912–). Studied with Cowell, Weiss and Schoenberg; at first much concerned with percussion instruments, for which he wrote a series of works (amongst others *Construction in Metal* for a large number of percussion instruments made exclusively of metal). His research in the field of sound proper then broadened to the piano; he modified the sound of the strings by attaching diverse "preparations" of various materials, such as rubber, metal and wood. These materials, carefully placed at some point on the vibrating string, entirely modify the resulting sound, either in timbre or amplitude; moreover, the dynamic level is largely reduced. Already influenced by Oriental ideas in the thinking and form of his early works, he has recently started from the discovery of chance in composition, and, to pursue this research, he has taken as his basis the book of Chinese oracles, *I Ching*. He has also tried to construct non-instrumental works, with electronic sounds or non-musical (properly speaking) sounds, effecting montages with the sounds recorded on magnetic tape. Chance has manifested itself in the very materials with which he composes, since he was able to write *Imaginary Landscape* for 12 radio sets, where the "sound" is provided by the different existing broadcasting channels. However his adventurous research with chance is viewed, C. remains nevertheless, in his works for percussion or for "prepared piano", a musician who is very gifted in research in the field of sound proper. Among his works may be mentioned several *Imaginary Landscapes* for diverse sound materials, *A Book of Music* for 2 prepared pianos, *Sonatas and Interludes* for prepared piano, *Music of Changes* for piano (not prepared), *Construction in Metal* for percussion, pieces for generally restrained groupings.

PB

---

[1] *Encyclopédie Fasquelle*, vol. 1 (1958) p. 474; the only entry by Boulez not reprinted in *Stocktakings*.

48

Letter from Pierre Boulez to John Cage[1]
5 September 1962

---

baden-baden
kapuzinerstrasse 9

my dear john,
i received your letter[2] only today, 5 september, for it was addressed to me at the dear old rue beautreillis; but i haven't lived there for a long time . . . for it is a long time since i left paris. (soon 4 years!!) to tell you the truth, i was fed up with the place, where you couldn't do a thing, and where the "political" situation became so unpleasant that i was finally better off trying to live elsewhere!

eventually, i landed up here, for various reasons, the first being, of course, my involvement with the südwestfunk.[3]

so i have almost lost touch with what is going on in that noble city of light, fast becoming the city of darkness and obscurantism. i only go there 4 times a year, solely to conduct the "domaine", and don't stay a day longer than necessary!

which is to say that my means are more than limited when it comes to possible "influences" for getting you there.

if you had written to me a little earlier, i could easily have got you to come to the "domaine musical". unfortunately, our programmes are entirely complete, printed, and contracts signed for the whole season. further, the dates for your stay in europe are very awkward, since they fall around easter; and with our slender resources, we cannot give concerts in the period immediately preceding, or which follows that fateful date of easter.

we have, as you can appreciate, fairly limited financial means, and, once the "budget" for the season is set, we are absolutely obliged to shut up shop, save for extra pennies.

i am going to write to philippot – perhaps you met him in paris? –, who now has an official position at the radio; and to françois bayle, one of stockhausen's pupils, who is a member of schaeffer's team, which is forever in metamorphosis – and always the self-same!

---

[1] Boulez's letter, the only one in the collection to be typed, does not use any capitals. This typography has been preserved.
[2] Cage's letter has been lost.
[3] Thanks to Heinrich Ströbel, Boulez was invited to work at the Südwestfunk in Baden-Baden in June 1958, then as composer in residence from January 1959.

I hope, without expecting too much, that one at least of these two contacts will bring some result.

you asked me what is going on in europe? ordinary life, in the most ordinary sense. i now live very isolated in this little super-provincial town, and i only meet my colleagues on very rare occasions.

i am trying to deepen what i do and think ... it isn't always easy, and always requires more isolation! perhaps i shall end my days in some cell, still trying to look behind a non-existent mirror?? to surprise reason??

if you are going to be 50, i have got to 37 – the age you were when we met for the first time in paris ... which at least leaves me with the hope, to judge from your example, that i have a lot of things to discover before i get to 50, when you will be 63!! and so on, until we become (which i doubt) hypercentenarians when the relative difference will tend towards zero, although even then, i am sure, the absolute distance will remain constant!!

another idea – relativity of space, not time, this one – i will be in new york first at the end of january (in fact, i have to conduct the n.y. philh.[4]); then i shall be at harvard from 15 february to 30 june.[5] after which, i don't know ... i would have fancied going to mexico – if only to buy an obsidian knife, unevenly black and dangerously jagged – but the obligation to earn some money, and not to shirk certain debts of friendship (darmstadt, amongst others) will no doubt push me back towards our good old continent "with its pale, water-heater sun".[6] and the obsidian will remain in splinters, still always hypothetically ... black suns, once again, would not have made me a son of the light!! those are the few couplets of my "ballade" – not former time, nor recent time, nor time henceforth, nor time to come, but time fixabolished, fixploded, mirroreflected, etchcized, spellbeamed, narcoselected, foundlost, lost! lost? what? yes![7]

oh well, for your jubilee (which, to go back to my calculations, means that you were exactly twice my age in 1938 – a year of especial grace since it saw munich, and chamberlain-pépin, and daladier – a bull who let himself be had by that king of foxes, the beloved adolf – a period when you were 26, and i 13 — nothing to worry about, it's an amusing algebraic problem put forward in all the good introductory scientific magazines. better ones follow: what age

---

[4] This plan did not come to pass. Boulez first conducted the New York Philharmonic as guest conductor on 13 March 1969, and his début as principal conductor was on 15 April 1971.

[5] During this time, Boulez gave six Harvard University Appleton Lectures, in English, entitled "Nécessité d'une orientation esthétique" on their French publication in the *Mercure de France*, April-May 1964 (personal communication from Sophie Galaise). They were given again at Darmstadt the following summer. The first part of these is published in *Orientations* (pp. 63–83). The second part is found in the *Revue de musique des universités canadiennes*, no. 7 (1986), pp. 46–79.

[6] A quotation of unknown origin. (RS)

[7] This sequence of Joycean neologisms is untranslatable. The French reads, "*temps figeaboli, fixe plosé, miroirefleté, ensorcelirradiant, narcosélu, trouvéreperdu, perdu! perdu? quoi? oui!*" (RS)

will cosmonaut x be ... if he goes to, then returns from, uranus, at a constant speed equal to thirteen times the speed of light! the answer is more abstruse than it seems at first sight. but this is nothing: i read very recently that they are going to make time values, where particles will be constrained by this damned obligation to get older! which allows me to return, in kindness, and by a neat transition, to your imminent jubilee), i hope that you receive (maybe from kennedy?? he likes "the arts", so they say ... but they say so many things; one is badly informed, it's well known, rimbaud is largely out of date; it isn't love which has to be reinvented, everyone knows that, it is information which has to be reinvented, but no-one knows it) a time valve. apparently the inside spins very quickly, and there is a high tension (which you often look for in music): thousands of millions of volts – but not of faces; oh! the heavenly word games. the essential thing, in everything, to make non-sense without a programme! bah! pooh! non-sense programmes, fine, just right for piggies! in any case, thank the lord for making us so intelligent, so good, so gifted, so strong, so solitary, so "strong and silent" so "go it alone", so herd-like, so blackening, finally, yes, finally, if six saws saw six cypresses, sixty-six saws saw sixty-six cypresses[8] (there is a less poetic variant than that given here, frightfully more materialistic; i give it only to communicate horror and violent repulsion to you: if six saws saw six sausages, sixty-six saws saw sixty-six sausages;[9] but i am almost ashamed to have given you this second version, so basely interested ... even the calculations must be absolutely disinterested; otherwise, where are we going?? for my own humble part, i have chosen irrevocably: between the cypress and the sausage, i go for the big vegetable sausage, which at least you don't eat ... leave that for painting – see vincent. as for the saw, it is obligatory; without that, the joke lacks bite, if i dare venture that tremendous comparison!)

and there you have it, ladies and gents! should i have made you smile looking forward to that half-century mark?

whilst waiting – not at all whilst i await your smile by post; at least you have the ability of alice's cat – you will gather from this letter, either that i have grown up considerably, or that i have returned to infancy. that's the message i would like to leave in closing, in these hard relativist times.

as always, despite the obvious lack of the rue beautreillis, i remain a capuchin[10] who thinks fondly, if not helpfully, of you.

PB

---

[8] The French tongue-twister reads, "*si six scies scient six cyprès, six cent scies scient six cent six cyprès*".

[9] Boulez adapts the tongue-twister, substituting "*saucissons*" for "*cyprès*": (RS)

[10] A reference to the street where Boulez was living in Baden-Baden (cf. the head of the letter).

Biographical glossary

The following notes are offered as a guide to the names most frequently encountered in the letters and documents.

AJEMIAN, Maro (b. 1927): American pianist. She made the first recording of Cage's *Sonatas and Interludes* for prepared piano (1951, DIAL 19/20). Performed extensively with her sister Anahid, a violinist. Works written for them by Lou Harrison, Henry Cowell, Alan Hovhaness, Wallingford Riegger, and John Cage.

ARDEVOL, José (b. 1911 in Barcelona): Cuban composer. Studied conducting with Hermann Scherchen. Took part in the Cuban revolution and became Musical Director for Cuba. Composer in a nationalistic and neo-classical style, then influenced by Webern in the 50s. Later turned to aleatoric techniques.

BABBITT, Milton (b. 1916): Hugely influential American composer and theorist. Taught at Princeton from 1948, and at the Juilliard School and Darmstadt, amongst other places. Member of the editorial board of the journal *Perspectives of New Music*. Fascinated by the combinatorial possibilities of the elements of the series.

BARAB, Seymour: French cellist. He took part in the Cage-Cunningham spectacle of 15 January 1950, and the performance of *Pierrot Lunaire* conducted by René Leibowitz. (Communication from Robert Piencikowski)

BARRAULT, Jean-Louis (b. 1910): French actor and theatre director. Formed the Compagnie Renaud-Barrault with Madeleine Renaud in 1947. The company specialised in the performance of new works. Writings include *Réflexions sur la théâtre* (1959) and *Souvenirs pour demain* (1972). (RS)

BAYLE, François (b. 1932): French composer. Studied with Stockhausen in Darmstadt and Messiaen in Paris. Joined the Groupe de Musique Concrète in 1960. Director of the Groupe de Recherches Musicales from 1966. A disciple of Pierre Schaeffer, he has devoted himself exclusively to electro-acoustic music, which he has renamed "acousmatic" music.

BEYER, Johanna (1888–1944): American composer. A small number of works, published by *New Music Edition*.

BROWN, Earle (b. 1926): American composer. Closely associated with Cage, Tudor, Feldman and Wolff from 1952 onwards. Influenced by Pollock and Calder. Developed graphic notation (*November 1952* and *December 1952*) and "open works" (*Twenty-Five Pages*, 1953) hard on the heels of Cage.

BROWN, Merton (b. 1913): American composer. Studied with Wallingford Riegger and Carl Ruggles. His works employ the system known as "dissonant counterpoint". He was a member of Cage's circle in New York until 1949, when he moved to Rome (he returned to New York in 1967).

CASANOVA, André (b. 1919): French composer. Studied at the École Normale de Musique. One of Leibowitz's first pupils in 1944. His *Concertino pour piano* (1952) was first performed by Yvonne Loriod in 1959.

CHAR, René (1907–88): French poet. Perhaps the most important poet of the surrealist movement. The works of his that most interested Boulez at this period were *Le marteau sans maître* (1934), *Fureur et mystère* (1948), *Le soleil des eaux* (1949), and *Les matinaux* (1950). His *Œuvres complètes* were published in 1983 (Paris: Éditions de La Pléiade). (RS)

COPLAND, Aaron (1900–90): American composer. With Leonard Bernstein, the most popular of the "traditional" composers. Particularly known for the works *El Salon Mexico* (1933–6), *Appalachian Spring* (1943–4), and *Rodéo* (1942).

COWELL, Henry (1897–1965): American composer, pianist and essayist. Produced nearly a thousand works. Essentially an experimentalist. Wrote *New Musical Resources* (1916–19, published in 1930). Inventor of the "string piano" and rhythmicon with Lev Termen. He was the first to insert foreign objects inside the piano. Derived much inspiration from music of oral traditions. Coined the term "cluster".

CUNNINGHAM, Merce (b. 1919): American dancer and choreographer. Met Cage at the Cornish School in Seattle, and became a lifelong friend and collaborator. Formed his own company in 1953, and school in 1959. One of the most original choreographers of his generation. Has also worked with Brown, Feldman, Tudor, and Wolff.

DALLAPICCOLA, Luigi (1904–75): Italian composer, pianist and writer. Pioneer of the serial technique in Italy. Enormous output, including most notably the operas *Volo di notte*, *Il prigioniero* and *Ulisse*, and the *Canti di prigionia*, and *Canti di liberazione*, indicating his political inclinations.

De SCHLOEZER, Boris (1881–1969): French composer and essayist, better known for his writings. His *Introduction à Jean-Sebastien Bach* (Paris: Gallimard 1947) was the first work of French musicology inspired by Gestalt psychology. Wrote *Problèmes de la musique moderne* (Paris: éditions de Minuit, 1959) with Marina Scriabine. Sub-editor of the *Revue Musicale* and columnist with the *Nouvelle Revue Française* from 1921 to 1957.

DÉSORMIÈRE, Roger (1898–1963): French conductor linked with the École d'Arcueil and Les Six. Musical director of the Ballets Russes until 1925 and principal conductor of the Opéra comique from 1937. Made a classic recording of Debussy's *Pelléas et Mélisande*. Conducted the première of *Le soleil des eaux* (18 July 1950; cf. no. 8, note 11, and no. 24). Considered, with Scherchen and Rosbaud, to be one of Boulez's models as a conductor; Boulez devoted an essay to him in 1966 ("I Hate Remembering", in *Orientations*, pp. 500–13). This essay contains notes left by Désormière: "The aim is to achieve the greatest possible sobriety; to rid oneself little by little of everything inessential."

DEUTSCH, Max (1892–1982): Austrian composer, teacher and conductor. He conducted the first performances of several works of the Second Viennese School, in particular Berg's Chamber concerto (1927). He wrote several operas, among them *Die freudlose Straße* and *Der Schatz*. Acclaimed as a teacher of the highest order.

DUHAMEL, Antoine (b. 1925): Pupil of Messiaen and Leibowitz. An active member of the Club d'essai at the R.T.F. (the first *musique concrète* studio).

EIMERT, Herbert (1897–1972): German composer and theorist. His *Atonale Musiklehre* (1923) was the first description of a twelve-tone technique. Founder of the West-Deutscher Rundfunk electronic music studio at Cologne (1951) and Director until 1962. Developed the idea of *elektronische Musik*, using entirely synthetic sound sources (as opposed to *musique concrète*). Editor of the journal *Die Reihe*, which published early articles on electronic and new music. (RS)

FANO, Michel (b. 1929): French composer. Studied with Nadia Boulanger and Messiaen. His Sonata for two pianos and *Études pour quinze instruments* were first performed in 1952 at Donaueschingen and Darmstadt respectively. Devoted himself thereafter to film music, particularly for the films of Robbe-Grillet. Author of a book on *Wozzeck* with P. J. Jouve (1953).

FELDMAN, Morton (1926–87): American composer. Met Cage in 1950 and was associated with him from that time on, along with Brown, Wolff, and Tudor. His graphic conception of musical works – which left Boulez sceptical (cf nos. 31 and 35 – shows the influence of the abstract expressionist painters (cf. no. 32).

FIZDALE, Robert (b. 1920): American pianist, duettist with Arthur Gold. Their career began with *A Book of Music* and Three Dances for prepared piano, composed for them by John Cage. They gave the first performance of Luciano Berio's Concerto for two pianos in 1972.

FREUND, Marya (1876–1966): Soprano, specializing in German romantic lieder and twentieth-century music. Sang in the first performance of Schoenberg's *Gurrelieder*, and the French premières of his *Pierrot Lunaire*, *Das Buch der hängenden Gärten*, and Second String Quartet with soprano solo.

FROIDEBISE, Pierre (1914–62): Belgian composer, organist, and musicologist. Professor of harmony at the Liège Conservatoire. Works include *De l'aube à la nuit*,

Trois poèmes japonais, Cinq comptines, Auvercoeur, and *Stèle pour Sei Shonagon.* Style shows the influence of Stravinsky and Webern.

GATTI, Armand (b. 1924): French playwright and theatrical producer. His best-known works, of revolutionary inspiration, date from after the period that concerns us here: *La Crapaud-Buffle, La vie imaginaire de l'eboueur Auguste Geai,* and *V comme Viètnam.* On Gatti's collaboration with Boulez, see no. 36, note 6.

GOLD, Arthur (b. 1917): Canadian pianist. Renowned as a duettist with Robert Fizdale (q.v.), whom he met at the Juilliard School in New York.

GREEN, Ray (b. 1908): American composer. Author of a *Bibliography of Music Therapy* (1952). Eclectic style, attempting to create an authentically American style. Recorded works include *Festival Fugues, Holiday for Four, Sunday Spring Symphony.*

GRIMAUD, Yvette (b. 1920): French pianist and composer. She gave the first performances of Boulez's *Notations* (Jameux no. 1), *Trois psalmodies pour piano* (no. 2), the First and Second Piano sonatas (nos. 6 and 11) and, with Yvonne Loriod, the complete version of the first book of *Structures* for two pianos (no. 14). She also gave first performances of works by Nigg, Jolivet, Honegger, and others. Works include Piano Preludes, *Quatre chants d'espace* for non-tempered quarter-tones and *Chant de courbe* for two pianos. As an ethnomusicologist, she worked on Bochiman and Pygmy music.

GUSTON, Philip (1913–80): American artist. At first influenced both by the Italian masters Ucello and Piero della Francesca, and by the cubism of Picasso and Beckman; between 1947 and 1950 his style evolved towards abstraction, giving him a place in the Abstract Expressionist school. He taught at the Washington Square College of New York University from 1951 to 1958. Cage's and Boulez's interest in him may stem from exhibitions in New York at the Peridot gallery (1952) and the Egan gallery (1953). (RS)

HARRISON, Lou (b. 1917): American composer. Pupil of Schoenberg and Cowell. Inventor of several musical instruments, such as the "tack piano". Conducted the première of Ives's Third Symphony in 1947. Has composed for non-European instruments, particularly the Gamelan.

HENRIOT, Nicole (b. 1925): French pianist. Studied at the Paris Conservatoire, winning first prize in the Concours Marguerite Long. Her international concert career has been devoted to the German Romantic repertoire and to contemporary French composers.

HENRY, Pierre (b. 1927): French composer. Studied with Nadia Boulanger and Messiaen. Joined Schaeffer's studio at the R.T.F. in 1949, and led the Groupe de Recherche sur la Musique Concrète from 1950 to 1958. He later united *musique concrète* and *elektronische Musik* principles in many electronic works, including music for film, TV, and radio. (RS)

JARRE, Maurice (b. 1924): French composer. Pupil of Honegger. Percussionist of the group of musicians conducted by Boulez in the Compagnie Renaud-Barrault, then composer with the T.N.P. After several "art music" works, radically serial in technique, he opted for film music and became internationally famous with his scores for *Lawrence of Arabia* (1963) and *Doctor Zhivago* (1965).

JOFFROY, Pierre: Writer. Author of *Les prétendants* (short stories; Paris: Seuil, 1966); *L'espion de Dieu, La passion de Kurt Gerstein* (Novel; Paris: Grasset, 1969); *La punition* (play; Paris: Grasset, 1971); *Vingt têtes à couper* (novel; Paris: Fayard, 1973). Wrote a book on Winston Churchill with Armand Gatti (Paris: Club des éditeurs, 1961).

JOLIVET, André (1906–74). French composer. Early influences were Schoenberg and, more importantly, Varèse. His works were never strictly serial, but show a concern for method, especially in rhythmic organisation, within an eclectic modernist language. He became well-known in the 40s and 50s through a series of substantial works, notably the Concerto for Ondes Martenot (1947).

JUTRAS, Claude (1930–87): Canadian film-maker. Acknowledged as the leading figure in avant-garde cinema in Quebec, with *Dément du lac Jean-Jeune* (1947), *Mouvement perpétuel* (1949), and *Pierrot des bois* (1956). Later released the box-office hits *Mon oncle Antoine* (1971) and *Kamouraska* (1973).

KIRCHNER, Léon (b. 1919): American pianist, composer and conductor. Had a great success with his Piano sonata (1948, first performed 1949). His dramatic and eclectic style unites the influences of Hindemith, Bartók, Stravinsky and the Second Viennese School.

LEIBOWITZ, René (1913–72): French composer, musicologist, teacher, and conductor. Pupil of Schoenberg, Webern and Ravel. Taught privately on the Second Viennese School between 1945 and 1947, when his pupils included Boulez. Perhaps better known for his theoretical works than his musical ones: *Schoenberg et son école* (1946), *Introduction à la musique de douze sons* (1949), *L'Artiste et sa conscience* (1950), *L'Évolution de la musique de Bach à Schoenberg* (1952), *Histoire de l'opéra* (1957), *Schoenberg* (1972). One of Boulez's *bêtes noires*, in articles and the present correspondence (see, for example, no. 3, note 5).

MARTINET, Jean-Louis (b. 1912): Pupil of Messiaen, Koechlin, Munch and Désormière. Attended classes with Leibowitz. His stylistic methods derive from the work's content and the feelings to be expressed.

MASSELOS, William (b. 1920): American pianist. Known for his commitment to contemporary music and famous for his unorthodox programmes. Gave the first performances of Ives's First Piano Sonata (1949), Copland's *Piano Fantasy* (1957), and Ben Weber's Piano Concerto (1961).

MCLAREN, Norman (1914–87): Canadian film-maker. Inventor of the technique of engraving directly onto the film, and founder of the animation studio at the Office National du Film in Montreal.

MESSIAEN, Olivier (1908–92): French composer. Arguably France's greatest composer and teacher of this century. His pupils included Boulez and Stockhausen, and his presence at the Darmstadt summer schools in the 1950s was influential on a whole generation of avant-garde composers. His own music flirted with total serial techniques at this period, before returning to the intensely personal combination of modal techniques, spiritual inspiration, and birdsong-derived melody which was the foundation of his style. (RS)

MONOD, Jacques (b. 1927): French composer, pianist and conductor. Studied with Messiaen and Leibowitz, then at the Juilliard School, where he became assistant to R. F. Goldman. On 8 May 1951 he conducted the first concert entirely devoted to Webern. Made his début as a pianist in the concert for Schoenberg's seventy-fifth birthday, conducted by Leibowitz (see no. 4). Played or conducted the premières of Schoenberg's Songs Op. 48, Webern's Songs Opp. 17 and 25, Berg's *Schließe mir die Augen beide* (second setting), and Babbitt's *Widow's Lament* and *Du*. Principal conductor of the BBC Symphony Orchestra between 1960 and 1966.

NABOKOV, Nicolas (1903–78): Russian composer, who emigrated to the United States in 1933 and lived mainly in Paris from 1950. Pupil of Busoni and cousin of the famous author. Much involved in the organization of several music festivals: "Congrès pour la liberté culturelle" (1951), "Chefs-d'œuvre du XXe siècle" (1952), "Musique de notre temps" (1954; see no. 44), and "Rencontres musicales Orient-Occident" (1961). Wrote dance music, including *Ode* (1927) and *Union Pacific* (1934), and a book on Stravinsky (1964).

NIGG, Serge (b. 1929): French composer. Pupil of Messiaen and Leibowitz. A contemporary of Boulez at the Paris Conservatoire. Strongly committed to the extreme Left at the time of the "Prague Declaration", which made him turn away from dodecaphony. His works at this time include *Le fusillé inconnu* (1949) and *Pour un poète captif* (1950), Works of symphonic scope and concertos approaching neoromanticism. At present professor of orchestration at the Paris Conservatoire.

PHILIPPOT, Michel (b. 1925): French composer. Pupil of Leibowitz, composer of serial works. Has held several administrative posts in French radio.

POUSSEUR, Henri (b. 1929): Belgian composer and theorist. Writings include *Fragments théoriques I sur la musique expérimentale* and *Musique, sémantique, societé*. Works include *Scambi* (1957), *Répons* (1960), *Trois visages de Liège* (1961), *Votre Faust* (1960–7, in collaboration with Michel Butor), and *Les éphémérides d'Icare II* (1970). His music explores the possibilities of intervention by the performer, quotation, and chance processes. Currently Director of the Liège Conservatoire.

RENAUD, Madeleine (b. 1900): See BARRAULT, Jean-Louis.

ROLDAN, Amadeo (1900–39): Cuban composer, violinist, orchestral leader and teacher. His works often inspired by Afro-Cuban folklore. They include the ballet *La Rebambarama* and *Ritmicas V & VI* for percussion ensemble.

RUSSELL, William (b. 1905): American composer, active in the 40s and 50s.

SABY, Bernard (1925–75): French painter and member of Boulez's circle. He produced several cover illustrations for the Domaine Musical programmes. He was given a retrospective exhibition in 1986 by the Musée d'Art Moderne de la Ville de Paris (12 February–13 April), for which Boulez wrote an untitled testimonial on page 113 of the catalogue.

SCELSI, Giacinto (1905–88): Italian composer. His stylistic orientations were eclectic throughout his life; however, influenced by Scriabin's esoteric and theosophical preoccupations, he devoted himself to research into sustained sounds, microintervals and minimalist variations which have given him a belated popularity in certain sections of contemporary music.

SCHAEFFER, Pierre (b. 1910): French composer and theorist. Conducted the first experiments in *musique concrète*. Founded the Studio d'essai at the R.T.F. in 1942, and later the Groupe de Recherches sur la Musique Concrète, which he reformed in 1958 to create the Groupe de Recherches Musicales. Writings include *A la recherche d'une musique concrète* (1952) and an influential study of sound morphology, *Traité des objets musicaux* (1966). (RS)

SCHERCHEN, Hermann (1891–1966): Conductor. Deeply involved with twentieth-century music. Worked with Schoenberg on the première of *Pierrot Lunaire* (1912). Founded the *Neue Musikgesellschaft* and the Scherchen Quartet in 1918, and the journal *Melos* in 1919 (with Souvtchinsky). Conducted the first performances of *Three Fragments from Wozzeck* (1924, Frankfurt), *Matka* by Hába (1930, Munich), and the Dance of the Golden Calf from *Moses und Aron* (Schoenberg), the first extract to be performed in public (1951). Wrote a *Manuel de direction d'orchestre* (1933). Taught at Venice and Darmstadt. Refused to use a baton. Founded an electronic music studio at Gravesano and the *Gravesaner Blätter* in 1954. Boulez wrote an obituary notice for him (*Orientations*, p. 499).

SCRIABINE, Marina (b. 1911): Russian musicologist, daughter of the composer Alexander Scriabin; she settled in Paris in 1927. Author of *Introduction au langage musical* and *Le langage musical* (Paris: éditions de Minuit, 1961 and 1963), and, with Boris de Schloezer, of *Problèmes de la musique moderne* (Paris: éditions de Minuit, 1959).

SEKULA, Sonya (b. 1918): painter and friend of John Cage. She was born in Lucerne, and studied in Switzerland before moving to America. She had an apartment in the same building as Cage, and is the subject of several of the anecdotes found in *Silence* (see e.g. pp. 56 and 193). (RS)

SOURIS, André (1899–1970): Belgian composer, conductor and musicologist. Studied conducting with Scherchen. Founded the journal *Polyphonie* in 1947. The influence of Gestalt psychology, phenomenology, and the work of Bachelard is evident in his *Conditions de la musique, et autres écrits* (Éditions de l'Université de Bruxelles et du C.N.R.S., 1976).

SOUVTCHINSKY, Pierre (1892–1985): Russian critic and writer, who emigrated to Paris in 1927. Met, early on, Prokofiev and Stravinsky. Founded the journal *Le contemporain musical* in Russia, then *Melos* and, in Prague, *Eurasie* in partnership with the linguist Troubetskoy. Assisted with the writing of Stravinsky's *Poetics of Music* (1952). Close links with Pasternak (a long correspondence), Artaud (took part in the first performance of *Les Cenci*), and Munch. Worked at the N.R.F. Author of *Un siècle de musique russe* and editor of the two volumes of *Musique russe* (P.U.F. 1953) in which Boulez published his analysis of *The Rite of Spring*. Was crucially important in the founding of the Petit Marigny and Domaine Musical concerts. Was general editor at the Éditions du Rocher of a series under the title Domaine Musical which included uncollected letters by Debussy, the Nietzsche-Gast correspondence edited by Schaeffner, Pousseur's translation of Berg's writings and a collection of essays on Roger Désormière.

STOCKHAUSEN, Karlheinz (b. 1928): German composer. The most celebrated European *enfant terrible* of the 1950s avant-garde. In common with Boulez and Luigi Nono, he developed the use of total serialism, and experimented with electronic techniques. His concept of "moment form" has been influential on many subsequent composers. His own works since the 1970s have shown the influence of Japanese philosophy and American minimalism; his seven-opera cycle *Licht* is the most ambitious "work in progress" of any contemporary composer. (RS)

STRANG, Gerald (1908–83): Composer and teacher. Pupil of Schoenberg, Toch, and Koechlin. Composer of instrumental works, then electronic and computer-created pieces.

STROBEL, Heinrich (1898–1970): German critic and administrator. Director of the Südwestfunk in Baden-Baden, to which he invited Boulez in 1959. Director of the Donaueschingen festival. Took over the editorship of *Melos* on its revival in 1946. Boulez wrote two obituary tributes to him (*Orientations*, pp. 519–22).

TÉZENAS, Suzanne (d. 1991): Organizer of the sponsorship that enabled Boulez to found the Petit Marigny concerts in 1953, and subsequently the Domaine Musical, of which she became the first president.

THOMPSON, Virgil (1896–1989): American composer and critic. Lived in Paris from 1925 to 1940. Although his aesthetics remained neo-classical and he drew inspiration from specifically American musical characteristics, he exhibits a constant interest in his many writings for Cage and Boulez. He wrote two operas to libretti by Gertrude Stein: *Four Saints in Three Acts* (1927–8) and *The Mother of Us All* (1947).

WEBER, Ben (b. 1916): American composer. His works use serial and twelve-note techniques.

WOLFF, Christian (b. 1934): American composer; born in Nice but emigrated to the United States in 1941. Studied Classics at Harvard. Self-taught in music.

Associated with Cage, Brown, and Feldman, his research in the 50s emphasized the interaction of performers, the role of silence and the value of each sound considered in isolation.

WOLPE, Stefan (1902–1972): American composer born in Germany. Atonal style. Studied orchestration with Webern. Held a number of teaching posts in America and had some influence on Shapey, Feldman and Tudor. His sonata for violin and piano dates from 1949.

WORONOW, Vladimir (1903–80): Belgian composer born in Russia. Works based on serial techniques.

WYSCHNEGRADSKY, Ivan (1893–1979): Russian composer, living in France from 1920 onwards. A pupil of Sokolov, much influenced by Scriabin. Experimented with quarter-tone, sixth-tone, and other tuning systems, constructing a quarter-tone piano. His earliest quarter-tone works date from 1918. (RS)

Index